ROCK OF GIBRALTAR

*To Daddy
Lots of Love
Suzanne xxx*

This book is aimed at people with an interest in racing or football, and those with none at all who just want to know more about an intriguing story. I have tried to explain as best I can the intricacies of racing in particular, and have included a glossary of racing terms at the end of the book to assist those who have no knowledge of the sport.

All distances for races are given in imperial measures, but I have included a conversion to the metric system in the glossary. Similarly, monetary amounts are given in the currency of the country in which the sum was spent, with conversion to pounds sterling as appropriate to that time.

ROCK OF GIBRALTAR

Ultimate Racehorse and
Fabulous Prize in a Battle of Giants

Martin Hannan

CUTTING EDGE

EDINBURGH AND LONDON

For luck
To Grace Olivia Atherton Campbell

Copyright © Martin Hannan, 2004
All rights reserved
The moral right of the author has been asserted

First published in Great Britain in 2004 by
CUTTING EDGE PRESS
7 Albany Street
Edinburgh EH1 3UG

ISBN 1 903813 05 0

No part of this book may be reproduced or transmitted in any form or by any means without written permission from the publisher, except by a reviewer who wishes to quote brief passages in connection with a review written for insertion in a newspaper, magazine or broadcast

A catalogue record for this book
is available from the British Library

Typeset in Giovanni and Univers
Printed and bound in Great Britain by
Antony Rowe Ltd, Chippenham, Wiltshire

Acknowledgements

The list of people I wish to thank for their advice and assistance in preparing this book cannot be completely stated. Many fellow journalists and other sources in racing, business and football circles spoke to me knowing I would never name them, and I never will. Nevertheless, my gratitude to them is undying. You know who you are, ladies and gentlemen, and you know this book would not have been possible without you.

At Cutting Edge, I would like to thank Bill Campbell for commissioning this work – this book is dedicated to his daughter who was born the day he signed me for the task; Peter MacKenzie for one piece of advice in particular; Graeme Blaikie for his supervision; Lizzie Cameron for her design of the cover; and above all Kevin O'Brien for his patience and diligent editing – and at least I have made one convert to the joys of racing from this process.

My most appreciative thanks go to Ester Barrett of the Three Sisters Gallery in Co. Limerick for permission to use her astonishingly lifelike portrait of Rock Of Gibraltar on the back cover of this book. I am convinced that Ester is going to become one of the biggest names in the growing field of equine art, and her work should be supported.

ROCK OF GIBRALTAR

I would like to thank Empics, John Grossick and Scotsman Publications for the use of their photographs; my photographer colleague Robert Perry for his superb work and his friendship; and I also wish to thank my friend, the freelance journalist Frances Anderson, for her pictorial advice.

There are many fans of Manchester United who assisted me, and I am grateful to them. I will single out Sean Murphy of United4Action who deliberated long and hard before deciding to speak to me. I wish to acknowledge his courage in so doing.

I wish to thank the writers and editors who gave their permission for the use of quotes from newspapers and other material.

All quotes in this book not sourced to a publication are taken from racing's bible, the *Racing Post*. It is simply the sine qua non for any serious follower of racing. In particular, I would like to thank Chris Smith, editor of the *Racing Post*, for permission to use the paper's material. It helped that Chris himself penned one of the best tributes to Rock Of Gibraltar, and his deputy editor, Howard Wright, has encouraged me in my career and I want to take this opportunity to thank them both for that help.

I have tried to find the copyright owner for every quoted source, and believe I have succeeded. If anyone has been inadvertently quoted without acknowledgement, then I apologise in advance and will rectify the matter in future editions.

I would especially like to thank Frankie Dettori, Lester Piggott and Mark Johnston for their contributions. Truly great men always find time to help others, and their words of tribute to Rock Of Gibraltar were very much appreciated.

I wish to emphasise that at no time did I receive any assistance from Sir Alex Ferguson or John Magnier or their employees, and therefore neither is in breach of their legal undertakings on confidentiality. Nevertheless, I feel this book is as definitive an account of Rock Of Gibraltar's life and the events surrounding him as could have been achieved in such circumstances.

I would like to thank my colleagues at *Scotland on Sunday* and elsewhere in Scotsman Publications for their help and support, and especially freelance journalists and writers Douglas Middleton and Jeff Connor for their advice and friendship. I

ACKNOWLEDGEMENTS

became ill during the final weeks of writing so I wish to thank Dr Stephen Murray of Inch Park Surgery and Pete Sochart of Evolve gym, both in Edinburgh, for their care which helped restore me to full fitness and enabled me to complete the book. May I also thank my mother Catherine for the use of the 'office', and her loving support over the years. Above all, I wish to thank my wife Isabel, my children Debbie and James, and all my family and friends for putting up with me and encouraging me in this task. Thanks even to those who said 'don't touch this with a bargepole' and 'watch your kneecaps'.

Since he cannot read, it may seem strange to thank a horse, but I really do want to thank Rock Of Gibraltar and all his fellows for the pleasure they have given me. It has been more than three decades since I first started following the sport of horse racing and in that time there have been many ups and downs, but there have always been two constant qualities – the beauty and the nobility of the thoroughbred racehorse species. God bless every one of them, even those who cost me a small fortune.

Contents

Preface		11
Chapter One	The Ultimate Racehorse	15
Chapter Two	Genes Worth Fighting For	34
Chapter Three	Fergie's Horsey Hobby	61
Chapter Four	The Beginnings	84
Chapter Five	The Gimcrack Craic	112
Chapter Six	The Triumphs	140
Chapter Seven	Those Two Impostors	
	(Triumph in Paris and Disaster in Chicago)	168
Chapter Eight	The Final Furlong	193
Chapter Nine	The Finishing Post	220
Chapter Ten	Objections and Inquiries	241
Appendix	Key to Race Reports	264
Glossary of Racing Terms		265

Preface

In the legends of King Charlemagne, there is a great deal that is purely mythological. One story is told of a horse called Bayard who belonged to the knight Renaud, also known as Roland, and his three brothers, the sons of Duke Aymon. As well as being a great charger, Bayard had the happy ability to elongate his body and accommodate all four brothers at once. He could also talk, which was most helpful for mediaeval chroniclers.

Not surprisingly, the great Charlemagne wanted the best horse around and was desperate to acquire Bayard, and though the legends vary as to whether he did so by hook or by crook or by straightforward means, the horse ended up in the King's hands. But the steed escaped. Some tales say that he was thrown into a great river by Charlemagne's henchmen because it was clear he would only obey his master, and that he swam to safety and made his way back to Renaud. To this day, in cities and towns across Europe – such as Dendermonde and Namur in Belgium or Montauban in France – they claim Bayard as their own and celebrate his speed, strength and loyalty to his master, while such was his fame that the word Bayard has long been used by writers as a generic term for a horse.

Fiction though it is, Bayard's tale is indicative of the esteem in which we humans have held horses, and still do. Ever since mankind first domesticated horses, men and women have always wanted to possess bigger, better, but mostly, faster animals. Over the last 300 years, the most famous species of horse on the planet has been the thoroughbred racehorse, and the Sport of Kings has seen a vast array of people, mostly rich men but also a few wealthy women, compete with each other to buy or breed the best.

We still tend to weave legends around the achievements of great horses. The modern equivalent of a chivalric saga is probably a movie, and such films as *Phar Lap*, *Champions* and the wonderful *Seabiscuit* have taken the stories of horses and made the animals something grander, something more fabulous, than merely winners of races.

Every so often, a racehorse appears who needs no artist to paint his glory – his deeds speak for themselves and public adulation follows. Very rarely, if ever, has such a famous racehorse then become the prize in a bitter duel between two celebrated and wealthy men.

The story of Rock Of Gibraltar is unique in the annals of horse racing. If he had 'merely' set a world record of seven Group 1 races in a row, he would have been worthy of a biography in his own right. What makes his story irresistible, however, is the extraordinary and very messy public conflict which erupted after he went to stud. The monumental row involved Britain's greatest-ever football manager, Sir Alex Ferguson, against John Magnier, the Irishman who revolutionised racehorse breeding and now owns Coolmore, the world's greatest stud operation. Standing alongside Magnier throughout was his billionaire friend J.P. McManus, probably the best-known gambler in Europe.

The conflict became nothing less than a game of poker – stud, of course – in which the stakes were the reputations of its players, plus tens of millions of pounds' worth of horse DNA and the future of the world's most famous football club.

To write a racehorse's biography is a difficult matter. For a start, since Bayard and television's Mr Ed are the only talking horses on record, you cannot exactly interview the principal subject. Although his races are the stuff of fact, and many other details of

PREFACE

his life are straightforward enough, a great deal of obfuscation lies in the path of anyone writing about Rock Of Gibraltar. Some facts can only be approximate, as the two principal human beings who fought over him have sworn a vow of silence, which they have maintained in the hope that a line has been drawn under the Rock Of Gibraltar Affair, as the matter became known. The silence of Ferguson and Magnier has been absolute, but the row rumbles on.

While researching this book, I travelled to Ireland, to Co. Tipperary and the small town of Fethard. In a public house there, I asked about the nearby Coolmore Stud and sought local opinions on the spat between John Magnier and Alex Ferguson, which was then past its conclusion, as far as the public knew. Given that Coolmore is the biggest local employer and that Magnier has spread plenty of largesse around the town, you can guess which side the vast majority of the local people supported. Perhaps curiously, that bias was not always evident elsewhere in Ireland.

As I rose to leave McCarthy's, a well-dressed middle-aged gentleman took me aside conspiratorially and said, 'You should know this – it is not over yet, and the repercussions of this matter will go on for a long time.' Nothing I have learned since then has contradicted this prediction.

Yet this book is not intended to prolong the agony experienced by those involved. Rather, it is aimed at investigating what happened and explaining how such events occurred. Hopefully, some people may learn some lessons and my conclusions may surprise you.

Above all, however, this is the story of a magnificent Bayard, the ultimate racehorse – Rock Of Gibraltar.

CHAPTER ONE

The Ultimate Racehorse

I shall call him Rocky. Others have their own nicknames for Rock Of Gibraltar, but I have called him Rocky since a few minutes after I clapped eyes on him, so Rocky he will be throughout this book. My name for him obviously owes something to Rocky Balboa, the fictitious 'Italian Stallion' heavyweight boxer played by Sylvester Stallone on the silver screen. As we shall see, though, this connection relies on more than just the simple facts that their names are similar and that both are 'stallions'. My other reason for calling him Rocky is slightly more unusual. Rock Of Gibraltar reminds me, in a strange way, of Marilyn Monroe. As this no doubt requires some explanation, I will come back to it a little later on.

I first saw Rock Of Gibraltar in the flesh at Doncaster racecourse on 14 September 2001. He was being led around the parade ring of the historic Yorkshire track just prior to the Rothmans Royals Champagne Stakes, a Group 2 race for two-year-old colts and geldings. The Champagne Stakes is one of Britain's top races for two year olds, long recognised as a trial for the following year's Classics. The Classics are the five historic races competed for annually by three-year-old colts and fillies. In order of when they take place, they are the 2,000 Guineas (for colts) and the 1,000

Guineas (for fillies), both over one mile at Newmarket; the Oaks (for fillies) and the Derby (for both sexes but usually only colts compete), both over one mile four furlongs at Epsom; and finally the St Leger, over one mile six furlongs at Doncaster. The Classics are so important in racing history that almost every country in Europe copies the same Classic pattern, and indeed Ireland even uses the same names. The winners of those Classic races usually, though not always, go on to enjoy pleasant careers at stud, while their owners win excellent prize money and gain lucrative fees from their champions' services as stallions and mares. This happy fate is also shared by the horses and owners that win what are known as Group races – the Champions' League of racing.

Though racehorses from different countries and continents have competed against each other for the best part of two centuries, it is only since the early 1970s that an organised system of classifying the best races has been recognised worldwide. Previous attempts at giving races in different countries a similar status were unsatisfactory, but now there is a tried and tested international Pattern system operated by racing administrators across the globe. The Pattern is supposed to standardise the top rank of races. In Britain, these races go on a 'List', hence the adjective 'Listed' which can be seen in the official names of that small percentage of races considered good enough to be on the 'List'.

These 'Listed' races are organised into four categories. From the top division down, they are Groups 1, 2 and 3, plus a Grade A 'Listed' division for races which just fail to reach Group status. Prize money is one element that decides the grouping of a race, and there are minimum prize levels in each group. But the tradition and history of a particular race also counts towards its status. It is common for races to be moved between groups by the administrators, depending largely on how well particular races are supported by trainers and owners. To add to the confusion, some races within the Pattern are termed 'championship' races, because over the years these races have tended to define the best horse in a particular category. The Epsom Derby, for instance, is recognised as Britain's championship race for three-year-old colts racing over one mile and four furlongs. Only in the past few years has there been an official World Championship Series of races – a sort of

Grand Prix circuit largely inspired by the most successful owner of horses in the world today, Sheikh Mohammed Al Maktoum of Dubai, about whom we will learn more later.

There are many grades of racing below the Listed category, but common to all levels is the system of calculating the weight a horse carries. That weight is the combination of the jockey's own poundage plus lead weights in a special saddlecloth which brings horse and jockey to their 'handicap weight'. All horses which have competed in at least three races are allotted a handicap rating by expert handicappers employed by the administrative bodies – in the UK that organisation is the British Horseracing Board (BHB) – and the handicap mark is supposed to show how high or low a horse is ranked. These handicap 'ratings' are always expressed in imperial pounds, so in a typical handicap a horse rated 126 would carry nine stones of jockey and lead put together. As in golf's handicap system, the idea of a handicap in racing is to try to equalise the contest, and the ideal handicap race would see a dead heat between every horse.

The rating varies in line with results over a period of time. Confusingly, the extra weight carried by a horse can also vary depending on the status of the race. All Group races are non-handicaps, and in these races horses compete against each other carrying the same weight with allowances only for age and sex. The older a horse is, the more weight it carries, and fillies and mares get an allowance because they are deemed weaker than the males. For example, in a Group race, a three-year-old filly would get a weight allowance of perhaps 10 lbs when competing against a four-year-old colt. Needless to say, the less weight a horse carries, the more chance it has of winning.

Unlike the vast majority of racehorses, which are not good enough to compete in Group races, Rock Of Gibraltar's entire career on track took place at Group level, except for his debut in Ireland which we will learn about later. It follows that in most of his races he faced horses carrying the same weight, except when allowances were made for age, sex and experience – a Group race winner sometimes has to carry a penalty in a subsequent race.

In the Champagne Stakes, Rocky was penalised for having won two earlier Group races at The Curragh and York, so he carried 9 st. while the other colts carried 8 st. 10 lbs. He was still fancied to win the Group 2-ranked Champagne Stakes at Doncaster, however, and it is always a very good prize to capture, even though other races have assumed more importance than the Champagne Stakes in the annual calendar, principally because Group 2 is only the second-highest rating. For two year olds in Britain, several other races such as the Racing Post Trophy, also run at Doncaster, and the Middle Park and Dewhurst Stakes at Newmarket – remember the latter – have become more important, as they are top-ranked Group 1 races. But the Champagne has the kudos of tradition and the list of winners shows that it has often produced champion racehorses, including Classic winners, in the past. It still does.

That day at Doncaster, Rocky was in a field which included a potential superstar in Dubai Destination, owned by Sheikh Mohammed, who, as well as being the absolute ruler of oil-rich Dubai, is also the head of the mighty Godolphin operation dedicated to owning, breeding and training only the best horses. But Rock Of Gibraltar was the centre of all the attention. For this was Rocky's second race in Britain in which he would be wearing the scarlet colours of the most famous football club manager of the day, Sir Alex Ferguson of Manchester United – a man admired by many football fans, detested by others for his success and his occasional behavioural lapses, but utterly adored by millions of United fans worldwide for his skills as a manager and for his constant, unremitting defence of all things Red. They truly love their Scottish general, Stonewall Ferguson, at Old Trafford. So they should – no man other than 'Fergie', not even the late, great Sir Matt Busby, could have taken Manchester United to the pinnacle of European football and made it, quite simply, the biggest club in the world.

Having apparently bought a half-share in the horse from the Irish multi-millionaire owner of Coolmore Stud, John Magnier, Ferguson was having his colours worn by Ireland's seemingly perennial champion jockey Michael Kinane. Kinane is the jockey for Ballydoyle stables in Co. Tipperary, run by Aidan O'Brien. Coolmore Stud and Ballydoyle stables have been formally linked since the 1970s, and though Coolmore owns Ballydoyle and is the parent half of the operation, it was the success of the stables under the legendary trainer Dr Vincent O'Brien from the 1950s to the 1970s which really began the rise of Coolmore–Ballydoyle to its present world-leading status. Vincent O'Brien and his namesake, Aidan, are related only through genius. Vincent was known as the Master of Ballydoyle, and it seemed that no one could ever usurp that title, but such have been his successor's achievements at a comparatively young age that Aidan is known to me and many others as the Maestro of Ballydoyle.

There was a larger than usual press corps at Doncaster that day in 2001, and not all of them were the highly professional racing correspondents who serve the British racing public so well. The interlopers were there for the simple reason that Alex Ferguson was involved, and everything to do with Manchester United and Ferguson is news. Racing was strictly his hobby, but even that is big news. The knight from Govan and his horse's co-owners would later find out that anything even remotely attached to the magic name of United is worthy of media attention – public demand makes it so.

The combination of Ferguson's colours and a potential champion racehorse was irresistible to some editors. By the end of that racing season, some newspapers would be speculating about Ferguson leading in a Derby winner at Epsom, and, of course, by the end of Rock Of Gibraltar's first year at stud, no newspaper in the land could avoid the story of Rocky and his 'connections': that succinct racing term which just means his owners and trainer.

I will confess now that I had not travelled to Doncaster to see Rocky. I was actually in pursuit of Ferguson, in order to interview him for my newspaper, *Scotland on Sunday*. I knew he had owned or co-owned horses for three or four years up to that point and had enjoyed some success, though not at the very highest level. Now that he owned a 'proper' horse, I was fascinated by the idea that Ferguson, who had announced his forthcoming retirement from his managerial position, might be on the verge of increasing his racing interests, as he had hinted he might do. Could this man who had been so successful in one sphere of sport then repeat the dose in another, entirely different pursuit? Would the 'Fergie' approach to managing Manchester United also work when he applied his formidable talents to horse racing, which, in its own way, is very much a team sport? The answer to my question about his future would have to wait for a few weeks. I didn't get close to Ferguson that day, for the simple reason that he is never easy to grab when his mind is on other things, such as a bet. Yet, though I'm no Mountie, I did eventually get my man.

It was not the first time I had seen Rock Of Gibraltar or backed him, however. Thanks to satellite television in my local bookmaker's shop, I had seen Rocky run at Royal Ascot and York. I wish I could say that I had followed his career from the off, but his first race, a maiden stakes at The Curragh, had not been on my list of 'must see' races – I've lost far too much money betting in Britain to lose even more on juvenile races in Ireland.

Before Royal Ascot, an Irish friend had tipped him to me as a good each-way shot in the Coventry Stakes, and though I was not convinced Rocky could beat the hot favourite Meshaheer, I decided to go with the tip. I had my usual few quid each-way on him at 10–1 – generous odds for an O'Brien horse, I thought – just before the off. Rocky was bumped rotten after only a furlong and got trapped behind a horde of flailing colts and fillies in a very rumbustious race. He just couldn't get out, but still showed pace inside the final furlong to finish sixth behind Aidan O'Brien's supposed second string, Landseer. I made an appropriate mental note to send my Irish pal to Coventry for failing to alert me to the chance of Landseer. It was worth the loss of the money, however, to put Rocky in the notebook as a sure-fire winner in future, maybe even next time out. Unfortunately, his 'next time out' had been at The Curragh in early July and I had been on holiday, so had missed the Group 3 Anheuser Busch Railway Stakes in which Rocky had hacked up by two lengths at the short odds of 1–2.

The next race was the historic Gimcrack Stakes at York. By then, the deal had been done for Ferguson to co-own Rocky with John Magnier. Mrs Susan Magnier's striking plain dark blue colours are normally used on jockeys riding horses which the Magniers own, but part of the co-ownership deal with Ferguson was that he would have his colours carried by the jockeys on board Rocky. For the first time aboard Rocky, Kinane rode in the manager's distinctive red and white silks.

THE ULTIMATE RACEHORSE

Football always comes first for Ferguson, though, and United had a match that night against Blackburn Rovers, so preparing for that encounter took priority. He did keep the team bus waiting while he watched the race, however.

That afternoon at York was to be payback time for Royal Ascot, I thought, but I couldn't make it to the Knavesmire, the majestic course in that beautiful city, because the next day I was heading to Finland to cover their round of the World Rally Championship and interview Scotland's former world champion Colin McRae. In my local bookmaker's shop, I was sure enough to invest a whole crisp 'pinkie' – my term for one of those £50 notes I rarely see – on the nose. I managed to get on at odds of 5-2 and thought I'd got a bargain, only for Rocky to drift to 11-4, meaning I would win only £125 when I could have had £137.50 if he won. Just my luck, as usual.

I can honestly say that this was one of the few occasions in my betting life when I didn't have to panic or even get excited. I can recall with some clarity that, as I watched Rocky breaking from the starting stalls at York, I didn't even whisper a 'come on, boy' or 'get moving, Mick' because I knew with absolute certainty from about, oh, the second furlong that Rock Of Gibraltar was going to win and win handsomely, which he duly did.

I felt sorry for Linda Perratt, the Scottish trainer I knew and had often written about, because her horse Ho Choi did very well to finish second, and she rarely had horses good enough to contest juvenile Group 2 races. But a win's a win, and if you've bet the winner you don't really care – it's your horse and hang the rest as long as the notes are in your hand. I also knew that plenty of Linda's followers, not to mention Ho Choi's gentlemanly owner Alan Guthrie, a Scot with strong links to Hong Kong, would have had a goodly sum each-way on a colt whose starting price was 33-1.

While decent horses floundered in his wake, it seemed to me that Rocky had won with a lot in reserve, and he was definitely a fast horse able to cruise along and then kick into top gear – a very valuable asset in a colt who would clearly be aimed at the one-mile Classic, the 2,000 Guineas, the following year. I made a mental note to follow him, and not just because he was now running for Sir Alex Ferguson.

ROCK OF GIBRALTAR

A few weeks after York, in that Doncaster parade ring, I cannot honestly say that Rocky stood out from the rest of the magnificent colts at first glance. But as he moved around, I noticed that he was indeed different from the others. I could not quite put my finger on it, but after a while I was entranced. He was in gorgeous condition, supremely fit, as you would expect from any top horse trained by O'Brien at his world-beating Ballydoyle stables. The muscles moved rhythmically under a sleekly burnished bay hide. This light skin colouring contrasted pleasingly with pronounced darker areas on his face and legs, as is common in bay horses. His gait indicated that he had a surfeit of barely controlled vigour, which gave a curious sense of oversizing to an animal that was clearly in perfect proportion. Somehow, he just seemed bigger than the others, even though he wasn't really that much taller or heavier than most of them.

If you are not a fan of the racetrack yourself, you may think people are daft to sit and gawk at a horse doing nothing other than walk, but watching a horse being led round a paddock and parade ring is one of the sport's simple joys. It can also be very instructive, just as you can often tell something about a human from the way they walk.

In Billy Wilder's classic film comedy *Some Like It Hot*, for instance, there's a memorable scene that tells you a lot about men and the way they often look at women. Tony Curtis and Jack Lemmon play musicians forced to dress up as women and join a female band to escape gangsters. They are standing in drag on a Chicago railway platform when Marilyn Monroe walks ahead of them. The word 'walk' doesn't do justice to her way of putting one foot in front of the other, though, as the activity has never looked so good on celluloid. Monroe walked the way Michelangelo sculpted – perfectly.

Curtis and Lemmon become utterly captivated, and the latter utters Wilder's immortal description of Monroe's seductive wiggle – 'jello on springs'. This, believe it or not, was the feeling I got when I watched Rock Of Gibraltar parading for the first time. His name, combined with his walk, conjured images of Marilyn Monroe's classy chassis rocking from side to side, and I knew from this moment that 'Rocky' was going to be something special when he got onto the track. He just had a perfect rhythm – he bounced, he sprang, he *sashayed* around that ring.

Before the race itself, as Rocky trotted away down the track to the start, I was surprised to notice that his hind quarters were larger than I expected in a horse whose future was expected to be in mile races or further. I remember thinking he had the big muscular backside of a 'sprinter'. Like humans, horses are usually programmed by their parents' genes as to what distance they can run. On the Flat, a sprinter is a horse that can only compete over five or six furlongs at most, while a miler like Rocky will campaign at seven furlongs or a mile, and a middle-distance horse is best at ten to twelve furlongs and a 'stayer', as the name suggests, goes over longer distances from one mile six furlongs to as much as two miles six furlongs, the longest distance of any race on the Flat in Britain. Over the jumps, there are similar divisions, with some horses just managing to last the minimum distance of two miles over hurdles or steeplechase fences, while others can 'stay' all day. Bizarrely, some sprinters eventually become stayers, and the best-known example is Red Rum, who was fast enough to win over six furlongs on the Flat yet won three Aintree Grand Nationals and was second twice in that marathon, which is the longest race in Britain at four miles and four furlongs. Many racehorses defy their DNA and race as sprinters or stayers when they should be the opposite, but as you will see later, racehorses are often *sui generis* and the study of them is not an exact science.

In the Doncaster ring, Rock Of Gibraltar looked almost like a sprinter to me, but the reports from Ballydoyle and my own observations had convinced me he was going to be best at a mile. Perhaps he would be that rare creature of wonder, a horse with sprinting speed that could stay a mile.

He definitely had a delicious movement. He did not have too much of an exaggerated wiggle, which is sometimes the sign of a horse with an ungainly running style, but there was an obvious, almost jaunty, swing in his walk. It was something about his attitude, however, which made me lean over the parade ring rail and really study the horse.

It is always dangerous, even foolish, to ascribe human qualities to horses. Although they can be moody, lazy and downright cussed, just like us, horses usually have a reason for such behaviour, perhaps because of physical pain, while the human species never needs an excuse to be objectionable. Yet I thought Rocky looked as if he had an air about him of a particularly athletic class of human being I have come to know well in my trade as a sportswriter – the professional boxer.

Like horses, boxers have to be supremely fit to do their job well, and the very best exponents of the fistic arts have an intensity about them, a focus, which is displayed at its most public in the moments when they make their way into the ring. At such times, the best boxers are not unconscious, but they are, as Americans say, in 'the zone' – that private and secret place that top sportspeople inhabit when their concentration is total. Boxers do hear the crowd's roar, they always pay attention to their cornermen, and some even listen to what the referee tells them about keeping the Marquis of Queensberry's rules. But mostly they are intent on only one thing – getting the job started in the most dangerous arena in sport.

Prior to all his races, Rocky was always alert and watchful. Sometimes, he got too frisky, for he knew where he was and what he was going to have to do – race, and win.

That day at Doncaster, I saw his eyes taking in the scene around him with some intelligence. The superb portrait which adorns the back cover of this book is by the brilliant young Irish equine artist Ester Barrett, one of three painting sisters with their own gallery in Co. Limerick. Ester has perfectly captured the look I saw in his handsome face that day. Some horses have 'dead' eyes before or after a race. As Ester shows, however, Rocky's eyes are the kind that never glaze.

As he pulled his way around the ring and cantered down to the start, I also got an impression of his sheer latent power, like a Ferrari engine idling in neutral awaiting Michael Schumacher's foot on the pedal.

Before some of his earlier races, Rock Of Gibraltar had reportedly misbehaved and displayed that nervous-aggressive behaviour that is called coltish – even when fillies do it. Two year olds are, after all, the equine equivalent of teenage brats, and are inclined to act the goat, especially in public. At Doncaster, Rocky was again on his toes and acting the monkey, all right, but I also noticed that, like a champion boxer, he was partially reining himself in, keeping himself ready to race, a prizefighter conserving his energy for the opening bell. I knew, I just *knew*, he was going to win. The famous catchphrase of the boxing ring announcer Michael Buffer – 'let's get ready to rumble' – came into my mind and, misbegotten soul that I am, I abandoned my contemplation of this beautiful prodigy in favour of the pursuit of filthy lucre. I dashed headlong in the direction of the bookmakers' ring, because I was sure that Rocky was a heavyweight champion who was going to topple any four-hooved challenger.

Watching him pulling up at the start on the Doncaster turf, nothing changed my nascent view that Rock Of Gibraltar was hugely impressive in the flesh. I now made Rocky my banker bet of the whole Doncaster meeting – if he lost, I was finished with punting that day – and had managed to get on at 5-4 before he went off the 11-10 favourite.

Something nagged me, however, about the only possible danger I had seen in the parade ring, which was Dubai Destination, owned by Sheikh Mohammed and trained by David Loder, who at that time prepared the Sheikh's horses as two year olds. The best of them went on to Sheikh Mohammed's elite Godolphin stable where the trainer is former policeman Saeed Bin Suroor. Many of the Godolphin horses become champions before going off to the Sheikh's studs, just as Ballydoyle prepares champions for Coolmore. Frankie Dettori was on board the colt, and the normally ebullient Italian superstar of racing was pensive before the race, which is always a sure-fire sign that he is up to something.

Frankie and Loder were indeed up to a ruse, and Rocky came off the worst as their plan worked perfectly. They were going to use a pacemaker, a horse from the same stable which sets the correct pace at the front of a race to ensure that a better horse from the stable gets the exact galloping speed it needs to show its best turn of foot. With the wily old fox Willie Ryan in its saddle, Loder's other entrant, a no-hoper called Ice And Fire, set off to make the running as pacemaker. Ryan has carried out this thankless role so often in his career he could do it in his sleep, and he is a supreme judge of pace. In his capable hands, Ice And

Fire did exactly what he was supposed to do – dictate the race speed for Dubai Destination to come from behind and win in the final furlong.

Which is precisely what happened. I could see it coming even as they turned into the straight. Rock Of Gibraltar cruised into the lead but Kinane would have had a fit if he could have seen what was happening behind him. Frankie was moving stealthily forward with Dubai Destination on a tight rein, and then he pressed the button and Rock Of Gibraltar and my hard-earned cash were toast. Dubai Destination went to the front right through the pack like a long jumper vaulting clean over the pit, and though I knew my money was lost, I couldn't help but go 'whoosh' as Dettori's horse accelerated.

I'd better explain what a 'whoosh' moment is. In June of that year, 2001, I had been in the press gallery at Epsom for Derby day. I was standing next to the peerless Hugh McIlvanney, who was covering the race for the *Sunday Times*. Hugh McIlvanney and his mentor, John Rafferty of *The Scotsman*, are largely the reasons I became a sportswriter, as their elegant prose and inspirational passion for sport made a huge impression on me more years ago than I wish to contemplate. After many years in various forms of journalism, I had still hankered after the chance to write about sport, and when an opportunity eventually came my way in a roundabout manner, I thought of Rafferty and McIlvanney and went for it. So a few years later, there I was standing beside the great man watching the Derby from the best vantage point other than Her Majesty's box. As you do.

Hugh loves his racing and truly appreciates great horses and horsemanship, though he'll admit to coming off worst against the bookmakers on occasion. He also had a wee problem with his laptop computer that day and I was able to help him, and we ended up preparing to watch the Derby side-by-side and chatting about a mutual friend, my former boss, the nonpareil Scottish journalist Andrew Fyall, who is one of Hugh's great friends. Hugh is also a long-time admirer of both the O'Briens of Ballydoyle, and Aidan O'Brien had a wonderful colt in that Derby called Galileo. I suspected Aidan and the mighty Vincent would both have told Hugh to bet the Ballydoyle contender, but if Hugh had the information he wasn't telling me. The fact is, though, I strongly fancied that year's 2,000 Guineas winner Golan, who was an early favourite for the race. I'd also bumped into Galileo's jockey, Mick Kinane, just as an Irish journalist asked him, 'Is he up for it?' Kinane's knowing smile said everything we needed to know and gave me a real quandary – Galileo or Golan?

The binoculars were up as we watched Galileo canter easily down to the start. The impressively handsome colt was then 11–4 joint favourite with Golan, who looked in the pink, and for once in my often senseless betting career, I thought out my plan. So by post time, I didn't care which of the two won as long as one finished in first place and the other came second, because I had invested my pocket money on a bet known as the Reverse Exacta on the Tote, racing's national 'pool' betting system. With the Reverse Exacta bet, you just have to pick first and second in either order. Sounds easy, but it is often fiercely difficult. For purely aesthetic reasons, I ended up wanting Galileo to win – I just didn't fancy seeing another headline about 'Golan hitting the Heights', while surely there was plenty in the life of Galileo Galilei to inspire any newspaper sub-editor, even those who had not heard of the play by Bertolt Brecht.

As the race started, the concentration was intense in the press gallery high above the finishing line, and as the Derby field rounded Tattenham Corner and entered the straight, Kinane had manoeuvred Galileo into prime position to deliver a winning run. He was lying in third place, cruising at a decent pace, while trainer Barry Hills' pair, Mr Combustible and Perfect Sunday, were ahead of him. It seemed to us all in that press room that it was just a question of when Kinane would set his horse loose.

Some two-and-a-bit furlongs out, Kinane said 'go' and Galileo took off. It was an astonishing surge of acceleration, a demonstration of power and class and all the ingredients that make a top-class racehorse a thing of sheer animal beauty. In the space of a few dozen yards, he had sprinted by the first two and was clear of the field and in a different gear, on a different planet, from those behind him. As Galileo blasted off, beside me I distinctly heard Hugh McIlvanney exude a noise of wonder and awe that was somewhere between a 'phwoar', a 'whoof' and a 'gosh', so the rules of onomatopoeia determine that it must be rendered as 'whoosh'.

Galileo was poetic in his stylish domination. He sauntered home in the second-fastest time ever recorded for the Blue Riband, and was immediately and correctly hailed as a superstar, and I picked up £286 for my massive £40 outlay with the Tote. Ever since that Derby day, when I see a horse quicken up spectacularly and leave his opponents for dead, I think of Galileo and Hugh McIlvanney, and call it a 'whoosh' moment.

Three months or so after the Derby, the problem for Rock Of Gibraltar in the final furlong of the Champagne Stakes was that Dubai Destination had whooshed right by him and, though Kinane tried to conjure up a late run from Rocky, it was Frankie's day – damn and blast him! I cursed my luck for all of a few seconds and then deduction and reason took over. Punters always need to make intellectual excuses for themselves when they have backed the wrong horse, rather than admit that they just got it plain wrong. 'Dirty trick of Loder and Dettori, using that pacemaker when Rocky didn't have one,' was one train of thought. 'Kinane will really need to get spectacles for those eyes in the back of his head,' was another. The truth was that, on the day, the better horse and jockey combination deservedly won the race. But had Rocky's bubble burst? Was he going to be an also-ran in the big races that lay ahead of him?

On watching the replay over and over again later on the Doncaster racecourse video recorder, I saw something that stuck in my mind. I became convinced that Rock Of Gibraltar would be a better horse over longer distances because he stayed on so strongly in the final furlong despite the fact that he was obviously going to lose the race. Way back in its history on the plains of Asia, Arabia or wherever, the ancestor of the thoroughbred racehorse was a herd animal, and it's amazing how quickly many horses, even refined thoroughbreds, revert to type and give up the chase when the leader of the pack races by them. Not Rock Of Gibraltar – this guy was obviously a fighter, and there did not seem to be any sacrifice of his basic speed as the race went on.

From that Doncaster day onwards, I took much greater interest in Rocky, and it was not just because he won me some goodly sums that I became a fan of the colt, as did so many other people. Perhaps it was his speed, his courage and just the way he went about his racing that attracted us and made him a hero. Or perhaps it was something intangible, maybe a feeling that you are somehow attached to greatness when you alight on a particularly wonderful horse and follow its career to glory.

Yet there was something else, apart from his obvious winning habit, which made Rock Of Gibraltar so popular. And yes, part of that was to do with his celebrity, the media attention, and his glamorous connection to the most famous football manager probably of all time. To truly understand Rocky's appeal, however, you have to put him in the context of what happened to racing in Britain early in each of the two years in which he raced – 2001 and 2002.

Rocky began his career in April of the former year, and his arrival coincided with a national release from the purdah caused by an outbreak of foot-and-mouth disease. Britain was under a cloud in the spring of 2001 – literally so, in many parts of the country. Foot-and-mouth disease spread like wildfire through the nation's cow and sheep population, and the drastic measure of destroying healthy and infected livestock alike in all the areas in which it appeared was taken to quell it. The disease ravaged entire rural communities and set 'city slickers' against 'country folk', as if the latter were somehow to blame for the former's demand for cheap food, which, as with mad cow disease, was the underlying cause for the unhygienic practices that spread the epidemic. For fear of humans transmitting the disease by carrying it out of infected sites on their shoes or clothing, parts of the countryside became virtual no-go areas. Consequently, many aspects and fixtures of rural life ground to a halt – not least of all horse racing. The annual highlight of the National Hunt season, the Cheltenham Festival, was called off, because the racecourse was close to an infected area. Driving down to Aintree for the Grand National, which itself at one point had been under threat of postponement or cancellation, I was appalled when the acrid smell of burnt meat hit me on the M74 north of Gretna. On the M6 in Cumbria, I could see entire dales lying under a dread-inspiring pall of grey-blue smoke, and the stench was sickening. It was like a scene from some documentary on the aftermath of a bombing raid, only this inferno had been fuelled by flesh. Only then did I realise the full extent of the horror that foot-and-mouth had brought to rural Britain. The television pictures could not do justice to the abyss into which decent farming folk had been plunged. If more people from towns and cities had actually visited the bonfires constructed of perfectly healthy animals, then sympathy would have been more forthcoming.

That year's Grand National went ahead, though many people wished it had not done so. It was quite simply the worst running of the National in years. The rain poured incessantly all day and turned the course into a bog. Any other race would have been called off, but there is only one Aintree National a year and vested interests, i.e. those with monetary income depending on the great race, would have screamed blue murder if the race had been cancelled.

There was nearly death on the track as a result of the misguided decision to let the race proceed. Horses fell, slipped up, brought down others and just simply became exhausted in the bottomless ground. Only four horses finished and two of them had to be remounted after falling, while Red Marauder, who was well known for loving the mud, won as he liked at the bookie-pleasing odds of 33–1. I had gone to the Canal Turn to watch the race, and saw a dreadful pile-up on the first circuit happen right in front of my stunned eyes. That no horse or jockey was seriously injured in that grotesque mêlée was a miracle. I also ruined a perfectly good pair of boots walking to the press centre where I appeared to the denizens like Nanook of the North caught in a rain shower on a melting polar ice cap.

It wasn't a good time to be in racing – indeed, it wasn't a good time to be in Britain, period. Misery was played out across the television screens every night. At least the farmers and agricultural businesses got some financial compensation for their losses. Shamefully, racing did not receive anything of any note from the Government, and though some racecourses were able to claim insurance for cancellations, many trainers and jockeys lost large sums of money and owners were unable to race their horses. Trainers, jockeys and owners alike received not a single penny of worthwhile compensation, and not a few people simply left the industry there and then.

Foot-and-mouth was gradually conquered and, in the early part of the 2001 Flat season, the search was on for superstar horses to capture the public's imagination and get them back to the racetrack, though at most courses you still had to traipse through disinfectant upon entry. At Hamilton Park, I swear I saw a woman take off her brand new shoes and walk barefoot across the chemically loaded mats. She had somewhat missed the point.

Fortunately, British and Irish racing was about to witness one of the best seasons in living memory. It was full of fantastic horses, and the quite incredible feats of Aidan O'Brien made it into a vintage year. By the end of the year, he had set a new world record by winning 23 Group 1 victories in 5 countries, and his position as the finest trainer in Europe was unquestionable.

The horses from Ballydoyle and elsewhere were just sublime: Golan in the 2,000 Guineas; Imagine in the Irish 1,000 Guineas and the Oaks; Galileo in the Derby, the Irish Derby and the King George; Black Minnaloushe in the St James's Palace Stakes at Royal Ascot; Royal Rebel winning the first of his two Ascot Gold Cups for Mark Johnston; Noverre winning the French 2,000 Guineas (he lost it later after a failed dope test) and the Sussex Stakes; Mozart's red-hot dash in the July Cup; Nayef's marvellous Champion Stakes; Fantastic Light and Frankie Dettori in the Prince of Wales's Stakes, plus his win over Galileo in the Irish Champion Stakes; Milan's St Leger; and Frankie again aboard Sakhee in the Juddmonte International and, above all, the duo's wonderful performance in the Prix de l'Arc de Triomphe. And those were just some of the horses and Group 1 races which enthralled us.

The other big races were just as special – Mediterranean's Ebor Handicap and Continent's Ayr Gold Cup wins spring readily to mind. As for the two year olds, that season was to produce not one but three superstars, all from one stable. To paraphrase Shakespeare, one was born great and showed it as a two year old, the second horse achieved greatness at two and three through the speed of his hooves and the size of his heart, and the third had greatness thrust upon him almost accidentally at four.

The second of the trio was Rock Of Gibraltar, which neatly

points up the conundrum which had many observers, such as myself, quite confused when I first began to seriously follow his career in the autumn of 2001 – why was he only the third-rated of O'Brien's juvenile hopes? The top two year old of the 2001 season by some way was reckoned to be Rocky's stablemate Johannesburg. Sired by Hennessy, a Grade 1 winner in America, and a grandson of prodigious sire Storm Cat, Johannesburg blew away all opposition as a juvenile. Running in the colours of Michael Tabor, the former East End bookmaker turned millionaire partner of John Magnier at Coolmore, Johannesburg won his maiden race at Fairyhouse in Ireland at odds of 1–3 – obviously the jungle telegraph had sung about his potential. The Norfolk Stakes at Royal Ascot and the Anglesey Stakes at The Curragh were won at a canter, and the Group 1 Phoenix Stakes was taken in astonishing fashion, the colt winning by five lengths easing down.

The Group 1 Prix Morny at Deauville followed, despite Johannesburg losing a shoe in mid-race. The Group 1 Middle Park Stakes was another easy success, and then came the magnificent seventh, a breathtaking display in the colt's juvenile race at the Breeders' Cup at Belmont Park. Even the normally grudging American trainers fell over themselves to praise a European raider who looked every inch a world beater. Bob Baffert, who held the world record for Group 1 wins (though the top races are known as Grade 1 in the USA) until O'Brien beat him that year, said, 'You could see the greatness in the way he moved. For him to come over and just toy with our colts – our Breeders' Cup horses – like that, shows he is above the rest.' But in the *Racing Post*, their race reporter after the Middle Park proved almost prophetic with his verdict by writing, 'It is also worth noting that he is by no means the strapping sort of colt you would expect to be better at three than two.'

And brilliant though Johannesburg was, he wasn't actually the fastest two year old in O'Brien's armoury at that point. That horse was Hawk Wing, one of the finest and unluckiest horses to emerge in these isles in recent years.

Hawk Wing is a very handsome horse and beautifully bred. His sire, Woodman, was a champion at stud and his dam, La Lorgnette, was a granddaughter of Nijinsky, the last British colt to win racing's ultimate challenge, the Triple Crown. La Lorgnette was a Classic winner in her own right in Canada. Hawk Wing was nothing less than sensational as a two year old, breaking the seven-furlong track record at The Curragh, not just for two year olds but for all ages – an astonishing feat by a juvenile.

In Chapter Ten, I will explain why Hawk Wing is the true pointer to the greatness of Rock Of Gibraltar. For neither Hawk Wing nor Johannesburg became the ultimate racehorse. Instead, that title would go to the horse which had once been ranked behind them.

When I first saw him in the flesh, Rock Of Gibraltar was already pretty special, but no one knew how fantastic he would be for the sport of racing. Nor would anyone have dreamed of the plot that would make him famous far beyond the narrow confines of racing. Why did this horse become so great, and why did he end up as the fabulous prize in a battle between giants?

For a partial answer to those questions, you need to understand how Rocky's very essence is at the heart of this story. As you will see in the next chapter, he stands at the end of a long line of ancestors stretching back more than 300 years, and he is the careful product of centuries of human-managed evolution of a beautiful species.

As we shall also see, Rock Of Gibraltar would go on to make history, but we have to proceed by stages if you are to properly realise why he was able to break records, and why he became worth a king's ransom. And let's start at the very beginning. For as Messrs Rodgers and Hammerstein once wrote, it's a very good place to start.

CHAPTER TWO

Genes Worth Fighting For

To understand why the stallion Rock Of Gibraltar became the ultimate racehorse and the fabulous prize in the biggest game of 'stud' poker ever played in these islands, it is necessary to know about his most precious commodity – his genes. Even before he was born, they were worth millions, and now that he is at stud in Ireland and Australia, they are worth tens of millions. Welcome to the strange and expensive world of horse breeding.

For the avoidance of doubt, this brief explanation of breeding largely concerns horses that run on the Flat. The breeding of National Hunt horses obviously uses the same basic procreational process, but foals intended to go over the jumps are often kept away from sales to mature at stud farms or training stables. Owners who specialise in National Hunt horses are some of the most patient people you will meet in sport, happy to wait until a horse is four or five or older before letting it loose on the track.

That humans 'breed' horses has always been a mystery to some. As with any arcane science it has its own nomenclature, but breeding is actually pretty straightforward. You peruse the stud books (catalogues of stallions and mares) and check out the ancestry of the potential mum and dad – their bloodlines – to see

GENES WORTH FIGHTING FOR

what pairing of stallion and dam might best produce a champion over the distance you have in mind. You choose a mare – or perhaps you already own it – and send it to a stud to mate with your preferred stallion. There are all sorts of fees and payments and sharing arrangements involved, but that is up to the humans. The horses just get on with nature, and never complain. At least, not in writing.

The actual deed should happen preferably in the spring. As all horses share the same notional birthday of 1 January (in the calendar year in which they are born), it is vital to have a colt or filly born as early in the late winter or early spring as can be risked. Too early – as in any time before 1 January – and the horse will be classed as one year older than one born any time on or after 1 January. Given that horses can and do have premature births, most breeders allow two or three months to cater for this and aim for a foal to arrive in February or March at the earliest. As the gestational period of a horse is 11 months, and since stallions can't read calendars, most of the enjoyable bit of procreation needs to be forced to happen in the spring. This apes nature, as horses have been programmed by evolution to be happier when they see sunshine. It is worth remembering, next time you are betting, that a bit of sun makes a male horse run faster, but can lend jet propulsion to the hooves of a reluctant filly.

Life being too short, we'll omit such subtleties here as secondary bloodlines and out-cross breeding, and we'll not even dare mention artificial insemination, which is still taboo in thoroughbred breeding. (If you really want to get into breeding, call the BHB or check their website: www.bhb.co.uk.)

When the mare is ready to mate, she is often introduced to a 'teaser'. This is usually a substitute stallion, though he can be a gelding who has kept his sex appeal despite losing the necessary equipment. It's not the worst job being a teaser, because you do get to meet a lot of nice females – it's just that you don't get any of the real action.

The teaser's job is to do the equine foreplay and get the mare all hot and bothered and ready to meet the love of her life (usually a different one each year, but hey, who said horses were fussy?) with the substitute usually staying on the other side of a fence when the consummation occurs, like bishops during the reign of King Henry VIII. The 'main man', then, does what comes naturally, though sometimes with human help. The greatest sire of recent decades, Northern Dancer, about whom we will learn more later, was the Alan Ladd of breeding, and, like the diminutive film star, the vertically challenged sire famously needed to be positioned on a platform to stay in shot, so to speak.

Most stallions and mares manage perfectly well, and after the deed is done the mare is packed off back to her home, while the stallion presumably goes for a beer or a smoke or something, to await the next arrival. There are 10,000 mares in Britain and only 430 stallions – it's good to be a sire!

Having been in 'touch' with its father for precisely as long as the moment of conception, the foal usually never sees dear old dad again, unless he ends up in the same stud, which happens but rarely, as with the ill-fated Danehill and Rock Of Gibraltar, and Sadler's Wells and his sons Galileo and High Chaparral. And yes, fathers, sons, brothers and half-brothers in some studs will occasionally share the odd 'girlfriend' or two, not that there's anything wrong with that in the equine moral universe.

Fertility rates of even the best sires and mares can often be just 50 or 60 per cent – and it's always the female's fault, of course. If all goes well, though, the mare will soon be found to be 'in foal', at which point you had better see the bank manager as you will then be liable for the stud fee. The standard arrangement is no foal, no fee, and you pay up on a given date, which, in the case of Coolmore Stud is always 1 October following the foaling date. Anything that happens to mare and foal after that date is your problem.

All being well, around 11 months after the indelicate transaction, out will pop a foal.

Sometimes, the stud will do a deal with you, as some insist on retaining shares in the foal, especially if there are top stallions or mares with renowned bloodlines involved, but usually it's up to you to decide what to do with your expensive acquisition, often with the advice of a trainer or bloodstock agent. If it is 'well made' and has decent bloodlines, then you can sell the foal immediately or wait until it becomes a yearling, i.e. after its first 1 January

GENES WORTH FIGHTING FOR

birthday. Or else you keep it for racing, in which case you get to give the horse its name – anything up to 18 characters including spaces but no swear words or rude bits.

You then send it to a trainer, who usually employs a specialist to 'break in' the horse and teach it to carry a human, after which it lives a life of luxury interrupted only by the tiresome business of training on the 'gallops' at its stables, and occasionally going to the racecourse. Racing it or selling it, either way the horse will make you millions, or at least that's the theory. The horse then retires to stud and the lucky owners, which may well still be you, live off the proceeds. Simple, really, so what's all the fuss about?

To the uninitiated, which is the vast majority of us, the science of breeding is a secretive rite conducted almost in a vast global monastery. The brotherhood – though many breeders are 'sisters' – keep their knowledge to themselves and many only emerge into the glare of daylight at places such as Keeneland in the USA or Goffs in Ireland, which are the great auction pavilions of the racing world. These establishments are the sporting equivalent of Sotheby's or Christie's, except that the goods will often bite and kick as they are led into the sale. The prices, too, can often rival anything found in the very best fine art sale.

Conducting the business are auctioneers who rarely, if ever, miss the nod, wink, nose-touching or raised hand that signifies a bid. The fact is that the best and most experienced of them know exactly whom the bids will be coming from, and they can usually guess exactly how much of a price they can wring out of the often quiet and intense men who act as agents for the chief monks – the owners and trainers – sitting in their pews several rows back from the action. Does that mean that horse auctions are fixed? Not a bit of it, as the world found out one hot July day in 1985 at an unforgettable yearling sale.

The yearling sales are the most important auctions of horses. As the name suggests, when colts and fillies are a year old, if an owner thinks they can make a profit at that stage, they will be packed off to the auction barns. The buyers are often people who think they can spot a bargain in an untried horse that is still a year away from even seeing a racecourse. It is a huge risk. As thousands of owners and millions of punters have discovered to their cost after the event, many horses turn out to be useless at actually racing and simply want to be left alone to roll about in the hay or gambol in the fields.

Research is all-important before the purchase takes place, and in no sense would any sensible buyer be like a motorist walking up to a garage and buying a car on its looks alone. On the contrary, most buyers of yearlings or older horses will have spent weeks and often months studying the lots coming up at auction, poring over the vital stud books produced by the breeders, which give details of the horse's entire ancestry back through many generations. In general, a buyer, usually an expert bloodstock agent or a trainer on the lookout for horses for clients, will have a budget with which to work. The agents or trainers are usually acting for owners often thousands of miles away but in constant touch by telephone, though sometimes owners will take a rather more 'hands on' approach and attend the sale in person, not least because they may be about to spend a lot of money and because sometimes the sales are genuinely exciting, with rounds of applause greeting the most spectacular prices.

In July 1985, in Lexington in Kentucky, USA, the prices were not just spectacular – they were stratospheric. Two years previously, at Keeneland, a new world record had been set for the price of a yearling, when agents acting on the instructions of Sheikh Mohammed and the Maktoum family – the royal family of Dubai whose oil-based wealth is a licence to print money – went against a consortium led by British multi-millionaire Robert Sangster in the bidding for a son of Northern Dancer. Sangster was the public face of a group which included the world's top trainer, Vincent O'Brien, and one of the world's richest men, Greek shipping magnate Stavros Niarchos. They had money to burn, while the Maktoum family had a veritable inferno of oil money after the vast escalation in prices of crude in the 1970s.

At the Keeneland sale of 1983, the bidding just kept going up and up, and the Maktoums eventually won with a bid of $10.2 million, equal to around £7 million in UK sterling. Headlines around the world heralded the sale and not a few newspapers commented that the horse was a symbol of the greed-driven times and the profligacies of the Arab Sheikhs. Many pundits spoke and

GENES WORTH FIGHTING FOR

wrote of the clash between East and West, but it was really an egotistical bidding duel about the need to get hold of that vital Northern Dancer bloodline – the colt was later named Snaafi Dancer, in a nod to his illustrious forebear. Two years later, on Tuesday, 23 July 1985, Sangster and the Sheikhs came back for round two at Keeneland, but this time there were other bidders set to join the party – and what a party it became! In charge of the auction was Tom Caldwell, arguably the best horse auctioneer in American history, whose family were steeped in the business and who had joined Keeneland in 1957. Caldwell died at the age of 72 in 2001, after 25 years in which he never missed a Keeneland sale as its director of auctions. The obituaries all mentioned his role on that extraordinary day in 1985.

Bidding for Sangster and his consortium, which comprised Vincent O'Brien, John Magnier, Stavros Niarchos and their American partner – stable-owner and millionaire Danny Schwarz – was Joss Collins. He died of liver cancer at the age of 56 in February 2004, mourned as the most respected bloodstock agent of his generation. In 1985, Collins was already well known in the world's auction rings as he had bought such horses as the great stallion Nureyev, who made his purchase price of $1.3 million many times over for Stavros Niarchos. He represented the British Bloodstock Agency for 30 years, and one of his trademarks was to wear brightly coloured shirts – no auctioneer could miss them, it was said. His obituaries also centred on that day at Keeneland.

With Collins as the front man and Vincent O'Brien working behind the scenes, the Sangster crew entered the fray early in the sale and bought a few yearlings, as did the other big hitters around the ring. But things hotted up very quickly when their principal target entered the ring – the 215th out of 295 horses in the catalogue for that July sale.

Opposing Collins were the Maktoums, who by that time knew that Snaafi Dancer was not going to be their best-ever buy, and may have been cautious as a result. Also known to be interested was the very rich owner Allen Paulson, the former pilot and founder of the Gulfstream jet company who would later go on to own Cigar, America's favourite horse of the 1990s, which won nearly $10 million in prize money. Paulson died in 2000 at the age of 78 and it is safe to say that he is the only major racehorse owner ever to have set 35 international flight speed records.

Another bidder was former advertising executive Cothran 'Cot' Campbell of Dogwood Stable, then located near Atlanta, Georgia, but now based in South Carolina. Campbell was the pioneer of the 'group ownership' concept, which is now the way in which most owners get involved, either through racing clubs such as Elite in Britain or by buying into partnerships often run by stables.

The principal other bidder, however, was Californian trainer D. Wayne Lukas, revered as one of America's top handlers over several decades, who was a former baseball coach and loved that sport so much he often spoke in baseball parlance. He was bidding on behalf of three very rich men: Eugene V. Klein, then the owner of the San Diego Chargers grid-iron football team; Melvin Hatley, a successful breeder with his own stables; and Texan millionaire Bob French.

The colt was stunningly handsome. He was the son of the legendary Nijinsky, who won the Triple Crown in 1970. The British Triple Crown – it's a nominal honour which carries no actual trophy – is captured only by colts who win the 2,000 Guineas over a mile, the Epsom Derby over one mile four furlongs and the St Leger over one mile six furlongs. Not surprisingly, it is a feat that is not regularly achieved, and indeed no colt has managed it since Nijinsky, although Oh So Sharp won the fillies equivalent of 1,000 Guineas, Oaks and St Leger in 1985. The colt was also in demand because his mother, My Charmer, had already produced Seattle Slew, America's champion racehorse of 1977. Another of her sons, Lomond, had won the 2,000 Guineas for Sangster and O'Brien in 1983.

There was a noticeable buzz of anticipation as the colt was shown to the crowd. Then the bidding began, with the prices being called by Caldwell and shown immediately on an electronic display on the wall of the sales hall. Caldwell started the bidding at $1 million and accepted bids that rose at intervals of $500,000. It was a feeding frenzy, with the Maktoums, Paulson, Campbell, Collins and Lukas all concentrating intensely as the price rose in the space of 60 amazing seconds to an astonishing $8 million.

On it went as even the mega-rich Dubai princes pulled out. The price reached $9.5 million before everyone took a breath, and it looked as though the top bid had been reached. Not a bit of it. Though the price now rose at $100,000 a time, the sale was still on. Now only the big two were left after Cot Campbell bid $10.1 million – by several millions, it would have been the most he would ever have paid for a horse – and pulled out after it was immediately topped by Wayne Lukas. As the bidding reached $10.3 million – the new world record – there were loud exclamations from the audience. Up ahead, the ringmaster in this hyperbolic circus, Tom Caldwell, could not resist a quip: 'You ain't seen nothin' yet!'

He was correct. Collins and Lukas pushed up the price to $11.1 million, at which point Lukas conferred with his clients before carrying on. The electronics couldn't keep up as the price rose inexorably to $12.5 million. Even the greatest of horse auctioneers could not keep going at this rate in such a rarefied atmosphere – 'How about $13 million and we can stop this?' said Caldwell. It was a clever move. In one leap, the price rose by $500,000 as Lukas took the hint and bid the sum that Caldwell was suggesting.

Joss Collins apparently did not bat an eyelid as he trumped the Americans by bidding $13.1 million, at that time something approaching £10 million in UK sterling terms. Gasps and oohs and aahs greeted the bid. It was a new world record price by $2.9 million. The Lukas camp was split, and the majority decided enough was enough. Lukas signalled it was over. The entire sale from start to finish had taken just ten minutes. Robert Sangster and his crew had their colt and amazingly it was for a price he and his cohorts had been prepared to pay – only later did it emerge that Sangster had predicted that the yearling would sell for anything up to $15 million.

As Caldwell declared the bidding closed, there was stunned awe in some sections of the hall, head-shaking in others, but mostly loud cheers and applause – Keeneland's people could be forgiven their joy as the commission on that one sale was $655,000. Also pretty pleased, to put it mildly, were the trio who had bred the colt and put it into the sale – Warner Jones of Hermitage Farm in Kentucky, Bill Kilroy of Houston, Texas, and the third man in that successful sales team, one William S. Farish, a banker from Texas who owned his own stud farm in Kentucky and who, in 2001, was appointed as America's ambassador to Great Britain, where he indulged his love of racing by owning several horses. One of them – Casual Look, trained by Andrew Balding – won the Epsom Oaks of 2003. If he were not such a pleasant gentleman, people might get seriously jealous of Mr Farish.

Media interest in the sale exploded. Most non-racing people just thought it absurd, while some serious racing commentators called for such sales to be stopped as the breeding and owning market could not sustain such prices and the 'ordinary owner' would be priced out of the game.

Sangster's consortium and their rivals said they would carry on regardless. With typical understatement, Vincent O'Brien said the record-breaking colt was 'a beautiful specimen', but Sangster revealed that the main reason for purchasing the colt, named Seattle Dancer in honour of his illustrious grandsires, was because they had bought just about every other product of the dam My Charmer. 'Buying this horse is not a gamble,' said Sangster. Oh yes it was.

It was the most expensive yearling ever sold at auction and, even in 2004, despite some 19 years of inflation in the 'normal' economy since that July day at Keeneland, the $13.1 million price of Seattle Dancer has never been in hailing distance since. It was the biggest and craziest day in bloodstock history, and what drove the price was not greed or envy but fear.

The Maktoums were afraid that Sangster would soon possess all the best bloodlines, while Sangster was worried that the Sheikhs would end his domination of the bloodstock markets. Lukas told the astonished press at Keeneland that fear of losing the colt to Europe had been the inspiration for the bid. 'We've lost a large number of the big sales horses to Europe in recent years. We wanted to keep this horse here.' He could not resist a baseball analogy, saying, 'We had already bought a lot of singles hitters. This colt would have been our clean-up hitter.'

The remark by Lukas about the need to keep the best horseflesh in the USA signalled a real concern on the part of the Americans that their racing – the best in the world, according to them – would suffer over the years as rich men from Europe or the Middle

East snaffled all the best stallions and broodmares. Lukas and many other American commentators had warned of the rise of the two principal threats to the USA's ownership and domination of the best bloodlines – the oil-rich Arab princes and the leading European breeding and training operation, Coolmore–Ballydoyle.

It was a situation replete with irony. The fear that the best of the species would start to travel west to east mirrored the concerns several decades earlier of the largely British owners and breeders who had dominated the world of horse racing until some way into the twentieth century. Decades before Americans started to worry about coming second, the Brits had been scared that America would swallow up the sires and mares which represented the best bloodlines in the species.

Those bloodlines were largely created in the British Isles. Indeed, the species is often known as the English Thoroughbred Racehorse. It is undoubtedly a typically British creation. This has long been a manufacturing nation, bringing in raw goods from abroad and turning them into saleable commodities. So it was with the racehorse.

Ancient texts show that, as long ago as AD 210, the Roman Emperor Septimus Severus imported Arabian-bred horses into Britain and races were held between native animals and the newcomers at Wetherby in Yorkshire, where there is a racecourse to this day. It is not known for certain whether the foreigners beat the local nags but, given that the Emperor, with his power of life and death over his citizens, was betting on his Arabians, it is a fair conclusion that the home side probably didn't try too hard.

The racing of horses was common both across the Roman Empire and elsewhere in the world, and in pre-Renaissance Italy horseraces were haphazardly organised and called *Pallii* after the headgear worn by horses in those days. The Palio in Siena, the famous race round the city's main square, is just one example of the mediaeval practice of entire communities pitching their best steed against the prize horse of other towns or districts. In Siena's case, the *contrade* – areas roughly equivalent to local government wards – would often bribe opponents or even kill them to get the best horse, such was the rivalry. Visit Siena on Palio day and you are stepping straight back into the fourteenth and fifteenth centuries. The whole day, with all its spectacle of flag-tossing and cacophony of bands, is centred on a race that takes less than two minutes to run and can be won by a riderless horse – the jockeys are often thrown as the horses fail to take the sharp corners of the Piazza del Campo.

Like so many other sports, however, it was the British who gave horse racing its modern framework – its rules and regulations. Racing as we know it today first became an organised sport in England in the sixteenth and seventeenth centuries, the most important development being the establishment of Newmarket as the 'headquarters' of British racing. Newmarket's pre-eminence owed much to King Charles II and his love of his mistress Nell Gwyn – their trysts away from London at Newmarket meant that members of his court had to follow His Majesty's gonads to Cambridgeshire. To this day, Good King Charles is the only reigning British monarch to have ridden a winner in a recognised horse race, the Newmarket Town Plate of 1671, which he had founded six years earlier. Above all, Charles II made racing fashionable – the Sport of Kings – and the aristocracy took to it with passion, sometimes fighting duels over unpaid wagers and the possession of the best animals.

During his reign, the King's courtiers, who were the equivalent of modern-day 'racing managers', were trying to improve the best British horse breeds. Many of these horses were descended from heavy cavalry chargers and even cart-pulling Shire horses, while other genetic influences came from imported breeds such as Andalusians from Spain. In simplistic terms, they were good, strong horses, but not very quick, whereas the other great horses of the era – the Arabians, prized by rulers throughout Europe and the Middle East – had both speed and stamina but not sheer strength and size.

If any date can be said to be the year in which racehorse breeding really began, it is 1689, when King William of Orange celebrated his recent accession to the British throne by founding the Royal Stud at Hampton Court Palace. In that year, a Captain Robert Byerley brought a horse into England – an Arabian stallion that he had captured at the siege of Buda in Hungary the previous year. The dark brown, almost black, horse was known as the

Byerley Turk, because it belonged to a captured Turkish officer. The horse gained its fame when it won a well-publicised race in Ireland, where Captain Byerley was serving King William, during which time it may well have charged at the Battle of the Boyne in 1690.

Standing at Byerley's home, Goldsborough Hall, the Turk sired many fine colts, but more important were his daughters – the mares which became known as Byerley's Jewels. The various 'families' established by the Turk can be traced down through their descendants to this day.

In 1704, Mr Thomas Darley, a merchant, was in Aleppo in Syria where he acquired a colt either by purchase or by more dubious means, i.e. a bribe. The colt belonged to the local sheikh and was a pure-bred Arabian from the famous Muniqui strain. Darley shipped the colt back home to his father, James, and he arranged for good local mares to be covered by the Arabian, producing stout progeny with Arabian speed.

One of those horses sired by the Darley Arabian was Childers, whose extraordinary speed secured his sire's reputation as a stallion. In those days, races took place over heaths such as Newmarket's or laid-out courses such as Epsom Downs or Ascot. The races were often matches between two horses, with prizes effectively being the wagers struck by the owners while side-bets were struck by friends, camp-followers and increasingly by that much put-upon group, the punters. There were no bookmakers at that time – hurrah!

The distance of a race could be anything up to six miles or more, but a four-mile gallop became the most commonly run race. By 1721, the six-year-old Childers was a huge public favourite, and had been given the nickname 'Flying' before winning one of the best documented races of those early years – a colossal victory over Speedwell in a four-mile contest at Newmarket. The Flying Childers Stakes, an important race for two year olds, is still run at Doncaster in his memory.

The third important horse to come to Britain in the eighteenth century was the Godolphin Arabian. This stallion was originally called Shami and was imported to Europe as a gift to the King of France from the Bey (ruler) of Tunisia. Acquired by the Duke of

Lorraine, who later became the Emperor Francis I of Germany, Shami was apparently uncontrollable, and a well-regarded English merchant, Edward Coke, took the horse off the Duke's hands as a favour and brought it back to Derbyshire. Coke died young, at the age of 32, and bequeathed the Arabian horse, who had calmed down in the bracing English air and was already siring champions, to his friend, the second Earl of Godolphin. He moved the horse to his stables near Newmarket, which are still extant, and the Godolphin Arabian began to sire winners such as Lath and Regulus, while his grandchildren included Highflyer, whose fame is commemorated in various racing-associated enterprises which bear his name.

These three horses – two Arabians and a Turk – are considered to be the founding fathers of the Thoroughbred Racehorse species. They all mated with dozens of English-bred mares to produce animals that were big, strong, fast and blessed with prodigious stamina. About 30 of these dams have been traced and are recognised as the 'founding mothers'. One of the Godolphin Arabian's granddaughters was Spiletta, daughter of Regulus. She was covered by Marske from the Darley Arabian line, and the mixture of Godolphin and Darley Arabian genes produced Eclipse, the greatest sire of champion racehorses the world has ever known.

The breeder who had the idea of mixing the two lines to produce Eclipse was the Duke of Cumberland, England's army general who had defeated Bonnie Prince Charlie's Scottish army – in Scotland he is still known as Butcher Cumberland because of the slaughter of Highland prisoners and wounded clansmen. Cumberland knew about horses as well as fighting and bred many fine champions, but never saw his greatest breeding achievement race, as he died in 1765, a year after the colt was born during the solar eclipse of 1764, hence his name.

Eclipse was simply unbeatable. In 18 races, he was never close to being caught and his normal winning distance over a standard distance of 4 miles was 200 yards. The popular phrase of the day was 'Eclipse first, the rest nowhere', coined by gambler Dennis O'Kelly, who won so much money on the horse that he ended up buying him. At stud, Eclipse proved, if anything, to be even more prodigious than on the track. Owners and breeders queued up to have their mares impregnated by Eclipse, to the exclusion of a lot of other stallions, though his son Highflyer actually produced more winners across the different ranks.

The result of Eclipse's efforts at stud can still be seen in the breed 230-odd years later, as 90 to 95 per cent of all thoroughbreds contain the DNA bequeathed to them by Eclipse. The great stallion died at the age of 24 and in the scientific spirit of the age he was dissected to see if the secret of his speed and stamina could be discovered – his massive heart was given the credit. Eclipse's skeleton can now be seen at the National Racing Museum at Newmarket.

The Jockey Club started their self-awarded role as the masters of the rules of racing in 1751 – the name coming from a word originally used to describe those who managed horses rather than the riders. The mainly aristocratic members – the Club is still a bastion of the Establishment to this day – did not want to get their hands dirty with the actual administrative work and hired the Newcastle-born lawyer James Weatherby. In 1791, he published the first volume of the *General Stud Book*, the forerunner of every stud book in the world and still the essential reference work for the breeding industry. Indeed, a thoroughbred is only accepted as such if its ancestors appear in Weatherby's book.

It is almost incredible that, after 200 years and more, Weatherby's direct descendants are still the administrative managers of British racing and continue to publish the *General Stud Book*, which is updated every four years and currently records the details of 30,000 mares worldwide. The reason why they continue in the job is quite obvious – the Weatherbys are very good at it.

For a mob who are noted for their rapacious instincts and who normally never allow people to get ahead of them, the bookmakers were slow onto the racing scene. Most wagers were struck between individuals, but the first man to 'make a book' and offer odds to all and sundry was called Ogden, and he did not start operations until 1795. If only Mr Ogden had stayed at home, how happy we punters might have been.

While racecourses sprang up everywhere and major races

became the highlights during what was developing into the racing 'season', over in Co. Cork in Ireland in 1752 two clearly insane local men – Edmund Blake and Cornelius O'Callaghan – bet each other a cask of wine over a race to find which of their hunters was the faster. Their innovation was that the race was across the country – fences, walls, ditches and all – from Buttevant Church to the steeple of St Leger Church at Doneraile nearly five miles away, hence 'steeplechasing'. We don't know who won, but thanks to them and the Irish jumps racing tradition which these two men started, Ireland is by far the leading producer of steeplechasing horses in Europe to this day.

Britain adopted the new version of the sport only slowly, and it wasn't until 1839 that the first Grand National was run at Aintree, by which time the race we know as the St Leger, the world's oldest Classic, run at Doncaster, was already 63 years old. The Derby, the Guineas and all the other venerable races in the annual calendar date from the eighteenth and nineteenth centuries. It is Britain's horseracing history, then, which has evolved over the past 300 years, that makes British racing special and gives it a high standing on the world circuit. In the last century or so, however, innovative challenges to British superiority in the sport have been made by nations with a less hidebound approach to owning, breeding and training racehorses.

Quality breeding was almost exclusively a British pursuit until late in the nineteenth century, but now Britain lags well behind other countries in a global industry that really took off when the United States of America became involved. Organised racing in America dates from the Victorian era, with the three Triple Crown races – the most historic races in the USA – being founded between 1867 and 1875. These three races – the Kentucky Derby at Louisville, the Preakness Stakes at Pimlico in Maryland and the Belmont Stakes at the track of the same name in New York – are still recognised as the supreme test of American horseflesh, and if a horse can win the first two legs and head to New York with the chance of the Triple Crown, then an entire nation stops to watch that race. It happened in 2004 with Smarty Jones, who just missed out on history by finishing second in the Belmont.

The first organised races on a racetrack in America had been recorded in 1665 in New York colony, the course being named Newmarket in honour of England's racing headquarters. Before the War of Independence, British horses were imported for the sole purpose of racing, mostly by Southern landowners, and each of the fledgling states soon began to enjoy organised racing, especially after the Declaration of Independence. The greatest sire of the 1790s, Diomed, had been useless at stud in England but he flourished in Virginia and became known as the father of the American Thoroughbred. American racing and breeding evolved on quite separate lines from those pursuits in Britain, with such innovations as dirt ovals rather than grass circuits becoming the accepted racing surface. American breeding was dented by the Civil War, but the importance placed upon the Triple Crown races helped re-establish racing and breeding after the conflict.

Elsewhere, progress was also being made. Australia's most famous race, the Melbourne Cup, predates the American 'Classics', having been first run in 1861. The French have always done things their way and were quick to organise racing there – Longchamp racecourse in Paris was opened as long ago as 1857 and the Emperor Napoleon III himself instituted the Grand Prix de Paris, first run in 1863. Two years later, a French colt, Gladiateur, won the English Triple Crown. The rest of the world was catching up on Britain, but long into the twentieth century, British-bred horses were still seen as the best the species had to offer and were exported abroad regularly.

The writing was on the stable wall as far back as 1881, however, when the man who was possibly the greatest jockey of all time, Fred Archer, cajoled a winning run from Iroquois, which became the first American-bred colt to win the Epsom Derby. Archer's winning records stood for 50 years after he committed suicide in a fit of depression in 1886, and were only beaten thanks to the motor car, which allowed jockeys to travel to many more meetings.

In that same year of 1886, the winner of the Derby was Ormonde – a British-bred stallion who became the first Derby winner to be sold abroad at a higher price than he would have fetched at home. A famous race at Chester is named after Ormonde, who was sold to Argentina and then to California to stud. The international trade in racing bloodstock was well and truly established. In 1895, for example, the Duke of Portland sent all the way to Australia for a stallion, Carbine, who had been such a racing hero in Melbourne that he was given a huge public send-off. The Duke could afford it – his great sire St Simon had earned him in stud fees the equivalent of £25 million at today's prices.

The Russian court of the Tsars got involved, importing the staying champion Galtee More from Britain to improve their stock. Despite improvements in Irish breeding techniques, it was only in 1907 that the first horse to be bred and trained in Ireland won the Derby – the honour going to Orby. Sometimes, it seems like the Irish have been winning ever since.

American priggishness took a hand in New York in 1910, when an anti-gambling law forced the city's Jockey Club to close down and sell off their horses. Amid growing concern about the American 'pollution' of the English species, the Jockey Club in Britain passed the controversial 'Jersey Act' of 1913, which stated that a horse could not be included in the *General Stud Book* unless its parents' pedigree could be 'traced without flaw' to horses already in the book. This ludicrous piece of protectionism effectively barred many fine horses – and in particular, many American ones – because either their records were incomplete or other non-thoroughbreds such as quarter-horses had infiltrated the sacrosanct bloodline.

As the century progressed and developments in transport shrank the globe, the internationalisation of racing and breeding progressed and individual owners and breeders began to dominate the global scene. Some were prepared to race their horses in the best races anywhere. For instance, the Aga Khan, grandfather of the present Aga Khan, raced his horses in England, France and Ireland and won three Derbys in the 1930s to establish a tradition his dynasty maintains to this day. Italy's greatest ever breeder, Frederico Tesio, bred his country's finest stallion, Nearco, who was sold to Britain's Beech House Stud for a record £60,000 in 1938. Benito Mussolini himself approved the deal after it was claimed that Italian bloodlines would suffer if the horse went abroad. Mussolini's government also insisted on handling the cash. Did Signor Tesio ever get his full whack?

GENES WORTH FIGHTING FOR

The Continentals may have had the horses, but Britain still had the biggest races. Tesio himself once wrote, 'The thoroughbred exists because its selection has depended not on experts, technicians or zoologists, but on one piece of wood: the winning post of the Epsom Derby.' The great race's influence has never declined, not even when the Blue Riband suffered a loss of prestige and public support, now thankfully recovered, in the 1990s. The Epsom Derby remains the championship benchmark for three-year-old racehorses, and winning it automatically increases a colt's potential earnings at stud by several millions.

After the Second World War, British breeding declined during the austerity period. French-bred horses won the British Classics seemingly with ease – the Aga Khan's Gallic pair My Love and Masaka winning the Derby and Oaks of 1948. Over in America, Citation was winning his Triple Crown, and speed and course records were tumbling as breeding improved rapidly across the USA, the bluegrass state of Kentucky having become the acknowledged centre of breeding for America and later the world.

British-bred horses were no longer first choice for owners abroad, especially after Italy's Ribot won the Prix de l'Arc de Triomphe two years running in 1955 and 1956 and retired undefeated after 16 races. An American owner–breeder was reported to have offered a blank cheque to Marchese Incisa della Rochetta and Donna Lydia Tesio, joint owners of the wonder horse.

In the 1950s, a brilliant young Irish trainer, Vincent O'Brien, from near Cashel in Co. Tipperary, trained the winners of three Grand Nationals in succession. Switching to the Flat in the late 1950s, at a time when Americans were openly contemptuous of European breeding, O'Brien, the original Master of Ballydoyle, later teamed up with pools millionaire Robert Sangster, the world's most famous jockey Lester Piggott, and Coolmore Stud, then owned by Tim Vigors. Joining them at Coolmore was a youthful stud manager and bloodstock specialist, John Magnier. From then on, nothing in the world of breeding would ever be the same.

O'Brien had a revolutionary concept which has stood the test of time, so much so that he was recently acclaimed in the *Racing Post* as the most influential figure in racing in the twentieth century – some would argue that even King Charles II himself had less of an influence on the sport. Always an admirer of the American breeding industry, O'Brien broke new ground by travelling to Keeneland and other major sales rings across the Pond to buy yearlings and other unproven horses. This went against the established wisdom that success could not be bought, it had to be bred. In most years, the big races were won by horses bred and owned by men and women who had spent years building up their bloodstock resources and did not need to buy at auction – the Aga Khan and Her Majesty the Queen are just two who spring to mind. O'Brien did not like established wisdom and proceeded to stand such 'wisdom' on its head.

After he won his second Derby with Nijinsky in 1970, O'Brien was convinced that Nijinsky's sire, Northern Dancer, a Canadian-bred winner of the Kentucky Derby of 1962, was already on its way to becoming the greatest stallion of the age. O'Brien persuaded Sangster and his rich friends to back a strategy of buying the progeny of Northern Dancer and his descendants, then letting him train the horses to Classic success, selling on the best animals usually, but not always, to American syndicates who would take the stallions to their studs. Sangster raised the cash, O'Brien did the training and John Magnier – having taken control of Coolmore Stud – researched the bloodlines and the sales markets and managed the project with unparalleled skill. Such directly linked breeding-cum-training operations had been tried successfully in the past, most notably by the Aga Khan, but the Tipperary trio made it work as no one had ever done before. It helped that Charles Haughey, later taoiseach (prime minister) of Ireland, had worked either a visionary miracle or a fast dodge, depending on who you believe, during his spell as finance minister in the late 1960s. Haughey made stud earnings tax-free in a bid to boost Irish racing and breeding, and the Irish bloodstock economy has never looked back.

At first, however, the Coolmore–Ballydoyle plan faltered as American stables and owners constantly outbid them. But Sangster came up with the idea of syndicating stallions, effectively giving owners and breeders the chance to share in their success.

GENES WORTH FIGHTING FOR

Typically, a champion such as the great Alleged, twice winner of the Prix de l'Arc de Triomphe, would be syndicated with 40 'shareholders' who paid up front just to own the right to nominate a mare to be covered by the stallion, before being charged five-figure sums for the privilege.

In this way, Sangster began to turn in profits of up to £3 million a year per horse for the finest stallions. He and O'Brien would sometimes buy back the horses sired by their stallions to preserve the bloodlines, usually of Northern Dancer, who by then was recognised as the world's leading sire bar none.

Such Northern Dancer family members as The Minstrel, Nijinsky's son Golden Fleece, Secreto and El Gran Senor – first and second in the 1984 Derby – proved O'Brien's instincts correct and throughout the 1970s and early 1980s, Robert Sangster was rewarded for his courage as an investor by becoming Britain's leading owner several times in that period. Not even the richest American owners could match the wealth and determination of Sangster when he was committed to obtaining a horse.

The Minstrel was a classic example of the Sangster–O'Brien method. Bought as a yearling for $200,000, O'Brien trained the horse to win the 1977 Derby, though the decision to run it in the Blue Riband was largely influenced by the greatest jockey of the age, Lester Piggott, whose brilliance in the saddle that day at Epsom is still talked about. A week before the race, Sangster was offered £1 million for the horse. He turned down the offer and a few months later sold The Minstrel to stand at stud in America for $9 million. Only much later, when they were cash rich and Magnier became more of a driving force, did the group's policy turn to holding on to a stallion for Coolmore rather than selling it for a fortune to the USA.

From the early to mid-1970s, Sangster and company usually had it their own way at auctions, but after the Yom Kippur War of 1973 led to soaring oil prices, the arrival of Arab princes on the European racing and breeding scene led to a quite extraordinary inflation of bloodstock prices. Prince Khalid Abdullah of Saudi Arabia was the best known of the 50 or so Arab sheikhs who descended on British racing and were welcomed with open arms for their money but also, in some quarters, with snooty distaste for their culture and religion, which included a ban on gambling.

The Maktoum family of Dubai were absolute rulers of their part of the United Arab Emirates. Sheikh Mohammed – who is now Crown Prince and effectively head of state – and his three brothers were Anglophiles in racing terms. They were also determined to succeed in what was not just a hobby but a family obsession passed on to them by their father, Sheikh Rashid, who taught them all to ride and also instructed them in the ancient art of falconry. Sheikh Rashid died in 1990, by which time his sons were recognised as the world's leading family of owners. Though Sheikhs Hamdan Al Maktoum and Maktoum Al Maktoum became internationally renowned owners and breeders in their own right, it was their younger brother, Sheikh Mohammed bin Rashid Al Maktoum, who would eventually be nominated as ruler of Dubai and who controlled the family's racing fortunes from the outset.

An intriguing mix of Bedouin prince and westernised sporting gentleman, Sheikh Mohammed was taught to speak English at Bell's Language School in Cambridge in the mid-1960s, and while there he experienced his first British race meeting. His official biography records that in May 1967, he and Sheikh Hamdan saw Royal Palace win the 2,000 Guineas under the Australian George Moore, who was also in the saddle when Royal Palace later won the Derby. During a discussion with his hosts in Cambridge, Sheikh Mohammed learned about the Godolphin Arabian of ancient history being one of the three founding fathers of the breed. He would remember that name long after he completed his education at an officer cadet school in Aldershot.

With their fabulous wealth and a curiously old-fashioned approach to the business, the new Arab paymasters of British racing were not inclined to go to the USA and take on the Americans with their best horses, or try to emulate American breeding methods. Instead, they concentrated on taking on Sangster and company in the sales ring to acquire the best horses and send them to the finest trainers such as Henry Cecil.

The speed at which the men from the Middle East swooped into the bloodstock markets of the world can be demonstrated by the fact that their spending in Ireland in 1980 was around £400,000 and that was less than 10 per cent of the breeding industry's turnover, but by 1983 they were the biggest spenders in Ireland, bigger even than Sangster, with around £6 million spent. That year of 1983 also saw Sheikh Mohammed set a European record by paying 3.1 million guineas for a son of Shergar, the ill-fated Derby winner owned by the Aga Khan, which had only recently been kidnapped from Ballymany Stud in Co. Kildare. The Sheikh also set the world record when buying Snaafi Dancer. Just like Russian oil billionaire Roman Abramovich and his spending at Chelsea FC, the Sheikh didn't seem to care how much he spent as long as he got results.

At sale after sale, the Maktoums went for the Sangster–O'Brien jugular, trying their best to buy into the Northern Dancer line for themselves, as well as snapping up the best progeny of other leading sires as they set out to create a new stud empire, eventually to be based at Newmarket and increasingly now back home in Dubai. In the meantime, however, Sheikh Mohammed was simply happy to own the likes of the flying filly Oh So Sharp, the fillies' Triple Crown winner in 1985.

The Americans' insularity in the breeding world is renowned, but then perhaps they do not need to import many stallions when their own are perfectly excellent. From Bold Ruler in 1963 onwards, no stallion imported from abroad has led the list of champion sires in the USA – such lists are compiled annually to show which stallions are creating the most money-winning colts and fillies. As we have seen in the Seattle Dancer contest, there was genuine fear at one point that the Europeans and Arabs would corner the world market in the best bloodlines. Leading American owners such as Allen Paulson tried to compete, but probably the only man who could have taken on the Arab Sheikhs – the Texan oil magnate Nelson Bunker Hunt – had lost a fortune in his abortive attempt to control the silver bullion market and he even had to mortgage his massive stock of horses in the early 1980s. This was less than a decade after he had been Britain's leading racehorse owner thanks to the magnificent filly Dahlia.

Most owners and breeders in the USA, which was and is by far the world's biggest national racehorse market, were convinced that the Maktoums and Sangster would fail to keep the cash rolling in as both groups were known to be uninterested in actually racing in America, where the big money prizes were located.

'There's much less strain on the legs training on grass than on the hard dirt tracks in America,' Sangster told the *New York Times* in 1981. 'I'm just not prepared to train horses in America.' Interestingly, the Maktoums shared that philosophy, and it took the vast rises in already sizeable American prize money, and specifically the millions available in the Breeders' Cup series, to make them change their minds and occasionally race their horses in the USA.

In those heady days from 1980 onwards, some American owners did pile into the sales rings in case the rising prices were a long-term trend. Northern Dancer and his sons kept pushing the prices up themselves with their success at stud. For four years running in the 1980s, the winners of the 2,000 Guineas – Lomond, El Gran Senor, Shadeed and Dancing Brave – were 'Northern Dancer' colts sired either by himself or his sons Nijinsky and Lyphard. In 1983, Lomond, Shareef Dancer, Caerleon and L'Emigrant all won Classics. They, too, were Northern Dancer's sons or grandsons.

Demand for the Dancer's DNA was at fever pitch. The effect on the bloodstock market was massive inflation, with more than one commentator predicting that this 1980s version of the South Sea Bubble would burst spectacularly. In 1980, the average price per horse at the Keeneland sales was $196,863. In 1984, that average had risen to $544,681.

Sangster had previously been rivalled only by Stavros Niarchos, but now the two men and American millionaires such as Danny Schwarz joined forces to combat the Sheikhs. It was all to no avail. The 1985 record purchase of Seattle Dancer can now be seen as the moment that Sangster and O'Brien over-extended themselves. The sale also convinced American big hitters that Sangster and the Maktoums would nullify each other's long-term plans for world domination, so they pulled out of the race, which helped to bring prices crashing down. With the market collapsing around them, Robert Sangster met with the Maktoum royal family and a truce was declared with Sheikh Mohammed in particular. Apart from prodigious wealth, the two men discovered they were similar in one other respect – both genuinely loved racing and horses. There was one difference, though – Sheikh Mohammed is an expert horseman who went to his wedding standing on horseback and still takes part in gruelling long-distance cross-country races, while Sangster has bred many famous horses but is not too fond of riding them.

Rapprochement gained, they made a sporting declaration to carry on racing their horses against each other. They also agreed that they might just do business with each other in the future, as indeed they did. Sheikh Mohammed also paid a sort of tribute to O'Brien and Sangster by copying their groundbreaking move. In the early 1990s, he quietly set up his own breeding and training operation and called it Godolphin – that name he had first learned almost three decades previously. It was to become the biggest and best of its kind in the world by the late 1990s, when John Magnier got Coolmore–Ballydoyle going again, with a new man, Aidan O'Brien, at the stables and himself and his vastly rich business partner Michael Tabor in overall control. The rivalry between Godolphin and Coolmore–Ballydoyle is intense and has been wonderful for racing – they will be fighting for supremacy for years to come. They have even had jousts in the auction pavilion again, particularly over the progeny of a Northern Dancer grandson called Storm Cat (Johannesburg's grandfather, if you recall), who now has the world's highest stud fee at around $500,000 a pop. In a touch of the 1980s, between the two camps they spent $20 million on Storm Cat's descendants in the space of just a few days in September 2001. It was seen as a good investment by Coolmore – one of Storm Cat's sons was the 'Iron Horse', Giant's Causeway, who was champion of 2000. Sheikh Mohammed has also shown that he is either a sentimentalist or a supreme judge of horseflesh – he has tried to buy the entire 40-odd offspring of his favourite champion, Dubai Millennium.

Back in the late 1980s, that undeclared truce between Sangster and the Sheikhs was only one factor in the devastating collapse of the global bloodstock market, which has only recently recovered thanks largely to new money coming from Japan and elsewhere in Asia, but is still nowhere near the turnover of that frantic period. Money and a supply of rich new owners and breeders simply ran out, while existing owners who had shelled out millions for stallions and mares were suddenly left with animals fetching only 20 or even 10 per cent of their supposed worth. Yearling prices plummeted, as did stud fees, and whereas a stud nomination for Northern Dancer had retailed at a reputed $1 million, the fees for even the best of his progeny such as Sadler's Wells – owned by Coolmore, who won't declare the price – are even now reputedly less than a fifth of that seven-figure sum.

Sangster's pact with the Sheikhs was also timely because Vincent O'Brien's seemingly endless production line of champion after champion from Ballydoyle came to a halt in the late 1980s. The great trainer's powers were on the wane, just as the supply of Northern Dancer colts dried up. Stavros Niarchos also pulled out of the partnership and many of the horses he co-owned with Sangster's crew were sold. Ironically, Coolmore Stud was thriving and O'Brien's son-in-law, John Magnier, and Robert Sangster then pulled the master stroke which has made Coolmore Stud the pre-eminent breeding operation in the world today. At a time when many European breeders regarded the way in which Coolmore aped American studs by making stallions mate up to 70 times a year as akin to a form of cruelty to animals (did anyone ever ask the stallions themselves?), Coolmore also began to transport some of its stallions to Australia by air for a 'double shift'. This was founded on the simple premise that when their stallions were not in action in the Northern Hemisphere, they could be put to use in the Southern Hemisphere. Coolmore's revolutionary tactic was to send stallions to stables which they had swiftly acquired down under, where the sires enjoyed several months of procreation duties. The move proved spectacularly successful. Australian owners clamoured to send their mares to Coolmore stallions and, by the late 1980s, Magnier was transporting no less than £50 million's worth of stallions back and forth to Australia each year.

With Sangster again providing the money – he had sold Vernon's Pools for £90 million in 1989 – Magnier had brilliantly perfected a whole new approach to breeding known as 'the shuttle stallion'. At a stroke, Coolmore's potential income had almost doubled, and in the 1990s, Magnier came to own the stud having bought out Sangster's share. With wealthy partners such as Michael Tabor, and Ballydoyle thriving under Aidan O'Brien, business boomed. Just as with Vincent O'Brien some three decades earlier, the new Maestro of Ballydoyle made wonderfully bred horses into champions, and this time around, Magnier could afford to hold on to the very best for Coolmore. He already had Europe's top sires in Sadler's Wells and Be My Guest, and alongside those amazingly prolific stallions came the likes of Grand Lodge and especially Danehill, whose reputation as a sire grew throughout the 1990s as his sons and daughters won champion race after champion race. It was largely down to Danehill's unprecedented success at stud in Australia that the shuttle stallion concept became validated.

Coolmore's Ashford Stud in Kentucky and its now permanent Australian base have added millions to the group's worth. Coolmore is now the biggest breeding operation in the world, and its importance to the Irish bloodstock industry cannot be overstated. It is an industry which employs anything up to 20,000 people, and dwarves Britain's in terms of foals produced – in 2003, just over 5,000 thoroughbred foals were born in the UK, while the figure for Ireland was 10,574. Only the USA and Japan produced more foals.

As the stud which produces more high-priced yearlings than any other in Europe, Coolmore is the heartbeat of the Irish industry and, judging by the prices being paid for its produce in the last two years, it appears that Coolmore is well placed to rake in even more millions from its new crop of stallions. And the son of Danehill to whom everyone looks as the stallion who is best placed to help secure the future of Coolmore is Rock Of Gibraltar.

If any horse could be said to be a sure bet to succeed at stud it is Rocky, but breeding and owning horses has always been a gamble and the value of investments can soar or dwindle to nothing. Success is never assured. Proof? You will recall Snaafi Dancer and Seattle Dancer, the two colts purchased respectively by the Maktoums and Sangster's consortium in 1983 and 1985 at Keeneland, where the July sales themselves have been under threat of extinction because fewer people are prepared to invest huge sums in untried animals.

Snaafi Dancer was sent off to be trained by one of England's best trainers, John Dunlop, who soon discovered that the horse did not live up to his first name, which means elegant, and was also, to put it mildly, very slow. He never saw the racecourse. When Snaafi Dancer was taken off to stud to see if his DNA could at least produce a winner, he turned out to be useless at the most basic duty of a stallion. For years, it was rumoured that he was pulling a milk float somewhere, but more likely Snaafi Dancer was kept by the Maktoums. Philosophical gentleman and poet that he is – check out his own internet website – you can just imagine Sheikh Mohammed popping round to see the most expensive dud he ever bought, just to remind himself of the dangers of hubris and confusing your ego with your wallet.

Seattle Dancer at least made a decent go of things on the racetrack. He won a couple of Derby trials but did not go to Epsom, and he later managed to keep his end up at stud, unlike Snaafi Dancer. After spells at Ashford and Coolmore, he was shipped off to Japan for six seasons and in 2003 was bought by a syndicate of German breeders to stand at their stud farm, Gestut Auenquelle. His first crop included the 1991 Racing Post Trophy-winner Seattle Rhyme and he has also sired German Classic winners. But all in all, it was a poor return on $13.1 million. Funnily enough, no yearling has been bought for anything like that sum since 1985, so we can credit the two 'failures' with bringing some sense into the often crazy world of breeding and owning.

The new, more professional, approach to sales prices and stud fees has a downside – it means that stallions will have to be successful virtually from the off. And it really is not overstating the case to say that the future prospects of Coolmore, and racing and breeding generally, now rest on the shoulders of Rock Of Gibraltar and other fresh young stallions. It may well be that, like the two Arabians and the Turk, and like Eclipse of long ago, Rocky could be the horse to change his entire species for the better.

So much history, so much tradition, so much science and a whole lot of money are bound up in his ability to procreate. It was ultimately cash that led his owners to fight over Rock Of Gibraltar, but now you know why Rocky's genes are well worthy of a battle.

CHAPTER THREE

Fergie's Horsey Hobby

It was all supposed to be written in the stars. At the end of the 2001–02 football season, Sir Alex Ferguson's Manchester United side would crown a magnificent last season for the most successful manager in Britain by winning the Premiership before going on to lift football's greatest club prize, the European Cup. By a felicitous coincidence, the match which everyone presumed would be Ferguson's last in charge of United was going to be played in his beloved home city of Glasgow. In 2002, the final of the European Champions League, as the marketing gurus of UEFA would have us name it, or the European Cup final, as every sensible person still calls the annual highlight, was to be played at the superbly refurbished Hampden Park. It is a place that Ferguson once knew well as a player with Queen's Park FC, the resolutely amateur club which owned and ran Scotland's national football stadium until a controversial and costly refit funded largely by the National Lottery saw them all but elbowed aside, though it is still their home ground.

The script was this: Fergie would lead his troops onto the lush Hampden turf and walk off with the giant silver trophy, which would be captured after a titanic tussle against Real Madrid's galaxy of talent including such stars as Zinedine Zidane and Roberto Carlos. It would be a match to rival the greatest European Cup final of them all, also played at Hampden, when the Real Madrid of Ferenc Puskas and Alfredo Di Stefano put Eintracht Frankfurt to the sword in a 7–3 victory that featured some of the finest football ever seen in Britain. That magical 1960 final cast an inspirational spell over a whole generation of Scottish players and managers, among them Alex Ferguson. How apt that the culmination of Ferguson's magnificent career would be a simulacrum of that great final, with United confirmed as this generation's equivalent of Di Stefano's Madrid. Nothing, surely, could prevent this march to destiny by Ferguson and the team he had lovingly created. It would be poignant, too, that his active career in senior football would end in glory at the place where it began, the home of his first club, Queen's Park.

The man himself was actually quite philosophical about the prospect of not making it to Hampden. He told this writer in October 2001, 'I'm not going to let winning the Champions League become an albatross around my neck, because with what I've achieved in the game, well, you can't be greedy and say, "I deserve to be at Hampden." It would be wonderful if it happened, but if it doesn't it won't be bothering me too much. I'll be disappointed, very disappointed, but I'm disappointed every time we lose a game, whether it's a League game or a European tie.'

The Hampden ending didn't happen for two reasons. Bayer Leverkusen were nobody's idea of winners when they met United in the semi-finals of the Champions League. A 2–2 draw at Old Trafford and a 1–1 draw in Germany a week later saw the exit of the Reds on the 'away goals count double' rule. Trust those pesky Germans to go and spoil the show. It was a disappointing end to Ferguson's career as a football manager that he did not get the chance to contest the European Cup final again. Except, of course, Ferguson had not ended his reign at Old Trafford at all.

For, even as he was working his notice and supposedly running down to retirement at the age of 60, Alex Ferguson confounded friends and enemies alike by deciding that he would not, after all, be quitting the hot seat. United needed him to change his mind, because the early part of the season had been disastrous by the

FERGIE'S HORSEY HOBBY

Reds' standards. So, in February 2002, he signed a new three-year contract and roared back into battle, his change of mind coming too late to save that season but inspiring a rejuvenated United to yet another League title in 2002–03. It was a U-turn that would have made even the most thick-skinned of prime ministers blanch, but Ferguson didn't bat an eyelid and blamed it to a large extent on his wife, Cathy. She had made him do it, he insisted, because she couldn't stand the thought of having him under her feet at their home in Wilmslow in Cheshire. It would have sounded like one of the lamest excuses in history, except for the fact that it is at least partially true – those who know him say that Ferguson would not have changed his mind if Lady Catherine had not allowed him to, and, as he has stated, she may well have suggested the unexpected extension to his career.

Her generosity of spirit is even more remarkable because Cathy Ferguson was acutely aware that there was already a cautionary case of a football widow who saw her man driven to a fatal heart attack because of his refusal to stop managing football teams. That woman was someone the Fergusons knew well. On the evening of 10 September 1985, Mrs Jean Stein and her daughter, Ray, were telephoned at home in Glasgow to be told that their husband and father, the incomparable Celtic and Scotland manager Jock, had died of a heart attack in the moment of the triumph over Wales which virtually guaranteed the Scots a place in the World Cup finals of 1986.

The man who made that call from Ninian Park in Cardiff was Jock Stein's assistant that night, Alex Ferguson. Some 16 years later, Ferguson said that the death of the man he acknowledged as his master in the managerial trade was the sad inspiration for his decision to retire. 'I was there when Jock Stein died. Jean Stein always said to Cathy, "Don't let that happen to your man."' Yet within four months of saying that, and just a few weeks after he had reassured an old friend, *The Scotsman*'s venerable chief football writer Glenn Gibbons, that he was definitely retiring, Ferguson asked the United board if he could reconsider. Given the subsequent development of Ferguson requiring a pacemaker as a result of an irregular heartbeat, one can't help wondering if Cathy Ferguson might now prefer her husband to clutter up the carpet rather than go on under the pressure he has endured for so long. For, love him or hate him, it cannot be denied that no one, but no one, has soaked up more pressure on behalf of Manchester United than Alex Ferguson, and only the fans really thank him for it.

Prior to Ferguson's volte-face, his impending departure had caused many pundits to reflect on Ferguson's achievements, though the man himself swears – not too convincingly, it must be said – that he never looks back on his career. 'While I'm still in the game, I don't do that – I never look at what I have achieved. I just never look back,' he once told me. 'People say, "Look, you've won twenty-one major trophies here", but I couldn't have told you that unless I sat down and wrote them all down.' The number is now twenty-seven, beating Jock Stein's previous British record by one.

He may not think back over the long years, but the rest of us can easily conclude that he has had a quite extraordinary career and an utterly remarkable life. His own excellent autobiographies, *A Light in the North* and *Six Years at United*, and the later and more comprehensive *Managing My Life*, which was co-written with the inimitable Hugh McIlvanney, were a welcome and often acerbic change from the normal turgid football memoirs, and if read alongside Michael Crick's less than hagiographic biography *The Boss*, they provide considerably more detail about his life than there is space for here.

What is clear from all accounts is that Ferguson was a racing and betting man from his youth. Now a multi-millionaire, Ferguson really did start life on the mean streets of No Mean City. Glasgow, and more specifically Govan – one of those 'quaint little fishing villages on the Clyde', as the comedian Billy Connolly once described the shipyards' hinterland – bred tough people who also knew the value of sticking together as a community. Teamwork, you might call it. It has often been said of Ferguson that you can take the man out of Govan, but not Govan out of the man, but even if he could, Alex Ferguson would not dream for one second of eliminating Govan's myriad influences from his character. It remains a tough area, a land where survival is still wrought on a daily basis from the stretched wits of men and women alike, and it was many times worse in the post-war era. It is to his credit that Ferguson still has many friends from his Govan youth, and they will not hear a word said against him. He has also given of his most precious commodity, his time, to support such enterprises as the Govan Initiative and Harmony Row, the local amateur football club of which he was once a member.

Alexander Chapman Ferguson was born on 31 December 1941, at 357 Shieldhall Road in Drumoyne, to the west side of Govan. New Year's Eve is Hogmanay to Scots, and this calendar-inspired excuse for a party is celebrated in Scotland like no other country in the world. His father, Alexander Beaton Ferguson, hailed from Renton in the Vale of Leven in Dunbartonshire. Those of us from 'the Vale' are taught football in the womb and learn from an early age that, as long ago as 1888, the football team of Renton had been acclaimed as the Champion Club of the World after they beat West Bromwich Albion 4-1 in a special challenge match between the two Cup holders, at a time when both sides were acknowledged as respective champions of Scotland and England. Well, we Brits really did rule the world of football at that time, because we were just about the only people playing the game, so Renton really were champions of the world.

Perhaps it was that Rentonian tradition that made Alex Ferguson senior a footballing man. From an early age, he brought up his sons Alex and Martin, the latter being the younger by not quite a year, to play the game well and play it hard. Ferguson has often spoken about the huge influence of his quiet but occasionally temperamental father on his life, though he credits his mother, Elizabeth, for her legacy of willpower. His Cheshire home is called Fairfields, after the shipyard in which Ferguson senior was a respected timekeeper – and there weren't a lot of them on Clydeside.

It will seem almost ludicrous in this day and age to anyone outside Scotland and Northern Ireland that a person's religion would have anything to do with their choice of football team, but Glasgow has been a divided city for well over a century. Celtic are associated with the largely Irish-descended Roman Catholic community and Rangers are very much the Protestant and British unionist team. Sectarianism is a scar that defaces Scotland to this day and will do so until the guts of the last bigot are used to strangle the last apologist muttering 'It's only tradition' every time the fists fly.

ROCK OF GIBRALTAR

The Fergusons were different from the Green and Blue norm. Alex senior was a Protestant who married a Catholic and brought up his sons in his Presbyterian faith while following Celtic. His son also married a Catholic and has testified how that caused him great grief when he joined Rangers, where such an association was enough to make him fall foul of the club's thankfully long-since-abandoned ban on employing Catholic players. Ferguson was a staunch Rangers fan in the days when Glasgow's sectarian divide was near absolute, and it is one of his more endearing traits that he despises bigotry and has not only written about it but has spoken out on the subject when it would have been easier to remain quiet.

From his early childhood, Alex Ferguson's ambition was to be a professional footballer. He spent his teenage years playing for the local company of Life Boys, a junior department of the Boys Brigade, and then for his secondary school, Govan High. Though clever, he would never gain prizes for academic achievement or even effort, because he was just too consumed by football. After spells with the Harmony Row Boys Club and across the River Clyde with Drumchapel Amateurs, he joined Queen's Park in 1957. In 2003, BBC Scotland broadcast a television documentary tribute to Drumchapel Amateurs, the club which has produced more than 300 professional players and 29 internationalists in its 50-odd years – more than any other comparable amateur side in Scotland. The show focused on the club's remarkable founder, Douglas Smith – another figure credited by Ferguson as a major influence. Indeed, such is his admiration for Smith that Ferguson went out of his way to help publicise the show, calling me early one morning to ensure that I included his generous praise of Smith in an article on the Amateurs, which I was happy to do. The next time we spoke at Hampden Park a few weeks later, though, it didn't suit him to talk to me and he cut me dead in front of fellow journalists.

As a child, he was involved in another of his father's hobbies – betting. Having a punt, usually on the weekly pay day or the Saturday, was a part of working-class life in those days, even though it was against the law. For this was before the legalisation of bookmaking in the 1960s, and there was always an illicit thrill, not to mention the risk of arrest, in making contact with a street-

FERGIE'S HORSEY HOBBY

corner bookie. Fortunately for the Fergusons, the local bookie lived upstairs in their tenement block.

Ferguson has described his father as 'a hopeless punter' and gave as an example his backing of Devon Loch, the dramatic last-gasp loser of the 1956 Grand National. Ferguson's mother also liked a 'tanner Yankee' – a complex bet on four horses, consisting of six doubles, four trebles and an accumulator. If it came up, depending on the odds, a tanner Yankee could be quite lucrative, and the fact that the Fergusons knew about Yankee bets suggests they were quite regular and informed punters.

Sir Alex revealed to one journalist that his mother had a good system for her betting. As he told Richard Edmondson of *The Independent* in 1999, 'My mother would send me to the kitchen table to find out what he [his father] was backing. He would tell me two certainties and when I told my mother they would be the ones she avoided.'

Leaving school with no real qualifications, Ferguson aimed to combine senior football with a toolmaker's apprenticeship at the Remington Rand typewriter factory in Hillington, and there he famously became a shop steward and a strike leader. From 1960 onwards, he played part time, firstly as an amateur for St Johnstone, who were based 60 miles away in Perth. A combative centre-forward, or striker as we know them nowadays, Ferguson scored his fair share of goals for St Johnstone but was anxious to secure a move into the full-time ranks. All the travel to and from Perth was made worthwhile when Dunfermline Athletic signed Ferguson as a full-time professional in 1964, by which time he was 'going steady' with his future wife Catherine.

The couple were married on 12 March 1966, and their first son, Mark, was born in September 1968, by which time Ferguson had achieved his ultimate ambition – to play for the mighty Glasgow Rangers. A string of fine goal-scoring performances for Dunfermline, including some against Rangers, saw him signed by the Ibrox club's legendary manager Scot Symon for £65,000 in 1967.

In his first season, Ferguson became Rangers' top scorer, with 23 goals, and he was chosen to play for a team representing the best players in the Scottish League, scoring a goal in a 2–0 victory over the Irish League. But Jock Stein's Celtic were European champions and the top dogs in Glasgow – and it's never a good time to be playing for one half of the Old Firm when the other lot are in the ascendancy. Symon was abruptly sacked – he was asked to resign by the club's accountant – and was replaced by his assistant Davie White, for whom Ferguson could not hide his disregard. Ferguson had also fallen foul of the anti-Catholic element inside Ibrox, and the combination of a whispering campaign against him by bigots and his mutual antipathy with his new manager saw Ferguson leave the club he had idolised. In the intervening years, there have been many stories that he was going back to Ibrox to be the manager, but he has never done so.

In 1969, Ferguson moved to Falkirk for a fee of £20,000. White was sacked shortly afterwards and replaced by Willie Waddell, a known admirer of Ferguson who would certainly have found a place for him in the Rangers side which he rebuilt so successfully that they won the European Cup-Winners' Cup. Good timing and good luck are said to be Fergusonian qualities, but not on that occasion.

The highlight of his four years at Falkirk was the birth of his twin sons, Jason and Darren, on 9 February 1972. He was also involved in a players' mutiny against manager Willie Cunningham, who clearly held no grudges as he later appointed Ferguson first-team coach. As a player, Ferguson had already looked to secure a future in football management by taking part in the Scottish Football Association training courses for coaches, which were then recognised as innovative and trail-blazing.

Ferguson was always known to like a bet, and could often be found studying the racing pages of the daily papers after training, preparing for a trip to the bookmakers' shops. He enjoyed card schools with fellow players, but Ferguson did not have a reputation as a serious gambler, and though he did occasionally visit racetracks such as Hamilton and Ayr, he never displayed any sign that racing and horse ownership would become a consuming passion. Instead, he occupied himself with learning as much as he could about coaching and management, even going off to the English FA's managerial school at Lilleshall. One former footballer who attended a coaching course at Largs with Ferguson recalls that he seemed fascinated by money – 'but not betting with it, he just seemed too tight [parsimonious] for that'.

Ferguson himself told Alastair Down of the *Racing Post*, 'I was a punter until I finished playing with Rangers, but when I became a manager I was immediately so obsessed with the job that betting just disappeared off the map.' But not bookmakers, as we shall see.

In his 30s, and having already had troublesome knee injuries, Ferguson's career was waning and in 1973 he joined Ayr United on a two-year contract which was abruptly terminated on medical advice. Ferguson was suffering from enlarged arteries, then a common problem with footballers in their 30s, but also a possible indication of heart or circulation troubles to come in later years. His reputation as a future coach to note had circulated widely within Scottish football, and the man who joined him on that coaching course at Largs explains why. 'He just naturally took charge and bossed the younger guys like myself around, but you could see he had all the senior players' respect as well.'

At the comparatively early age of 32, Ferguson was offered the opportunity to manage East Stirlingshire in the summer of 1974. As in 2004, East Stirlingshire were then the worst senior team in the country, rock bottom of the old Scottish Second Division. Within months, he had them in contention for promotion, but even with such success, it was still a surprise when Paisley side St Mirren appointed him manager. He sacked most of the squad at the Love Street ground, rebuilt the team, and within two-and-a-half seasons St Mirren secured the First Division championship and entry into the Premier League.

Now that his playing days had ended, in time-honoured fashion for Scottish footballers, Ferguson opened a pub – Fergie's – near his old stomping ground of Govan. It was not the most salubrious of premises – the police were regular visitors, though Ferguson dealt with most troublemakers himself. He combined managing St Mirren with running Fergie's but gave up ownership of the pub in 1978, when he moved to manage Aberdeen.

That move would be the making of Ferguson, but it is often forgotten that his career in top-level management began in ignominious circumstances involving Ferguson's dealings with – strangely enough – a bookmaker. Also, it is a myth that Ferguson never backs down from a fight, as the events of 1978 showed.

Ferguson had actually been sacked by St Mirren, even as he was negotiating to join Aberdeen and, despite being advised not to, he sued the Paisley club for wrongful dismissal. The key issue was that the St Mirren directors had rather ungratefully fallen out with the manager who had brought the crowds back to Paisley and had trebled their club's income. But the board made allegations about Ferguson's conduct and at the industrial tribunal it was revealed that Ferguson had also given information about the club, albeit practically useless, to a local bookie – David McAllister.

James Neil, the editor of the *Paisley Daily Express* and brother of broadcaster and Scotsman Publications publisher Andrew Neil, testified on oath to the tribunal that he had seen Ferguson giving match tickets to McAllister and that the manager had told him that he and McAllister were friends and that he had given the bookie what proved to be correct advice that St Mirren would win an important game against Ayr United. Ferguson admitted McAllister was a friend but denied on oath that the conversation with Neil had even taken place, though he later admitted that he had indeed given the bookie the 'wire' about St Mirren beating Ayr. Friend to a bookie? That was something Ferguson would become again, much later in his career, and that relationship would end in trouble, too.

The tribunal sided with Alex Ferguson on the major and indeed career-threatening point of whether he had broken the strict code that managers and players do not give insider information to bookmakers. The tribunal rightly concluded that telling a bookie that your team is going to win is hardly a crime, after all. Their interpretation is obviously correct, but being seen even talking to a bookie, far less being friends with one, was hardly a sensible move on Ferguson's part, especially as he has subsequently admitted that he and McAllister often spoke about the matches on the weekly 'fixed odds' football coupon. No one has ever been able to tell Ferguson which friends he should choose or avoid, however, and McAllister had been a friend since their schooldays. That Ferguson sense of loyalty overrode any considerations of his image.

Ferguson's hero and mentor, Jock Stein – a strict teetotaller whose one vice was gambling – was also extremely friendly with bookmakers. Indeed, Stein was returning from holiday with one well-known bookie, Tony Queen, when he suffered his near-fatal car crash in 1975. Ferguson probably should have been more circumspect than to advise McAllister on football, and the evidence shows that Ferguson still kept in touch with the gambling world while running St Mirren. Yet it really militates against everything Alex Ferguson has ever stood for to think that he would even contemplate his side not winning.

The tribunal found against him on crucial issues, however, such as his obvious contempt for the directors. Modern industrial lawyers call it the irretrievable breakdown of the necessary relationship between employer and employee, but in plain English the bosses had fallen out with a man who they felt had become too big for his boots. It was a very bad loss for Ferguson – one that humiliated him at the start of his career at Aberdeen, and one that could have been avoided had he listened more closely to advice.

After the tribunal findings were published, it was clear that there were serious doubts about St Mirren's case against him, and Ferguson was advised that he would win an appeal if he took the case to the civil courts. But his father was seriously ill at the time – he died early in 1979 – and Ferguson backed down and accepted the outcome of the tribunal, albeit with no grace whatsoever. It was a fight he could have won, but Ferguson stepped away from the legal ring and got on with his career, which duly began to blossom spectacularly.

After initial problems, Ferguson led Aberdeen to the first of three Scottish championships in four years in season 1979–80, then won the Scottish Cup in 1982 – a trophy they retained for the next two seasons. The greatest victory of all came in 1983 in the European Cup-Winners' Cup final in Gothenburg, when Aberdeen defied a monsoon to beat Real Madrid 2–1.

The Old Firm's domination of Scottish football was, for a brief period anyway, smashed by Ferguson's Aberdeen and, to a lesser extent, Jim McLean's Dundee United – the two clubs from the north-east were known as the New Firm. Ferguson was lauded with honours, including an OBE, and, after Jock Stein's death, was appointed caretaker-manager of Scotland for the 1986 World Cup finals in Mexico, where Scotland exited at the first stage yet again.

In November that year, Ferguson left Aberdeen to succeed Ron Atkinson at Old Trafford. His career stuttered at first, but club chairman Martin Edwards and the board stuck by him even as the hoped-for results failed to emerge.

Ferguson himself took action to tackle a particular problem at United. The manager had always detested football's boozing culture, and he cleared out several players who were fond of a refreshment, notably club legends Paul McGrath and Norman Whiteside. Despite saying that players indulging in betting would be equally unwelcome at Old Trafford, he did not tackle the admitted gambling problems of players like Keith Gillespie. Indeed, according to Michael Crick in *The Boss*, Gillespie was used as a 'runner' by Ferguson, putting on the manager's bets for him at the local bookmaker's shop. Gillespie recalled that these bets were up to £50 a go, but other players recall the manager betting hundreds of pounds himself and never taking his players to task over their gambling. He could hardly do so, since he was indulging in the practice, though never in any way that compromised his footballing standards.

After coming perilously close to losing his job because of United's lack of success, Ferguson's methods began to pay off. The FA Cup in 1990 was duly won and on 15 May 1991, United beat Barcelona 2–1 in Rotterdam to lift the European Cup-Winners' Cup. Another event occurred that year which has considerable bearing on this story – United went to the stock market and became a public limited company, though effective control stayed with Martin Edwards and his coterie, including club lawyer and director Maurice Watkins.

Two years later, United's 26-year wait for the English League title was over and, in 1994, United did the 'Double', beating Chelsea 4–0 in the FA Cup final and finishing eight points clear of second-placed Blackburn Rovers in the League. By the end of his tenth year with the club, United were confirmed as the biggest draw in the sport and Alex Ferguson had won the first-ever managerial 'double Double' with the same club, as both the FA Cup and League were won in 1996. In Barcelona in May 1999, Ferguson emulated Sir

FERGIE'S HORSEY HOBBY

Matt Busby's 1968 achievement when United won the European Cup in dramatic fashion, beating Bayern Munich with two goals in the final minutes. The feat completed a historic Treble of League Cup, FA Cup and European Cup in the same season, which gained a knighthood for Sir Alex Ferguson later in 1999 (although the Honours Office cited the European Cup alone as the official reason), adding to the OBE and CBE he had received earlier.

Since then, of course, the club have grown even bigger and are now without question the world's most successful football club in terms of financial worth and annual income. Much of that success is down to the drive, determination and skills of Sir Alex Ferguson.

The pressure on him has never relented. Building one successful team after another over nearly three decades would have killed many a lesser mortal, but rather than standing down in his 50s and 60s – the age when most active managers in any industry would be looking to retire – Ferguson has taken on increasingly greater challenges. Add the constant unremitting problem of controlling men with either egotistic fixations or attitude problems, and sometimes both together, and you have a combination of pressures that are frankly beyond the understanding of normal men. Just think of Steve Archibald (at Aberdeen), Gordon Strachan (at Aberdeen and United), Mark Hughes, Paul Ince, Andrei Kanchelskis, Jaap Stam, Lee Sharpe, Dwight Yorke, Fabien Barthez and, of course, the three most important players in his time at Old Trafford: Eric Cantona, Roy Keane and David Beckham. It should not be forgotten that Ferguson's man-management skills were at their finest in rehabilitating Cantona after his ban from the game for a kung-fu attack on a Crystal Palace fan. And for every player who has spoken out to criticise Ferguson, there have been four or five who would have died for him.

In all that time, he has had two hobbies which, by his own admission, have helped to keep him sane (along with becoming something of a connoisseur of good food and red wine). He enjoys a game of golf and was on the course at Mottram Hall near his home when he learned that United had won the League for the first time under him. The other hobby has been racing and his love of a punt, which became something more solid after he visited the National Hunt Festival at Cheltenham.

ROCK OF GIBRALTAR

For someone now indelibly associated with the Flat, it is often forgotten that Ferguson's first steps into ownership involved the other 'half' of racing. Manchester United fan Mike Dillon, the head of public relations for Ladbrokes, had invited Ferguson to the National Hunt Festival at Cheltenham and he and Cathy were guests in the Ladbrokes box. Other guests included Lord and Lady Andrew Lloyd-Webber.

Dillon told this writer, 'It was really to celebrate Alex and Cathy's wedding anniversary. Going racing was something they felt they could do together and they both enjoyed it immensely.' The Fergusons did indeed celebrate their 31st wedding anniversary by going racing, and also at Cheltenham that day was a fellow Scot, Raymond Anderson Green, who made his fortune in the financial industries and is now the owner of Scotland's largest string of racehorses. He and his wife Anita are also tireless workers for children's charities and once donated a valuable horse as the prize in a nationwide racecourse raffle. Anderson Green remembers that Cheltenham Festival well, because the day after the Fergusons' anniversary, 13 March 1997, brought him his most satisfying success as an owner until then – victory for his star horse in the Cathcart Chase.

Said Anderson Green: 'We were there because my best horse, Sparky Gayle, was running. We didn't actually get to meet him there, but we could see Alex was having a whale of a time in the company of his family. He was mostly with Mike Dillon and Hugh McIlvanney, and he was determined to bet a Scottish horse, so even though he left the course, he left instructions for a bet on Sparky Gayle, which duly won. I think that day really rekindled his love of racing in a big way, because we have met him several times at racecourses since then and he always remembers that Sparky Gayle won for him that day.'

Sparky Gayle was one of the most popular steeplechasers in Scotland and the North in the 1990s, and is now enjoying retirement in the paddock at Anderson Green's house in East Lothian.

At the end of his day out, Ferguson said to his wife, 'Why don't we buy a horse?' With considerable prescience, she said yes but predicted he would become obsessed and end up 'owning the whole of Newmarket'.

FERGIE'S HORSEY HOBBY

That Cheltenham trip and a later visit to the Derby in June 1997 were responsible for taking Ferguson's dormant love of the Turf as a punter and turning him into an owner with a new-found zeal for the sport. 'There are great similarities between racing and the passionate outdoor sport I've been involved with all my life,' he told *The Independent* in 1999. 'You can see the enthusiasm from the punters, owners and trainers when they get a result at Cheltenham. It's fantastic.'

Ferguson had obviously been exhilarated by the Derby, which was a hugely exciting race won by Benny The Dip by a short head from Silver Patriarch. He went on: 'When Benny The Dip won the Derby, I was in the parade ring before the race and you could feel that tension building up. You knew something big was coming.

'Football's like that. When the coach is going to a ground you can always tell by the atmosphere on the bus how big the game is. Going to a normal game, there is a lot of cackle on the bus but when it's a big one you can hear a pin drop. And in the parade ring at Epsom that day it was so quiet. All the owners were milling round and you could see the tension getting to them. There was a trepidation or apprehension about how their horse was going to do. There were big stakes there. That's akin to football. Those are all the feelings you get in our game.'

It was a feeling that Ferguson wanted to experience for himself. At that point, Mike Dillon's legendary contacts throughout the racing industry came in useful. Effectively, Dillon became Ferguson's racing manager, advising him on who to deal with and what to buy, and he used to frequently describe himself as such. Dillon did try to dissuade Ferguson from latching on to the messy and usually fruitless business of ownership. 'I tried to stop him,' he told this writer in 2001. 'I really did. I told him it is the quickest way of ripping up £50 notes known to man.'

Having had his salary vastly increased by United, Ferguson had plenty of 'pinkies' to spare, however, and was determined to move into ownership, both on his own account and in partnership with friends and in larger syndicates, such as the 11-strong group which owned the steeplechaser Yankie Lord.

Ferguson employed the well-known bloodstock agent Charles Gordon-Watson to do his buying and his first spending spree brought Ferguson instant success. The first colt he owned was named after a ship on which his father had worked, while the second was named after a district of Glasgow. Respectively, they were Queensland Star, who was sired by College Chapel out of a mare called Zenga (a granddaughter of Northern Dancer), and Candleriggs, who was sired by the star sprinter Indian Ridge, winner of the King's Stand Stakes at Ascot in 1989.

'They were young colts and I got them cheapish,' Ferguson told me. 'They did very well for me. Queensland Star was trained by Jack Berry [the famous Lancastrian trainer who has since retired] and won its first two races, one at Newmarket and one at Chester, while Candleriggs later proved a good handicapper.'

Ferguson admitted that at first he knew nothing about owning horses. But Gordon-Watson really did know his onions. He had snapped up Queensland Star for 17,000 guineas at the Tattersalls October Sales, Ferguson having given Gordon-Watson a sum of money and left the buying to him. In return, Gordon-Watson gave Ferguson useful advice that he should only buy 60 per cent of two horses, 'so that if anything went wrong with one, then he'd still be OK', as Gordon-Watson later recalled in the *Racing Post*.

As he has often done over the years, Ferguson roped in his mates to help him in his new pursuit. He became the majority shareholder in the Right Angle Club along with three friends from the fishing industry in Aberdeen, and Queensland Star won first time out for them in Ferguson's red and white colours, lifting the £4,000 first prize in the European Breeders' Fund Stuntney Maiden Stakes at Newmarket on 16 April 1998. To use a fishing metaphor, Ferguson had landed a winner with his first cast, and like every fisherman who does that trick, he became hooked on his new hobby. He was also lucky – many owners go through lots of horses before they get a win, and some never get a win at all.

When the colt took a step up in class and won his next race, the Joseph Heler Lily Agnes Conditions Stakes at Chester – almost Ferguson's local course – pundits began to talk of him as a potentially classy performer. Indeed, trainer Jack Berry spoke of aiming him at Royal Ascot. This time, the prize was nearly £7,500. In just two races, after deductions, Ferguson had won back half the price of the horse. Queensland Star did indeed go to Royal Ascot, but ran down the field in the Coventry Stakes and never hit the heights once forecast for him.

Candleriggs was trained by Ed Dunlop at Newmarket, and Ferguson enjoyed going to Newmarket to watch his horse and others ride out early each morning on the gallops which radiate out from the town. Candleriggs suffered feet problems as a two year old but at three he won first time out at Kempton, bagging the Milcars Ruislip Handicap on 3 April 1999. He would repeat the trick the following year, lifting a much more valuable race of the same name. That was his second and last victory, despite a number of placed runnings, and the horse was later gelded and sold. In 2004, it remained in training at the yard of David Nicholls.

From the outset, Ferguson was not prepared to lose money for sentimental reasons. Exactly how much he was spending on his horses has never been divulged. It is reasonable to assume that he bore his share of the expenditure, at least on his early horses, but with training fees at a minimum of £12,000 a year in the cheapest yards, plus race entry and jockey fees, an annual cost of around £20,000 per horse would be a fair assumption. Since Queensland Star and Candleriggs together cost at least 60,000 guineas, a figure of £100,000 expenditure in his first year or two would not be unreasonable. Ferguson did not demur when I put that figure to him in 2001.

'I said to my wife when I first started that hobbies always cost money, and though you pay for your fun you don't want to bankrupt yourself. At the moment, I have done well. You only hope you can make it pay.'

Ferguson had learned one thing straight away – horses who have fulfilled their purpose are disposable. Candleriggs and Queensland Star were sold in short order. Ferguson told me: 'The advice I got at the start was not to fall in love with the horses. I have been professional in that respect, so when I have had offers or I don't think they can get to Group 1, I've sold them on. For instance, I had a half-share in Chinatown with Ivan Allan and we sold that for good money. It's a wee bit like footballers: a manager shouldn't fall in love with them.'

With Gordon-Watson buying for them, the Right Angle Club took on more horses such as Ninety Degrees, which won at

Yarmouth on the day that Ferguson went to Buckingham Palace to be knighted. Jack Berry trained the horse on that winning day, and delighted in revealing that Ferguson had taken some time out of his big trip to the Palace to check on the horse's well-being before the race – presumably, Ferguson then had a bet on the horse which was backed into 6–4 at the off. Did he let his fellow racehorse owner in on the tip when he and Her Majesty had the traditional chat after the dubbing of the new knight?

After being introduced by Mike Dillon to the well-known owner and trainer Ivan Allan, who was based in Hong Kong, Ferguson went into partnership with him. Much later, Allan's 'interesting' love life exposed the owner–trainer to massive publicity. Loyal as ever, Ferguson would say nothing about his friend. The two owned Caledonian Colours, who was trained by Sir Michael Stoute, won a decent maiden at Haydock and was duly sold at a good profit to race in America. The same happened with Chinatown, who won a maiden at Newcastle and was later sold to race in Hong Kong. A pattern was being established in which Ferguson was clearly more interested in short-term profit than holding on to a horse for long-term, possibly sentimental, reasons.

As we shall see in more detail later, Ferguson was also developing a relationship with the best and biggest names in European racing – trainer Aidan O'Brien and Coolmore owner John Magnier. Other partnerships in which Ferguson participated included the joint-ownership of the successful sprinter Fairgame Man with two of racing's biggest owners – Robert Ogden and Jack Hanson. Fairgame Man was trained by Alan Berry, son of Jack, at Cockerham and whether it was Ferguson's influence or not, Berry soon attracted a famous footballing clientele led by Michael Owen of Liverpool and England. Owen is a very keen owner and racegoer and has also had horses with John Gosden.

Manchester United players also took to the sport, joining Ferguson at Haydock Park and elsewhere. Most of the first-team squad were spotted with him on a rainy day at Catterick, and when a race meeting was held at Haydock in tribute to Ferguson, the course was so busy that the doors had to be shut.

Alex Ferguson did indeed bring excitement to racing and, more pertinently, the manager encouraged fans to join him in the

FERGIE'S HORSEY HOBBY

Manchester United Racegoers Club (MURC), which had its first runners in 2000. The idea was for the MURC, which was run by owner and breeder Henry Ponsonby, to purchase a number of horses to run in club colours. The Manchester club had 700 members in its first year, and Ferguson played an active part, just as he did at first when appointed president of the national Racegoers Club. The Racecourse Association (RCA) set up the Club to encourage people to take up the best part of the sport – actually going to the tracks and watching racing live, and the RCA were very pleased to secure Ferguson's services as a figurehead. The MURC had five horses in training at the outset, and had a winner on its very first outing, which was to Naas, just south-west of Dublin in Ireland. Red Coral, trained by Aidan O'Brien, was the appropriately named horse, while the club also had the even more appositely named Kings Of Europe on its books.

Unfortunately, the club's horses did not enjoy real success and the membership never reached the 1,500 target which Ferguson had hoped for. Until the events of 2003, the biggest disappointment which Ferguson experienced in racing was the failure of the MURC in 2001. He said afterwards: 'We just didn't get enough members. We thought at the start we might get 5,000 but we struggled to get over 800. I thought it would be a fantastic thing, but maybe the United fans just didn't fancy the horses. The costs just kept building up and it wasn't fair to the guys who had financed it to keep going. If we did it again, we would do things differently, and we would also hope to avoid the injuries which happened to two of our horses.'

Those remarks reveal how Ferguson approached his racing. He was happy to let his name be associated with partnerships and clubs and provide his guidance. He saw that as his contribution – an important point in view of the facts to be revealed later in this book.

It should be remembered, however, that he first got into the sport as a punter enjoying an escape from the pressures of living in the global goldfish bowl that is Manchester United. As Mike Dillon said, 'It is great relaxation for him away from all the stress of his job, and he really does enjoy the company of the people and the characters who go racing.'

ROCK OF GIBRALTAR

The manager himself acknowledged to Alastair Down in their 1999 interview how important it was for him and his players to relax with a day at the races: 'My players aren't that interested in racing, but it is a great release for them and a different atmosphere. And I can go along and be left alone more than usual; a few people want an autograph, but most just say hello and get on with enjoying their own day. I don't want to talk football at the races; I am more interested in finding out what's going to win the next.'

The picture that emerged in 1998 and 1999 was of a man who began to take his hobby very seriously, and who at least had the considerable advantage of excellent contacts within the sport and who also took their advice on board. He may have become an owner by then, but at heart Ferguson was still a punter, though he was beginning to learn that owners and punters need to be different kinds of people.

He is still a punter, a gambler, and a Manchester United source says he now spends as much, if not more, money on this pursuit as he did ten years ago, though in these days of telephone accounts and internet gambling, it is difficult to track how much anyone spends on gambling.

Dutch striker Ruud van Nistelrooy told a soccer magazine in his native country that the United squad, as has been the case for many years, still enjoys a game of cards, just as Ferguson did in his playing days. 'The lads play on the train when we go to London, in hotels and on the plane and the manager is fine as long as he is winning,' said van Nistelrooy. 'He never misses a thing. The players call him The Hawk because nothing goes unnoticed.'

Van Nistelrooy set a racing record himself – he was the most expensive yearling sold at auction in 2001, costing John Magnier $6.4 million. That particular Van Nistelrooy is the stunning chestnut colt sired by Storm Cat and now 'scoring' at Coolmore Stud, not the handsome United player who is worth rather a lot more than the price paid for his namesake. And yes, in 2001, the horse was deliberately named after the player that Magnier's then friend Alex Ferguson had finally managed to sign for Manchester United.

Ferguson is also known to visit casinos. It is still a mystery why a man who cracked down hard on one source of addiction –

booze – can be less critical of another which may not be as damaging physically but which wreaks havoc on a person's mind and emotions. A psychologist interviewed for this book said: 'Sir Alex must know that an addiction to gambling is harmful, and may well take action if he sees a player developing a problem. As a "man manager" he no doubt weighs up the disadvantages of the risk of players developing such problems against the release from pressure which he and his players obviously enjoy when they have a day out at the racecourse. We know that some people have what are usually called addictive personalities and it is these people that must be watched.'

When launching his Sporting Chance clinic for men and women in sport suffering from various addictions, the former Arsenal and England captain, Tony Adams, told the *Evening Standard* that a third of the people who had contacted his charity were problem gamblers: 'Because of the number of tests available these days, it would be very difficult for any player to drink to excess or take drugs. It would be seen and detected straight away. Those with addictive personalities are now turning to gambling to get their buzz. More and more players are buying horses and with that comes gambling. It's hard to detect because there are no obvious signs like there are with drinking or taking drugs. The only real clue is in the players' faces or in their body language.'

After a spate of stories about top players gambling and losing five- and six-figure sums, and with players and ex-players 'coming out' and admitting they were problem gamblers or addicts – Paul Merson, Tony Cascarino, Eidur Gudjohnsen and Steve Claridge, to name but four – the Professional Footballers Association's chief executive Gordon Taylor felt obliged to say in a press release:

> Few people in the sport would be surprised to hear such stories because gambling isn't new. Perhaps the size of the losses being quoted would seem quite alarming to some but you have to remember that, with wages being so much higher for the top players these days, the stakes are higher and so the losses are going to be greater as a result. It is important, however, as with most things in life, not to allow the gambling to become excessive.

It is also important to keep things in perspective and remember that card schools, for example, have been part and parcel of football for many, many years. Players have to make long journeys and have numerous overnight stays in hotels, and these card games are a form of release. Although, as we have seen in the cases of people like Paul Merson, Eidur Gudjohnsen and Keith Gillespie, some individuals can take things too far and get into serious financial trouble.

It is down to club managers to keep control of card schools and the like, ideally through the club captain, and keep everything in proportion because, amongst other things, it can seriously affect team spirit if large amounts of money are owed by a player to a teammate.

Is that advice followed at Old Trafford? The United manager would never allow team spirit to be compromised and no one reads players better than Ferguson, so he is the first person at United to become aware and take appropriate action should any of his players develop the symptoms of a gambling problem. There is also no suggestion whatsoever that Ferguson himself has ever been addicted, and he has testified to long spells away from racing and betting. But Ferguson can often appear to be different people in the space of a few minutes. There is a wonderful Scottish word which perfectly captures Ferguson in one of his grim moods – he can be quite carnaptious when he wants to be. Say it slowly, 'kar-nap-shuss', and you can just about picture Ferguson's face in that near-snarl of bewildered defiance-cum-aggression, a look that says, 'Just because I'm paranoid doesn't mean they're not out to get me!'

Carnaptious and curmudgeonly he can be, but by all accounts he is wonderful company among family and friends, as well as being a raconteur of some style and a genuinely fun-loving creature. The tales of his loyalty, generosity and hospitality are legion. So, too, are the myriad occasions on which Ferguson has blistered walls and ears with his temper. He has often been called a Jekyll and Hyde character, but no one can remember Hyde at the racecourse, only a beaming Jekyll. Remember also that Doctor

FERGIE'S HORSEY HOBBY

Jekyll was a Scot and the story was written by a Scotsman who understood that the Caledonian psyche is a many-sided thing. It is something the Scots share with their Celtic cousins across the sea in Ireland, and though he had always had Irish players around him – 'he's virtually married to Roy Keane', as one United source mischievously put it – from around 1998 onwards, Ferguson would see a lot more of that country, its people, and especially its horses.

At first, the Irish dimension was wonderful for Ferguson, as he said to Alastair Down: 'I am very smitten by the Irish experience and can't see how anyone could go for an afternoon at The Curragh and not enjoy themselves. Mind you, the woman who sells "three bars for a pound" outside the gates always sees me coming. I gave her a fiver last time and she said, "Is that all you're giving?" so I gave her 20 quid. People tell me she's a millionaire – she soon will be at that rate.

'I like the feel of racing in Ireland. You see the important players mixing in with ordinary folk and there is none of that old landed gentry thing that we have in Britain.'

That phrase, uttered in 1999, is a major indicator of Ferguson's attitude towards the aristos and the blazerati, the buftie brigade who were perceived to be the amateurs running a professional sport in Britain. We will soon see how a prominent figure in the world of racing held that attitude in common with Alex Ferguson, and how this shared view was the root cause of what is now known as the Rock Of Gibraltar Affair.

CHAPTER FOUR

The Beginnings

No one really knows why the Irish as a people are so totally in thrall to the horse. Their myths, legends and ancient histories make no more reference to horses than most other European nations that can trace their lineage back to prehistoric times, yet it is commonly understood by the Irish people that they have been obsessed with horses since time immemorial, and they still are.

Official returns by Horse Racing Ireland, the sport's governing body in Ireland, show that this country, with its population of just under four million, has 3,373 individual registered racehorse owners, plus 1,217 syndicates, clubs and companies also in ownership. That is a ratio of more than one owner per thousand people. The comparable figure for active owners in the United Kingdom, according to the BHB's figures, is a little more than one owner per six thousand people – 9,762 owners in a population of 59 million.

The Irish do not own horses just to admire them – they race them. Ireland has 27 racecourses, or around one course per 150,000 people, while Britain had 59 courses in 2004, or one for every one million people. One of the Irish venues, Laytown, is actually a beach that features racing on a temporary track at low tide.

THE BEGINNINGS

The racing public in Ireland can at times consist of the entire population. When Ireland's most famous horse of all time, and the world's greatest-ever steeplechaser, Arkle, died on 31 May 1970, the announcement of this national hero's death was broadcast as the first item on the Irish radio and television news programmes.

With the possible exception of three-times champion hurdler Istabraq, owned by J.P. McManus, no horse since Arkle has enjoyed such celebrity. Though Irish-bred and Irish-trained horses have won Classics galore, no horse that runs on the Flat is ever likely to enjoy the kind of fame and adulation which Ireland reserves for its hurdlers and steeplechasers. For Ireland is the land where organised racing over jumps was invented, and it is still by far the country's favoured division of the two kinds of racing. For proof of that assertion, do not go to Ireland but visit Cheltenham during the National Hunt Festival in March. There you will meet tens of thousands of Irish people dedicated to following the sport, all hemmed into a corner of Gloucestershire which they have made their own. Many racecourse managers in Ireland would happily slaughter their grandmothers if doing so would get even half of the Cheltenham Irish crowd to visit their track for a Flat-only meeting.

Though it has the highest average prize money per race in the world, in neither Flat nor jumps racing is Ireland pre-eminent in Europe in any of the categories of total prize money, number of horses participating in the sport and quality races run on its tracks. But this small country does lead the continent in one vital aspect of the global sporting industry – the breeding of top-class thoroughbred racehorses.

Perhaps it's the temperate climate; perhaps it's the limestone-enriched lush, grassy fields; perhaps it is the tradition of handling horses passed from generation to generation which make Irish stud farms so successful. It is definitely due in part to the tax breaks introduced in 1969 which mean that income from stallion fees is exempt from all forms of tax. Over the past three decades, the Irish breeding industry has constantly continued to grow and Ireland now produces twice as many thoroughbred foals per year as Britain. But, as the majority of Irish studs' output goes to

National Hunt duty, the figures may appear skewed in any consideration of the respective nations' worth as a breeding centre.

The correct test of Irish superiority in the breeding stakes is the performance of the sires which stand in Ireland. In terms of money won by their progeny, in terms of championship races won by their sons and daughters and in terms of the prices their owners charge in stud fees, Ireland's stallions win every time. The two best sires in recent decades have been Sadler's Wells and Danehill. Both belong to John Magnier and Coolmore.

Seeing things through a media-generated fog often leads the public to take diverse views about celebrities. Tribal loyalties, such as which team or pop band you favour, also tend to colour whom we like and dislike among those who are cursed with fame. David Beckham, for instance, is either the handsomest demi-god of the age and the greatest footballer in recent English history, with a home-life considerably less torrid than that of our own dear Royal Family, or else he is an airheaded, overpaid, oversexed, 'better off over there', sarong-wearing swine who deserved all the opprobrium he got in early 2004.

Among those who care about such glorious trivialities as racing and football, one half of the public probably think that John Magnier and John Patrick McManus are rapaciously rich Irishmen who are determined to get their own way in everything and should leave Manchester United and Fergie well alone, while the other half no doubt consider that they are lucky broths of boyos who wouldn't hurt a fly and have merely been defending their own patch in their dealings over Rock Of Gibraltar and United. The truth about Mag and Mac, as they are never called, at least to their faces, lies somewhere between those two extremes.

John Magnier was born in 1948 into a family steeped in the traditions of stud farming. Land records show the Magnier family were in occupation of farms near Fermoy in Co. Cork in 1850. Two branches of the Magniers had possession of two different areas of farmland in Fermoy, while other Magniers of that period in Cork emigrated to America and some became Magners. There has been some discussion about the pronunciation of the Magnier name – some prefer the French version Man-yee-eh or a Dublin-sounding Man-yer but the local pronunciation in south-west

THE BEGINNINGS

Ireland is Mag-na or Mag-nerr. This is also how a well-known brand of cider, Magners, is pronounced, at least until you drink your ninth pint of it. Diligent broadcaster that he is, BBC Radio's racing correspondent Cornelius Lysaght once had the corporation's pronunciation unit check it out and they recommended Mag-na.

Magnier was educated at the all-boys Glenstal Abbey School run by the Benedictine order in Co. Limerick. He is listed in school records as being in the year group which left the school in 1964. The boarding school seems to have been a jolly place, as evidenced by photographs of that year's school play, *Macbeth*, which featured three particularly ugly witches. Magnier may have left the school by then as his father Michael died while John was in his final year at Glenstal. That 1964 group held their 40th anniversary reunion in April 2004. It is not known if Magnier attended.

On leaving school, Magnier helped run the family's Grange Stud. He was already steeped in bloodstock lore, but he must have been some kind of boy genius to have pulled off the trick with which he is often credited. It is sometimes reported that Magnier persuaded Charles Haughey, Finance Minister of Ireland, to pass the law which gave owners and breeders tax exemption on stallion stud fees. In one fell swoop, the myth goes, Magnier enriched Coolmore, where Haughey later had his horses bred. In Ireland of the conspiratorial whisper, some truths are as airy-fairy as a banshee, for the tax break, which has undoubtedly been the single biggest factor in the Irish breeding industry's growth and thus John Magnier's success, was first proposed by Haughey in early 1969 when Magnier was just 20 and, in his own words, 'still digging ditches' on the family farm. Much later, Magnier did have dealings with Haughey and it was the former taoiseach, impressed with Magnier's success and his views on the breeding industry, who nominated Magnier to the Irish Senate in 1987.

As reputable stud farmers, the Magniers had wide contacts in the horse industry in neighbouring counties, and they knew trainer Vincent O'Brien from Cashel in Tipperary very well. Indeed, Michael Magnier owned Cottage, Ireland's great sire of jumps horses in the 1930s and '40s, who fathered the immortal Cottage Rake, trained by O'Brien to win three successive

Cheltenham Gold Cups from 1948 to 1950. The Magnier farm in Co. Cork is 77 kilometres from Coolmore in Co. Tipperary and the N8 is a much better road now than it was back in the 1970s, but it was a journey made regularly by John Magnier after he was brought in to manage the Coolmore operation in 1974. The stud's original owner, Tim Vigors, who died in November 2003, was in partnership with Vincent O'Brien and the multi-millionaire Robert Sangster. In 1971, Magnier was becoming well known in breeding circles as a young man of considerable skill and drive. With the backing of owners in the syndicate system he was then developing, Magnier had paid 160,000 guineas for sprinter Green God. Two days later, it won the Sprint Cup at Haydock. The race was sponsored by the Sangster family company, Vernon's Pools, and Robert Sangster was impressed with the young Irishman's ideas about ownership and breeding – two activities in which he was already dabbling.

In 1975, Magnier married Susan, daughter of O'Brien, but this was not a case of the son-in-law also rises – John Magnier brought his own special bloodstock genius and his organisational skills to the group. What are now accepted practices, such as syndication, shuttling stallions to Australia and especially the buying of American yearlings for racing in Europe, were all pioneered by Magnier and his partners.

Robert Sangster died early in 2004, and Magnier attended the funeral of the most successful owner and breeder in recent British history – he bred Sadler's Wells, the greatest sire of the past two decades, which would be epitaph enough for any racing man. Back in the 1970s, it was Sangster's money and personal commitment which enabled himself, Magnier and O'Brien to transform the world of training and breeding by merging the two into a seamless operation. Buying mostly Northern Dancer's offspring from America, O'Brien trained them at Ballydoyle, Lester Piggott rode them to victory after victory and the trio sold them back to the USA for syndication as champions for much more money. It sounds so simple now, but back then it was a revolution. It became a money spinner with The Minstrel. Bought for $200,000 as a yearling, after winning the Derby under Piggott it was sold to America for syndication for $9 million.

THE BEGINNINGS

A friend of Sangster's who knew all three men over several decades described their triumvirate in the 1970s and 1980s as a perfect partnership. 'Vincent had the training genius, John had the knowledge of the bloodlines and the management expertise, and Robert had the money and the drive to make things happen.'

It took years for the concept to take off, and therein perhaps lies the difference between Magnier and Sangster which eventually led to the former buying out the latter in the early 1990s (Magnier took complete control of Coolmore, while Sangster concentrated on his Swettenham Stud, which has also been hugely successful). Magnier had a rare combination of vision and long-term ambition, and was known to be unhappy when Sangster sold stallions to the USA. A patriotic Irishman, he could see no reason why the very best stallions should not stand at stud in Ireland and also earn tax-free fees. For he had seen the possibilities that Haughey's exemption gave Coolmore and wanted to exploit them to the maximum.

Someone who has known Magnier for years said to me: 'He was very focused on trying to build up the bloodstock. Beforehand, there were all these Irish-trained horses that were very successful on the track, thanks to Vincent O'Brien, which they then sold back to the USA. Following this, they were going over to the States and buying their offspring. John thought this was crazy, we have to keep these horses. It has taken him all these years, but he has built up Coolmore on that idea. He had a vision even then.'

That vision was summed up by Magnier in a rare interview in *Time* magazine in 1982. Said Magnier, 'It all follows the semen. If you don't have the semen, you don't have the industry.' Straight to the point, and absolutely correct. It took Magnier nearly 20 years to build up Coolmore to its dominant position, largely based on the income from sires such as Be My Guest and especially Sadler's Wells, the Sire of Sires, who at one stage commanded tax-free annual stud fees of £40 million.

With another sire, Danehill, performing wonders as the world's first major shuttle stallion – he raked in the cash in both Australia and Ireland – and with a new partner in former bookmaker Michael Tabor, the only remaining piece of the triangle in 1994 was to find the new Vincent O'Brien. Along came the brilliant young Aidan O'Brien, like Vincent before him the champion National Hunt trainer of Ireland, and once again Coolmore–Ballydoyle became a leading breeding-cum-training operation, vying with Godolphin for the title of 'world's best'.

Magnier is happily married and has three grown-up sons and two daughters. He reportedly dotes on his children, most of whom are involved in the family business. His daughter Katie is married to trainer David Wachman – after his success at Royal Ascot in 2004 with his father-in-law's horse Damson, he will soon be a big name in training – and Magnier could not have been accused of stinting on their wedding in 2002. The beautiful Katie was married in the ancient abbey near Fethard and guests at the reception, which reportedly cost more than £1 million and featured Ronan Keating and Rod Stewart as entertainment, included the cream of Irish society, as well as Lord and Lady Lloyd-Webber and Sir Alex and Lady Ferguson.

Magnier is a collector of fine art, mostly by Irish artists. He is also generous to local causes in his Golden Vale of Tipperary – Coolmore sponsors local hurling and rugby teams – but he spends much of his time travelling and has a large home in Barbados called Laughing Waters, not far from the luxurious Sandy Lane Hotel owned by J.P. McManus and Dermot Desmond. Magnier is also believed to have a stake in the hotel which cost the Irishmen £40 million and much the same again to remodel it to their exacting standards.

Magnier's standards are also very high. His attention to detail is almost Ferguson-like. For instance, he was involved in the design of the custom-built Mercedes-Benz transporters which criss-cross Europe ferrying millions of pounds worth of horseflesh to and from Coolmore. He also insists on Coolmore being alcohol-free – two employees were once dismissed for having a glass of wine with lunch while on duty.

Magnier is a devout Catholic who had his son John Paul baptised by his namesake, the Pope, in the Vatican. Irish wags say the Pope must have been ill since he didn't fly to Ireland to do the ceremony. But nowhere in the Catholic catechism does it say 'Thou shalt not be ruthless in business'. And Magnier is a man who conducts his business well within the bounds of the law but with a will to win deals that is quite exceptional.

THE BEGINNINGS

'John Magnier does not pick fights with people,' one observer of his methods told me. 'If you bring a fight to him, John Magnier will take you on. He is fair, but very tough – very tough.'

He is also supremely professional at what he does. 'There is a major difference between the millionaires who dabble in this racing world and John,' said the source. 'They are in racing for a hobby, but racing and breeding is John Magnier's business. And every champion he breeds, every big race he wins, is like an extension to his factory.'

Magnier's professional approach to the business has made him some enemies, and on the few occasions he does speak out, he doesn't miss people and hit the wall. He supported the Irish Government's creation of a new national racing authority in 2001, which swept away a largely amateur administration of the sport in Ireland, and he ripped into the plan's critics. Among them were members of the Turf Club, whom he called 'a handful of amateurs' who were going to 'cost professional trainers, jockeys, agents and stable staff and a mass of others their livelihoods'. His speech was well timed – it came at the Irish Thoroughbred Breeders Association's awards dinner at which he had just been presented with its 'Hall of Fame' award.

He added, 'To be blunter still, there is a very small minority refusing to co-exist with Government, and never before have the decisions of so few amateurs affected so many professionals.' His words hit home hard, and Horse Racing Ireland came into being as a thoroughly professional organisation which benefits from Government grants and a levy on bookmaker profits.

Tough, ruthless and hugely successful he may be – his wealth is estimated at anywhere between £300 million and £600 million – but it is a myth that Magnier has been the King Midas of Irish racing. On at least two occasions, he has been involved in expensive ventures that flopped miserably. One was the plan to take over Phoenix Park Racecourse and develop it as Dublin's finest course, dedicated to showcasing Flat racing in Ireland. Along with Robert Sangster and Vincent O'Brien, Magnier, who was the junior partner, spent millions on acquiring the course, but it failed to attract custom and closed down in a protracted death agony in the early 1990s.

The second and most embarrassing failure was that of Classic Thoroughbreds, which was floated on the stock market in a blaze of publicity in October 1987, but which collapsed a few years later without ever achieving its aim of producing champion stallions and mares for sale or for Irish studs. Vincent O'Brien's reduced powers as a trainer and spotter of talent were perhaps largely responsible for that flop. But Magnier learns from his mistakes – all his ventures, such as an obscure investment in Scottish sausage-skin manufacturer Devro, are done from private resources and usually through Cubic Expression, the investment company based in the British Virgin Islands which he co-owns with J.P. McManus. Devro sources have nothing but praise for Magnier, who has been a supportive and interested investor as the company based in Moodiesburn, Lanarkshire, has grown to become a market leader in the supply of foodstuff casings.

It pains Magnier that he has occasionally been called on to testify to the various investigation teams which have looked into alleged scandals in Irish political life. He has never been found guilty of any offence or even questionable conduct. The only time when it looked as if he might appear in court was when Arrowfield Stud threatened civil action in Australia, and that matter was sensibly resolved. Magnier won, of course.

Yet, though he spreads his money wisely into other investments, Coolmore remains the massively lucrative engine room of Magnier's operations. 'He is successful in other spheres now, but it is racing that was and is his core business,' said an Irish journalist. 'And he's the very best in the world at it.'

In 2001, however, John Magnier had a problem. His greatest sire, Sadler's Wells, was getting close to the end of his stud career. Indeed, if the stallion had been human he would have been given a Zimmer frame to help him in his task. But alongside Sadler's Wells, Coolmore's other champion sire, Danehill, was in his equine prime at 15, and would guarantee income for years to come, by which time the colts that Aidan O'Brien had been turning into champions would be ready for stud duty, or so was the plan. Among the likely lot, however, there was no obvious successor to Danehill as a supplier of that sire's 'speed' genes. Yet just starting his two-year-old season was a Danehill colt called

THE BEGINNINGS

Rock Of Gibraltar, and Magnier liked the look of the handsome bay youngster.

Rock Of Gibraltar was foaled on 8 March 1999. He was bred by Aidan O'Brien along with his wife Anne-Marie and her father Joe Crowley. The latter two were much more involved than the maestro trainer in the science of breeding in the early years, and possibly had the biggest say in suggesting a union between Danehill and an obscure mare called Offshore Boom. Anne-Marie is the eldest of Joe's six daughters and is a brilliant horsewoman in her own right, being a top amateur jockey who subsequently turned to training and took over her father's yard in Piltown, Co. Kilkenny, when he 'retired'. One of a family of lovely women, Anne-Marie had done some modelling work as a girl but horses were her obsession. She had already met her future husband on the racing circuit before she took out a trainer's licence. She went on to become Ireland's first female champion trainer. In 1993, Aidan O'Brien took out his own licence for the yard, succeeding his wife.

Joe Crowley has since returned to the training ranks after his daughter Frances, who took over the stables when Anne-Marie and Aidan flitted to Ballydoyle, also left Kilkenny. Frances moved to The Curragh with her husband, the jockey Pat Smullen, who provided such valuable service to Rocky as the conductor of his pacemakers, but who is a very fine rider in his own right. Indeed, he won the Budweiser Irish Derby of 2004 aboard Dermot Weld's Grey Swallow.

Two of Crowley's other daughters have been involved at the Piltown yard – Breda was in charge of the office before marrying trainer Trevor Horgan, and Angela, an engineering graduate, was assistant trainer. The family was steeped in horse lore, but in O'Brien they had welcomed into their ranks a man for whom training and racing was a total obsession.

In recent years, Joe Crowley has enjoyed a spectacular comeback to training and has more horses than ever before. He has won prizes as prestigious as the Ulster Derby, and shows no sign of giving up the game. He also has a herd of prizewinning pedigree cattle to contend with, but arguably the greatest success he has enjoyed in his life was breeding Rock Of Gibraltar along with his daughter and son-in-law. Such is his modest nature that Crowley never went to the track to be seen in the winner's circle when Rocky was competing, and he had to be persuaded to go and collect the several awards from the various Irish breeders' associations which he earned because of Rock Of Gibraltar.

The most remarkable aspect of the whole story of Rocky's breeding is that Crowley had bought his dam, Offshore Boom, as a cast-off. She had been bred at the Moyglare Stud of well-known breeder Walter Haefner, and was a daughter of Be My Guest. At the age of 12, she was sold to Crowley at Goffs' sales in 1997 while in foal. There was nothing sensational in the mare's own career to suggest she would later give birth to a world beater – her best bit of form was a second place in a Listed race.

The filly she was carrying when Crowley bought her, D'Articleshore, was sold on and later turned out to be a huge star in that hotbed of international racing, Turkey, winning a very tidy £250,000 in her career. In 1997, though, none of Offshore Boom's progeny were remotely close to becoming champions, so Crowley must have been inspired when he took the plunge and bought her for 11,000 guineas. It now ranks as one of the biggest bargain buys ever in British or Irish racing. Crowley is rightly proud of the star he produced along with his daughter and son-in-law and admitted to journalist Michael Clower in the *Sunday Times* that though he did not go to watch Rocky's triumphs, 'naturally I took an interest because it would make the mare's future offspring much more valuable'.

The trio also got their breeding from her right first time, because it was in the 1998 breeding season that they sent Offshore Boom to Coolmore Ireland for her tryst with Danehill.

Rock Of Gibraltar's sire was already known to be a famous begetter of champions, it must be said. Coolmore had acquired all of him after a well-documented spat between Magnier and Jon Messara of Arrowfield Stud in Australia. Arrowfield owned more shares in the horse and wanted him to do more of his 'work' – some might call it that – in Australia, whereas Magnier wanted Danehill to stand more in Ireland. Even though Coolmore had a smaller shareholding, Magnier simply outmanoeuvred Messara, who had threatened a massive court case. In a closed auction,

THE BEGINNINGS

Magnier outbid his rival with an offer which effectively valued the horse at Aus$24 million.

Magnier had also acquired from Arrowfield the land at Jerry's Plains in Hunter Valley, New South Wales, on which Coolmore Australia stands. Such was Danehill's success at stud in both Ireland and Australia that Danehill has joined the 'founding father' of Coolmore's stallion success, Be My Guest, in having a bronze statuette sculpted of him. Be My Guest's imposing figure stands outside Coolmore Ireland, while Danehill's bronze can be found outside Coolmore Australia. If the stallions there could see him, they would look at Danehill and tremble at the prospect of living up to the sire's extraordinary record. For in 1999 alone, Danehill served 164 mares in Australia and had earlier covered 148 in Ireland, which works out at an annual average of nearly one a day, though the breeding season does not last a whole year. He must have had the constitution of an ox cross-bred with a Swedish porn star.

He did not look like equine beefcake, however. Australia's top writer on form and breeding, John Holloway, described in the *Sydney Morning Herald* in September 1998 how he encountered Danehill on a media open day at Coolmore Australia. He wrote:

> I saw Danehill again on Tuesday. He was one of 12 stallions Coolmore proudly displayed to a media contingent, and probably the most inauspicious of the dozen megastars. Quite frankly, if you weren't told he was Danehill you could be forgiven for wondering why this horse was so special. He doesn't look like a superstar, and just stood before the onlookers totally unfazed by the attention. That's probably the reason behind the phenomenon.

That's a typically perceptive remark by Holloway. Danehill's placid temperament was the principal reason why he was able to stand all that shuttling back and forth to Australia. A son of Danzig, which makes Rocky a great-grandson of the legendary Northern Dancer, Danehill was not a great champion on the track, but he was a winner whose four victories on the course included the Group 1 Sprint Cup at Haydock and Newmarket's July Cup, also a

Group 1 race. But it was at stud and as a shuttle stallion that he prospered. By the time he came to father Rocky, he had been champion Australian sire several times; once champion sire of France; and champion sire of two year olds in Europe three times. In all, he had sired 972 winners whose total earnings worldwide were more than £100 million. His 50 Group 1 winners would eventually include Landseer, Aquarelliste, Mozart, Desert King, Banks Hill, Dress To Thrill and Danehill Dancer. In turn, his sons had sired champions – Danehill Dancer, for example, is the sire of the amazing Australian sprinter Choisir, who electrified the British racing scene in 2003 with his victories at Royal Ascot and in the July Cup at Newmarket. This grandson of Danehill paid the greatest of all shuttle stallions the ultimate compliment when John Magnier stepped in to buy Choisir for Coolmore Ireland – the first Australian-bred stallion to stand at 'head office' in Tipperary.

Like every other stallion, Danehill did not know what he had sired when Rock Of Gibraltar came along. Neither, it must be said, did his breeders. Joe Crowley and his fellow breeders no doubt had the dam, Offshore Boom, more in mind when they gave the colt its distinctive name. At the time, there was huge media coverage of the troubles plaguing British and Irish bookmaking because several large concerns had located their telephone and internet gambling operations 'offshore' in tax havens such as Gibraltar, where the best known of these companies to relocate was that of gentleman bookmaker Victor Chandler. It looked as though the 'offshore boom' would never bust, and Chandler has certainly thrived despite the home bookmakers' fightback.

Magnier liked Rock Of Gibraltar from the outset and he was soon taken into Coolmore ownership in a deal reputed to have been worth £100,000 each to his breeders. Aidan O'Brien was also delighted to take the colt he had helped to breed into Ballydoyle. Tradition dictates that the names of grooms for particular horses are not given out at Ballydoyle, but Rock Of Gibraltar was clearly well cared for as he soon developed into a strapping colt, eventually standing 16 hands high, though he was light of frame at first. Under O'Brien's careful tutelage, the horse began to thrive

THE BEGINNINGS

as a two year old and there was a bit of a buzz about him in Tipperary as the time approached for him to go to work at the racetrack.

Rocky first saw the racecourse at The Curragh in Co. Kildare, headquarters of Irish racing and venue for all five Irish Classics, in April 2001. The First Flier Maiden Stakes is not the most prestigious race of its kind in Ireland but it usually attracts two-year-old colts foaled relatively early in the year. O'Brien had first won the race in 1999 with King Of Connaught.

The buzz about the horse made it to the bookmakers as usual, and they priced up Rocky as hot favourite for his debut. (Please see the Appendix for a key to this and all other race report details.)

> THE CURRAGH, 21 APRIL 2001, AT 2.15 P.M.
> The First Flier European Breeders' Fund Maiden for two year olds.
> Distance: five furlongs. Going: soft. Six ran.
> Prizes: 1. £8,387.10; 2. £2,451.61; 3. £1,161.29; 4. £387.10.
> 1. Rock Of Gibraltar, 9–2, M.J. Kinane, 11–10 fav, A.P. O'Brien.
> 2. Sandford Park, 9–2, S. Craine, 5–2, 2 l, Kevin Prendergast.
> 3. Mahsusie, 8–11, J.P. Murtagh, 10–1, 2 l, Francis Ennis.
> 4. One Flag, 8–11, K.J. Manning, 10–1, 7 l, J.S. Bolger.
> 5. Ayman, 9–2, P.J. Smullen, 11–4, hd, D.K. Weld.
> 6. Cifonelli, 8–1, D.J. Moran (10 lbs), 25–1, 1½ l, J.S. Bolger.
> Winner's time: 1 min 7.5 secs (slower than standard by 8.5 secs).
> Winning owner: Mrs Sue Magnier.

Rock Of Gibraltar's first visit to a racecourse proved to be highly satisfactory, if not totally scintillating. The soft ground at The Curragh was the only concern, as his trainer knew he had the beating of the rest of the field on sheer speed. Would that speed be blunted, allowing one or two of a field of largely untested maidens – only One Flag had run before – to cause an upset?

The other runners included a possibly decent colt in Kevin Prendergast's Sandford Park, owned by Mrs Isobel Foley, and a filly named Mahsusie. The former did not go on to enjoy huge success in his career, though he captured a decent handicap at Leopardstown as a three year old. Mahsusie, on the other hand, who was then owned by Mrs Norah Kennedy, went on to win her next two races, the second of them being the first Listed race for two year olds of the Irish season, the Setanta Media Marble Hill Stakes at Leopardstown – a good return on a filly who cost just 6,500 guineas as a yearling. She would later finish in front of Rock Of Gibraltar in the Coventry Stakes but did not fulfil that early promise, and was sold to run in England where she also failed to shine. Dermot Weld's Ayman briefly flattered to deceive in that race and in his career, but the trainer wasn't entirely unhappy as he and jockey Pat Smullen went on to enjoy a treble that afternoon at The Curragh.

Early in that season, punters had latched onto O'Brien's horses, which were all pretty far advanced in their training. Rock Of Gibraltar was sent off clear favourite, though he was not a totally guaranteed choice because of the ground. By the finishing line, all doubts had been eradicated and it was clear to all present that the Maestro of Ballydoyle had another fine young colt in his possession.

From the off, where there was some slight scrimmaging which didn't affect the outcome, Mahsusie wanted to get to the front and Johnny Murtagh was content to let her bowl along in front, with Ayman in second. Mick Kinane kept Rock Of Gibraltar handy behind the leaders but also took him to the outside of the small pack, clearly intent on making an uninterrupted late run.

Which is exactly what happened. As Ayman faded, Sandford Park came through to lead at the 300-yard mark but, at the furlong pole or thereabouts, Mick Kinane shook the reins at Rocky, who was cruising along merrily. For the first time outside Ballydoyle, the burst of acceleration which was to become his trademark was seen to good effect. In a few strides, he flew by Sandford Park and the race was over as a contest. Rock Of Gibraltar passed the post doing handstands, and though he had not obliterated the field as he could, and perhaps should, have done, nevertheless it was an

THE BEGINNINGS

impressive performance which had the experts in The Curragh stands purring. Sandford Park and Mahsusie both kept going to the line, but were flattered by their proximity to the future superstar.

Straight away, O'Brien and Kinane conferred, and the jockey's verdict was conveyed to the waiting press by the trainer. 'He's a smart colt and really put his head down and quickened when he was asked,' said O'Brien. 'Michael said he is a Royal Ascot horse, and if that is the case he will probably go there without another run. Bar the Marble Hill Stakes back here next month, there is really little or nothing for him.'

O'Brien left the Marble Hill to another of his potential hotpots, Wiseman's Ferry, who went off the 2-7 favourite for that race and finished a disappointing third behind Mahsusie. Wiseman's Ferry would enjoy a decent two-year-old career and at three he went to America and finished down the field in the Belmont Stakes before winning the West Virginia Derby. For Rock Of Gibraltar, however, the next stage would be as big as you can get in racing – Royal Ascot. Sadly for Aidan O'Brien, and ultimately for John Magnier too, things did not go according to plan.

His first race had been a straightforward victory, and Rock Of Gibraltar showed that at least he handled soft ground, winning as an 11-10 favourite should with no worries for his backers from some way out. Irish journalists who were there that day say he looked good but not a superstar, and to their credit none now say they spotted his vast potential that April day – honesty in journalism, whatever next?

It was O'Brien's first success with a two year old in what would prove to be an outstanding season with his juveniles. Michael Kinane clearly enjoyed the outing, as he jumped off Rocky and pronounced that he would like to ride him at Royal Ascot. (Later, he completed a double on the day for O'Brien aboard the filly Toroca.) Rock Of Gibraltar, meanwhile, went back to Ballydoyle looking as if he had been out for a Sunday stroll, but sadly his next visit to the racecourse proved to be far from a walk in the park.

99

ROCK OF GIBRALTAR

ROYAL ASCOT, 19 JUNE 2001, AT 5.30 P.M. (OFF 5.33 P.M.).
The Coventry Stakes, a Group 3 race for two year olds.
Distance: six furlongs. Going: good to firm. 20 ran.
Prizes: 1. £36,000; 2. £13,800; 3. £6,900; 4. £3,300.
1. Landseer, 8–12, J.P. Spencer, 20–1, A.P. O'Brien.
2. Firebreak, 8–12, K. Fallon, 14–1, nk, I.A. Balding.
3. Meshaheer, 8–12, L. Dettori, 2–1 fav, nk, D.R. Loder.
4. Redback, 8–12, R. Hughes, 20–1, ¾ l, R. Hannon.
5. Mahsusie, 8–8 (1 lb overweight), J.P. Murtagh, 2 l, Francis Ennis.
6. Rock Of Gibraltar, 8–12, M.J. Kinane, sh hd, A.P. O'Brien.
Also ran: Highdown, Twilight Blues, Million Percent, Dark Sorcerer, Lascombes, Wishmaster, Rehearsal Hall, Resplendent Cee, Western Verse, Triple Play, Mister Benji, Lake Verdi, Mister Waterline, Lady Dominatrix.
Winner's time: 1 min 15.62 secs (slower than standard by 1.32 secs).
Winning owner: Mrs Sue Magnier.

What a pig's dinner of a race this was. Yet given what happened afterwards, i.e. Sir Alex Ferguson being brought into the ownership of Rocky, it is interesting to reflect that if the race had been trouble-free and Rock Of Gibraltar had finished first or second, would he have gone to the Railway Stakes and then the Gimcrack? Would he not have gone straight to a Group 1 race? And would John Magnier have been willing to allow the name of anyone else on the horse's registration forms? It is a moot point, but the fact is that Rocky suffered a shocking reverse in this mêlée and that made a lot of difference to his future.

The field contained the usual sprinkling of high-class colts and only two fillies, one of which was Mahsusie, so comprehensively beaten by Rocky at The Curragh. The hot favourite was Meshaheer, Godolphin's big juvenile hope who had won well at Doncaster on his previous outing but who would ultimately fail to become the quality animal he threatened to be on this day at Royal Ascot. Ballydoyle was doubly represented as Rocky and Landseer were both in the field, though the latter was not expected to finish in front of Rock Of Gibraltar. Both horses were the sons of

THE BEGINNINGS

Coolmore's great stallion Danehill, so Rocky was racing against his half-brother.

Before the race, O'Brien told Mick Kinane that he would be better off on Rock Of Gibraltar, and in hindsight that was a blessing. For as the race turned into something of a rugby-style maul, Kinane showed all his experience and subsequent events confirmed that his actions in keeping the horse out of real trouble proved very much to Rocky's gain. Still, it would have been good to see Rocky really trouncing his rivals. He just never got the chance.

Everything bar Meshaheer was friendless in the betting market, and Rocky's antics prior to the off lost him support among the well-heeled punters on Berkshire's finest acres. He was coltish, according to observers, and did not appear to have his mind on the job. Consequently, he went off at 10–1, the second-longest price of his career, and third favourite behind Meshaheer and Henry Cecil's Western Verse. Landseer was seen as Ballydoyle's second string but more than a few people had a touch each-way on him at 20s or bigger, especially the family and fans of young Jamie Spencer, the 'coming man' of Irish jockeyship who would not forget this race at Royal Ascot.

Meshaheer, the mount of Frankie Dettori, was first to suffer misfortune, and was away slightly slowly so that he missed the chance to gain a good rails position. Frankie was forced to bring him the long way round the field and even then did not get a clear passage. Rocky was first badly hampered after only a furlong, and with a number of the colts showing their inexperience, the Coventry turned into a dodgem race at 30 mph with horses barging each other and jockeys frantically trying to find a way through the morass.

Rock Of Gibraltar was well to the rear of the field but Kinane was jollying him along as Frankie Dettori switched to try to find a path for his colt, who was clearly going to win if his rider could find daylight. None appeared until the final furlong, by which time young Master Spencer had Landseer out in front. The colt ran green, swerving left over a furlong out and Spencer tried to control him by switching his whip, which provoked his mount into a rightward movement so that he clearly caused interference to those behind him, which made a stewards' inquiry inevitable.

One of those hampered was Redback, trained by Richard Hannon and ridden by Richard Hughes, who eventually finished fourth and would meet Rock Of Gibraltar again. Firebreak was one of the few horses to avoid any real trouble and despite Kieren Fallon's urgings coming down the outside he could not catch the winner, going down by a neck or so and suffering one of only two reverses in an outstanding two-year-old career. The mighty Godolphin operation would later buy Firebreak and take him to Dubai where he would keep almost £700,000 of the stable's money in-house by winning the Godolphin-sponsored Mile race at the World Cup meetings in 2003 and 2004. Meshaheer simply never had the opportunity to charge until too late, but finished like a train to snatch third just two necks behind the winner. David Loder and most pundits were convinced afterwards that the horse would have won comfortably had he enjoyed a clear passage.

Arguably, Meshaheer was the unluckiest horse in the race, and his trainer David Loder said, 'He should have won but that's the way it goes. I just hope it doesn't go that way too often.' But Rock Of Gibraltar was equally deprived of the chance to shine. Kinane spent almost a half-furlong trying to find a way through the wall of horses in front and to the side of Rocky, but to no avail. Many another jockey might have tried to barge his way through or given the horse a thrashing but Kinane reasoned that there were many more races to be won by the animal underneath him and contented himself with a late and eye-catching flourish which suggested to his trainer and many more observers that he might have finished much closer to Landseer or even have caught the winner. The real proof that Rocky had been plain unlucky was that Mahsusie, the filly he had comfortably beaten in his first race, managed to finish one place ahead in fifth.

'It was unfortunate that he [Rock Of Gibraltar] got turned over early,' said O'Brien. 'But they are both smart colts and we'll look at the July Stakes at Newmarket and possibly the Phoenix Stakes at Leopardstown for Landseer next. He's a lovely tough colt with lots of pace who should stand plenty of racing.'

Landseer won the Coventry Stakes but never finished in front of Rocky again. As for Jamie Spencer, the stewards needed someone to chastise for the roughness of the race and the youngster copped

THE BEGINNINGS

the blame. The beaks decided that Spencer was guilty of two offences: careless riding as Landseer hung left, and then using the whip with excessive force as he tried to correct the horse's drift. A six-day ban from riding was the sentence. It was Spencer's first win at Royal Ascot, and he should have been celebrating, but sentiment has never played too much of a part in the machinations of stewards.

The Coventry Stakes had proven to be a horrible event for Rocky, but it took considerable courage for him to run as he did after being hampered after the start and also later in the race. When Kinane had brought him for his run, there was simply no way through the wall of horses. The jockey clearly decided not to risk putting Rocky into danger, which might have put him off his racing, and he eventually finished sixth.

So far, there had been nothing in either of his races to indicate that Rock Of Gibraltar was anything other than a decent colt off the conveyor belt of talent pouring out of Coolmore–Ballydoyle. But plenty of experts had been impressed by his unsuccessful tilt at the Coventry, among them Mike Dillon, the suave head of public relations of the world's biggest bookmakers, Ladbrokes.

There are two versions of what happened next. Either Mike Dillon said to Sir Alex Ferguson after the Coventry Stakes, 'This horse that has just been beaten in the Coventry is a potential star and you should buy half of him for £120,000, and it will make you a fortune' – that's Ferguson's recollection in a nutshell – or else there is another version of events. For the sake of brevity, we'll call the alternative version the Gimcrack Craic, and you'll find out why in the next chapter.

In addition to his recollection of Mike Dillon giving him the idea, Ferguson also remembered things slightly differently when he spoke to me on the record in October 2001, in that the offer of Rock Of Gibraltar had come direct from Magnier: 'John offered me a half share in it *before it saw the track* [my italics], so I said thank you very much.'

At that point in his career, Dillon had been in the public relations department of Ladbrokes for 22 years, starting as racing press officer and working tirelessly to promote his company, with considerable success. He is the affable son of a Manchester publican, spends his life with a mobile phone welded to his ear and has achieved the improbable cachet of being a public relations man that journalists actually like. He had started his career in racing as a bet settler with Ladbrokes before being plucked out of the desk job to become the racing press officer for the company. Dillon had been part of the Ladbrokes operation which ran the Grand National and that successful stint helped him to gain the promotion to front man for the company. He is renowned as a man who goes out of his way to help his company's clients.

Dillon's one great love in sport is not a horse but a football club – Manchester United. He had been friendly with key players at the club such as Bryan Robson before meeting Alex Ferguson. The two became good friends, and it was definitely through Mike Dillon that Ferguson met Magnier, J.P. McManus and Aidan O'Brien.

Dillon acted as a sort of racing manager for Ferguson, and it is highly likely that the two men discussed football just as Ferguson had done with David McAllister in Paisley all those years before. Undoubtedly, Ferguson could have advised Dillon on football matters, and Dillon certainly advised Ferguson on his horses. There is no suggestion of anything untoward, however, and neither man chose to conceal their friendship when they visited racetracks together.

From 1998 onwards, when he first started owning and co-owning horses, Ferguson had liked nothing better than to go down to Newmarket to Ed Dunlop's stable and he would get there very early in the morning to watch the horses on the gallops. His friend Dillon knew this and approached Coolmore and Ballydoyle, where he is undoubtedly well connected. In 1999, though Ferguson and Magnier had been introduced before, the two men met at a race meeting and were able to talk at length. It was all very informal and they got on well, and met again later, when they found that they shared a distaste for the Establishment in racing.

Ferguson was once asked what he disliked in racing and he told the interviewer that the one thing that really got his goat was when he, as an owner, would stand in the parade ring and a jockey such as the great Michael Kinane would come up to him and tip his hat,

THE BEGINNINGS

like some gardener doffing his cap to the Lord of the Manor. That sort of outdated class system stuff went against the grain for former shop steward Alex Ferguson of Govan and his views struck a chord with John Magnier, former ditch-digger of Fermoy in Co. Cork where airs and graces are actively discouraged. So in 1999, Ferguson began to make trips to Tipperary. An Irish source who knows both Magnier and O'Brien said: 'It was suggested by Dillon to Ballydoyle that it would be a great boost for both parties to let Ferguson visit Ballydoyle and see the cream of the crop, the best horses in Europe. It was definitely Ballydoyle he came over to first, travelling with Mike Dillon, because he wanted to see the stables rather than the stud. Ferguson and Aidan O'Brien hit it off.'

That makes sense. They are from very different backgrounds but are both quite undoubtedly driven men. Everyone knows how obsessed with football Ferguson is, and O'Brien is the same with racing. He is reported never to have taken a holiday since he went to Ballydoyle. They also have similar jobs in one respect – Ferguson can't go out and play the match with his players, and O'Brien's job is done once the horse and jockey are on the track. They are also in charge of big expensive squads and have to choose the right players for the right jobs.

Ferguson was certainly seen in Fethard, the town nearest to Coolmore and Ballydoyle, which, contrary to some misguided geographic views, are not actually next door to each other but are several miles apart with Fethard in between them. Fethard is about ten miles south-east of Cashel, the major urban centre in the region, which is dominated by a spectacular castle on Cashel Rock, which, though smaller in dimension, is every bit as dominating a feature as Edinburgh's more famous Castle Rock. Cashel is also a notorious bottleneck on the main N8 road which links Dublin to Cork. A by-pass round Cashel was under construction in 2004 when I last visited Co. Tipperary – and its opening can't come quickly enough for beleaguered motorists.

All around Fethard in this aptly named 'Golden Vale' of Tipperary are large numbers of stud farms. Fethard itself could be called a one-horse town were it not for the fact that around it are the stables and paddocks which are home to thousands of horses. Dominating the scene is Coolmore, the area's largest employer, which is why people were reluctant to say anything about the stud farm's owner. In the main street of Fethard, which dates from mediaeval times and was once an important market town, you will find McCarthy's Hotel, which advertises its services as 'Publican, Restaurant and Undertaker'. And no, you don't need to drink yourself to death at the bar to be buried by McCarthy's. Annette Murphy now runs McCarthy's and is circumspect about her famous clients – Lord and Lady Lloyd-Webber, George Foreman, Sir David Frost, as well as past guests such as Éamon de Valera and Michael Collins of sainted fame in Ireland. McCarthy's is a racing person's pub – the insignia on the sign above the door is a horse's head and John Magnier, Vincent O'Brien, Lester Piggott and Robert Sangster liked nothing better than a chat in McCarthy's in days of yore.

One denizen of McCarthy's remembered Sir Alex Ferguson: 'He came over a couple of times at his own request and sure the lads at Ballydoyle got a bit of a kick out of it. And why wouldn't you when he is who he is?' And sure enough, on the leaflet which promotes McCarthy's is a picture of a beaming Ferguson with an avuncular arm around the vivacious Annette Murphy.

There's no doubt that after visiting Ballydoyle, Ferguson soon gravitated towards the company of Magnier, and the Coolmore boss took Ferguson, very much a novice owner, under his wing. In football terms, it would have been a bit like the reserve-team coach of a Third Division side being given lessons by Ferguson himself. 'I have to say I've done well with my various partnerships,' Ferguson told me. 'John Magnier in particular has been very helpful to me, giving me the right advice, telling me not to get involved with too many horses because, as he said, "you'll just use up all your money".'

There was no chance of him doing so at Ballydoyle, as precious little money changed hands, at least not in the direction of Manchester to Tipperary. There were no contracts and no payments at the start of this relationship, even when racing business was eventually transacted. One thing that Ferguson was able to arrange was his contribution to a remarkable charity auction organised by J.P. McManus, in whose company – which he thoroughly enjoyed – Ferguson had been seen at Cheltenham and elsewhere.

THE BEGINNINGS

In July 2000, McManus organised a headline-grabbing auction for Limerick charities at the same time as his pro-am golf tournament, which also raises funds for his home city of Limerick. Among the 30 collectors' items sold at the auction at the Adare Manor Hotel in Limerick were four tickets for a Manchester United home game and drinks with manager Alex Ferguson and his squad. Ferguson had donated the item thinking it might raise a few thousand pounds. He was staggered when an outing that would have taken him a few seconds to organise was sold for an astonishing £250,000.

With every high-roller worth his salt in that hotel room and determined to fling his cash in the direction of charity, the United tickets were far from the biggest fundraiser. Joe Lewis, the billionaire brains behind the financial giant ENIC, bid some of his petty cash for a round of golf with Tiger Woods and his great friend, Mark O'Meara. The sum Lewis paid was £1.4 million.

Other items in the auction were a signed photo of U2 which went for a record £30,000 and the bowler hat worn by Captain Keith Brown, starter of the Aintree Grand National which ended in fiasco in 1993 after he declared a false start, which was sold for £10,000.

Ferguson was moving in the right circles, and long before the 2001 Flat season he had become so immersed in his new pursuit that board members of United had already asked him if he was not spending too much time worrying about four-hooved players. Ferguson himself admitted later in 2001 that he was getting very serious about racing, and as usual it was his long-suffering wife who spotted the signs.

He told me: 'Cathy enjoys going to the races, but now she says I'm becoming obsessed as usual, and that she's not enjoying watching me betting on it. I get the *Racing Post* every morning and study the form, but sometimes I just watch the racing in the afternoon and don't bother to bet. I love going to the races, however, especially at Chester, which is near us and is a lovely track. I also like Haydock and York. Going racing is just a great day out for all the family and I can relax and get involved in another world.'

And ownership was proving very satisfying to Ferguson, as he told me: 'I do like to bet if I get the right information, and I've had a few big wins. But the major enjoyment is to experience your own horse winning. I can still recall the excitement when Queensland Star won at Newmarket as if it was yesterday.'

He was certainly on a different stratum from the vast majority of racegoers and owners. To rub shoulders with O'Brien and Magnier is a dream beyond the vast majority of those involved in racing. And Ferguson loved the 'buzz' of circulating in such a rarefied atmosphere in racing terms, as he recalled much later in 2001 in an extensive interview with *The Sun*'s award-winning racing correspondent, Claude Duval:

> I absolutely adore racing – the excitement of it all, the chance to get out in the fresh air, and the excellent facilities at tracks like Newmarket, Ascot and York. Football is wrapped up in emotion and the rivalry between clubs and fans can be intensely fierce. Fans love chanting. That is what it is all about – tribalism. It's handed down from fathers to sons. But racing is very different. We are all there to enjoy the spectacle . . . and to beat the bookies!
>
> There is no better place on earth to stand than on the gallops at Ballydoyle or Newmarket in the morning. I think I am in heaven. There are no mobile phones ringing. And I love a breakfast of Newmarket sausages after seeing my horses work. There is a wonderful camaraderie amongst racing people that I've not found anywhere else. Every time I go to the gallops I meet new people. Every morning, I go to Manchester United's training ground, I see the same faces. With racing you meet so many different people but we all share the love of the sport.
>
> When March comes round, with all the pressure and intensity of European Cup nights, I can get away from it all with a trip to Cheltenham to watch the Gold Cup. Or I can go to watch horses working on Aidan O'Brien's gallops at Ballydoyle.
>
> It's funny to think back but I remember when Bryan Robson was captain of Manchester United. One year, he begged me to let him have the afternoon off to go to

THE BEGINNINGS

Cheltenham for the Gold Cup. I was far from happy and explained we had a big game on the following Saturday. I delayed the training session deliberately so that by the time we had finished it was too late for Bryan to get to Cheltenham!

Nowadays, we would both be in the car rushing off to the races. A lot has changed for me in the last few years.

Was Stonewall Ferguson, that carnaptious curmudgeon, truly mellowing? Friends say that in the weeks after he made the decision to retire, Ferguson went through a period of considerable introspection, and he was certainly quieter than usual, except when it came to defending his beloved United and his own reputation as the results just did not happen for the Old Trafford side late in 2001. It is difficult to avoid the conclusion that the first half of the season was well below par for Ferguson and, by extension, his team. For, in August 2001, something happened which would not only ensure that Ferguson was much more regularly in the company of racing folk, but also confirm his status as an owner of worth. His friendship with Magnier and O'Brien would move to a different level as Ferguson began his link to the horse that will forever be associated with his name. But that happened after the race which made many people in racing realise that Rock Of Gibraltar was a colt with a future.

> THE CURRAGH, 1 JULY 2001, AT 2.15 P.M.
> The Anheuser Busch Railway Stakes, a Group 3 race for two year olds.
> Distance: six furlongs. Going: yielding. Seven ran.
> Prizes: 1. £31,451.61; 2. £9,959.68; 3. £4,717.74; 4. £1,572.58; 5. £1,048.39; 6. £524.19.
> 1. Rock Of Gibraltar, 8–10, M.J. Kinane, 1–2 fav, A.P. O'Brien.
> 2. Hawk Wing, 8–10, J.A. Heffernan, 12–1, 2 l, A.P. O'Brien.
> 3. Daneleta, 8–7, K.J. Manning, 12–1, ½ l, J.S. Bolger.
> 4. Redback, 8–10, K. Fallon, 4–1, ½ l, R. Hannon.
> 5. Zaffrani, 8–7, T.E. Durcan, 20–1, 8 l, David Wachman.

ROCK OF GIBRALTAR

6. Master Papa, 8–10, S. Craine, 14–1, 1½ l, Kevin Prendergast.

Also ran: Let's Try It.

Winner's time: 1 min 14.4 secs (slower than standard by 2.9 secs).

Winning owner: Mrs Sue Magnier.

The Railway Stakes has been a favourite 'prep race' for Aidan O'Brien's juveniles, and Rock Of Gibraltar was attempting to give him a fourth success in five runnings of the race. O'Brien was doubly represented, with Hawk Wing having his second race after a narrow win in a maiden at Tipperary.

There was no doubt about the stable's first string, however, as Kinane sat aboard Rocky while the Curragh punters piled on the cash to send him off the 1–2 favourite. The sole English raider, Richard Hannon's Redback, renewed opposition to Rocky after finishing just over two lengths ahead in the trouble-hit Coventry Stakes, while a couple of Danehill fillies, Daneleta and Zaffrani, were also in the field. Neither would go on to enjoy real success, and certainly nothing as glorious as their half-brother. The field was completed by a couple of no-hopers, Let's Try It and Master Papa, though the latter had won a lowly five-furlong sprint at Leopardstown on its previous outing, which was also its debut. Master Papa later went over hurdles and was sold to run in England from the yard of Grand National-winning trainer Nigel Twiston-Davies.

The race was virtually a set-up for Rocky and he did not disappoint. Daneleta cut out the running almost from the start. She had comfortably won her maiden at Tipperary on her previous outing and as that race was over seven furlongs she was expected to stay the six furlongs well, even on ground described as yielding – that lovely Irish expression which is the equivalent of footballers saying that a pitch will 'take a stud'. In three races, Rocky had already encountered three different types of ground and he handled them all well.

He certainly handled the rest of the field in this race, which proved entirely uneventful, except for Hawk Wing swerving slightly at the start which cost him any chance of winning. Not

THE BEGINNINGS

that he had any, as his stable companion was never going to lose this race.

Perhaps mindful of being trapped in the rear as in the Coventry Stakes, Kinane took Rock Of Gibraltar almost to the front from the outset. Daneleta gave Rocky a tow, and Kinane merely had to shake a rein at his mount about 300 yards from the line to go by the filly and win easily, though Kinane gave Rocky another lesson about racing by riding him out all the way to the line.

Hawk Wing had come with a good run about the two-furlong pole and took second place behind Rocky as they entered the final furlong, but he never looked like catching the winner. Daneleta plugged on to take third while Redback at least earned some travel expenses by taking fourth, though he was clearly not liking the ground and subsequently never struck a blow on anything less solid than good going. Redback's next race was the Listed Weatherbys Superlative Stakes at Newmarket where he paid Rocky a big compliment by winning well.

O'Brien now began to talk up Rocky: 'He's a smashing colt: a big, mature sort and strong. We hope he'll get a mile and at this stage he'd be a possible for the Dewhurst.'

A theme that would recur over the next couple of years also surfaced at this point – how good was Hawk Wing in relation to Rocky? Diplomatically, O'Brien confined himself to saying, 'Hawk Wing has come on a lot and he is a beauty. He won't mind seven furlongs or a mile.'

Rock Of Gibraltar now had that most vital asset against his name – he had won a Group race, albeit not of the highest standard. Given his bloodlines, he would now have to flop seriously in his remaining career on the track to avoid being sent to stud. And as a Group winner, the only way for him to go now was into the very best two-year-old races in Europe and certainly all the recognised Classic trials were on his potential agenda. In mentioning the Dewhurst Stakes at Newmarket, O'Brien was stating his ambitions for the colt he had helped to breed, and they were lofty.

The Railway Stakes was also the last time that Rock Of Gibraltar ran in the familiar dark blue colours of Mrs Sue Magnier. Another owner was shortly to arrive on the scene.

CHAPTER FIVE

The Gimcrack Craic

It was supposed to be a joke. The whole story of Rock Of Gibraltar and Alex Ferguson and John Magnier and J.P. McManus and Manchester United began as a jest and then went horribly wrong. Two self-made millionaires, one from an Irish agricultural background, the other from a Scottish mean street, got together to wind up the British racing Establishment. Within 30 months, the greatest football club in the world was teetering on the edge of disaster, and the two men's friendship had disintegrated into a mutually self-destructive duel, with each fighting for what they saw as their honour, not to mention tens of millions of pounds.

Many years from now, fans of Manchester United will sit in the pubs of Manchester, Dublin, London and everywhere the Reds are worshipped, and people will say, 'Remember that fight between Fergie and Magnier? What was that all about?' The legends will be woven and the story will be embellished with every retelling and eventually people will forget the truth about this tale of two giants, which is that it all kicked off with a fabulous racehorse and a jolly jape.

'It was all done for a bit of craic,' I was told by someone who was certainly in a position to know. The Irish love to tell stories and

THE GIMCRACK CRAIC

jokes, and the 'craic' will often include mischief-making and 'extracting the Michael', as they politely term the telling of tall tales. The 'Gimcrack Craic' may seem an implausible version of events, except for the fact that there is documentary proof of much of the story. It goes something like this.

Coolmore faced a problem in the autumn of 1999. Mull Of Kintyre, a colt sired by Danzig and therefore a grandson of Northern Dancer, romped away with the Gimcrack Stakes of that year, beating a decent field without really coming off the bridle. Mull Of Kintyre, who cost Magnier $1 million as a yearling, was plagued by injury later in his career and never reached the heights, but now stands at Coolmore Stud.

The Gimcrack Stakes brings the winning owner the 'privilege' of addressing the annual Gimcrack Dinner on a racing topic. Some owners use the speech to lambast their enemies, but most get in a substitute who either makes a serious point or has the diners rolling in the aisles with laughter – and sometimes both simultaneously.

Technically, Mull Of Kintyre's colours were Sue Magnier's, but she has never been known to speak in public. Nor was there any question of John Magnier standing up in front of a room full of dignitaries and speaking. He was just not going to give the Gimcrack Speech. In his entire three years in the Irish Senate, he made an average of one contribution a year and put forward only one motion, and every source who knows him says exactly the same thing – that he is genuinely a retiring man who does not like to put himself forward for such duties, and only does so when he has something to say about his own patch, as when he took on the Turf Club in Ireland. Having personally seen him make his way through the crowds at Royal Ascot in 2004, it is easy to conclude that he is indeed shy. He walks quickly, his head down, but with his eyes scanning the crowd from under his trademark cream Panama hat.

In 1999, Magnier was not ready to speak at York, so a substitute had to be found. Enter the newly knighted Sir Alex Ferguson.

The suggestion did not emanate from the Coolmore camp, and once again Mike Dillon – though it may not have been him – is the man who gets the blame for what looked, on the face of it, to be a cracking idea. It would surely be good for racing if a man like Ferguson, who had been so successful in the world's most popular sport, could give his views on how racing could make itself more marketable. It would also be mutually beneficial – Manchester United fans who did not usually bother about racing would see their manager getting involved and perhaps conclude it was a sport worth looking into, while Ferguson could also use the speech to push the MURC. Magnier was enthused by the suggestion, since it got him off the job and he also genuinely felt that racing's top brass should hear the views of this very successful man who had come up the hard way and made it to the top.

The concept was checked out informally with someone at York who was snootily dismissive of the whole idea and made a remark to the effect that they didn't need to hear from the son of a Scottish shipyard worker. Had that blazered buftie engaged his thinking gear and encouraged the idea, and had the York committee been asked for and given its approval, then Sir Alex Ferguson would have delivered the Gimcrack Speech of 1999, and the probability is that he would never have been associated with Rock Of Gibraltar. He might well have continued and even developed his association with Magnier and O'Brien, and he could certainly have owned or co-owned horses with them, but Rock Of Gibraltar came his way because of Magnier's wish that Ferguson should give the Gimcrack Speech, and that didn't become possible until another two years of the Gimrack Stakes had been run.

Coolmore consultant Bob Lanigan eventually delivered the 1999 Gimcrack Speech written by Magnier in which he generously offered to sponsor a £50,000 race at York and also castigated the British Government for failing to encourage the racing and breeding industries – a favourite hobby horse, if you'll pardon the pun, of the Coolmore owner.

But Magnier had been riled by the patronising answer he had been sent by that York snob and became determined that Ferguson would give the speech sometime in the future. And what Magnier wants, Magnier usually gets. The Coolmore boss was someone who had come from the lesser ranks of racing – not many National Hunt stud farmers in Ireland are on the British racing Establishment's dinner invitation list – and had built up his business to world-beating proportions, not by wheedling his way up the society ladder but by dint of hard work and his own skills.

'John Magnier doesn't ask about your personal background, he just wants to know what you have done,' said one of his associates in Ireland.

Magnier shared his idea about Ferguson with Michael Tabor, who himself had risen from relatively lowly status to owning considerable wealth and holding a position of considerable influence in racing. An East End bookmaker is also usually not on the Establishment's Christmas card list, so Tabor agreed with Magnier that whatever horse they were going to put in the Gimcrack Stakes of 2000 would run in Ferguson's colours, which would require Ferguson to be listed as a co-owner.

Magnier had already tried to find his new friend a decent Group race-winning horse, as Ferguson himself said later. The first Coolmore–Ballydoyle horse of which Ferguson was registered as co-owner was Zentsov Street. He also had a share in another colt, Heritage Hall, but it was clear early in both of the horses' careers that neither would reach the highest class, though Zentsov Street ran third in the Dewhurst Stakes, and both were sold in late 1999.

Another piece of evidence which seems to confirm the Gimcrack Craic story is the bewildering ownership pattern of the colt Juniper, which documents at Horse Racing Ireland's registration department show was co-owned *several times* by Sir Alex Ferguson during its two-year-old season in 2000. A $1.5 million yearling, Juniper was a son of Danzig and was thus very well bred. When Ferguson was first registered as the co-owner in 2000, Juniper was a virtual certainty to be aimed at all the big two-year-old races, including the Gimcrack. But, while in training at Ballydoyle in the early part of his two-year-old season, Juniper was not entirely straightforward to train, even for a genius like Aidan O'Brien. At several points in the summer of 2000, it was not certain that Juniper would go to York and other races were considered for it.

People who do not know the dynamics of horse and stable management will also be unaware of how inexact a science it is. A horse may be thriving one day and down in the dumps the next, for no obvious reason. Most trainers know how to prepare horses for particular races – you might never guess it from the way some carry on, but most do know the business – yet all it needs is one or two days' missed work due to injury or adverse weather and a whole season's racing plans can go out the window, as happened at Ballydoyle in 2002 when the stable was hit by a virus.

A horse may also change ownership mid-season, and the new owner might ignore the trainer and decide that he wants his potential Group race winner to contest a selling event at a lowly track – that's an exaggeration, obviously, but you would be surprised how often owners beg trainers to run decent horses in a lowly race that it is bound to win, just for the pleasure of being a winner rather than a loser in the owners' and trainers' bar.

As the Ballydoyle plans for Juniper altered, so did its ownership. The horse made improvements in fits and starts, and each time that it showed signs of developing in its work, a form would go off from Coolmore–Ballydoyle to include Ferguson in the ownership. Horse Racing Ireland's registration department have confirmed that Alex Ferguson was listed as an owner, and then deregistered, on several occasions before the Gimcrack of 2000 and afterwards. Here are just a few examples of the changes, all taken from Horse Racing Ireland documents.

Juniper was registered on 11 April 2000 as an equal partnership between Mrs Sue Magnier and Michael Tabor. On 22 August 2000, the day before the Gimcrack Stakes at York, a form was submitted registering Sir Alex Ferguson as an owner of Juniper. On 11 September, Ferguson was taken out of the ownership but on 15 September he was put back in again. The following year on 9 March, Alex Ferguson was deregistered from ownership of Juniper but the forms show he was reinstated on 13 June 2001. On 7 August 2002, Alex Ferguson was deregistered from the ownership of Juniper again.

These forms prove that Ferguson was definitely listed as a co-owner along with Michael Tabor and John Magnier just in time for the 2000 Gimcrack, presumably so he could make the speech if it won. But that's when the plan went awry.

Juniper was making his racecourse debut when he contested the Gimcrack at York on 23 August 2000, ridden by Mick Kinane. He ran a bit green but still finished only a head and neck in third behind Richard Hannon's pair, Bannister and Zilch. Juniper might well have won had he not been hampered inside the final furlong. How different the recent history of Manchester United might have been had Juniper finished just five or six feet ahead of where he did finish in the Gimcrack. Ferguson would have given the speech a year earlier than he did, and would have been saddled with a horse who did not train on at three and simply flopped – there's no other word for it – on the racecourse, finishing down the field in the Cork and Orrery Stakes at Ascot and plum last in the July Cup at Newmarket.

The proof that Juniper was not 'Ferguson's horse' was that the horse on several occasions ran in the colours of Michael Tabor. Such chopping and changing of ownership is not entirely unusual behaviour on the part of Coolmore–Ballydoyle. An Irish racing source confirmed, 'It is almost as if the colours to be worn by their horses could be swapped around as they pleased.' Another source described the changing colours as 'a flag of convenience'.

It happened again in 2001, as the search for a Coolmore–Ballydoyle Gimcrack winner developed. At this point, a query arises over Sir Alex Ferguson's recollection that he bought into the horse after the Coventry Stakes. For it is an undeniable fact that Rock Of Gibraltar won the Group 3 Anheuser Busch Railway Stakes at The Curragh on 1 July 2001 and he ran that day in the colours of Mrs Sue Magnier. Horse Racing Ireland have confirmed that Sir Alex Ferguson was not registered as Rocky's co-owner that day, a full 12 days after the Coventry Stakes. Though the registration departments prefer three or four weeks' notice, a change in the registered ownership of a horse is almost an instant process in both Britain and Ireland as it can be done by fax. Perhaps Ferguson was using the football close season to think things over, or perhaps someone at Coolmore–Ballydoyle forgot to send in the change of ownership form – highly unlikely, because that is against the rules and, more importantly, the prize money is paid out to the ownership which was registered at the time of the race. Had Ferguson bought into the horse after the Coventry Stakes on Mike Dillon's recommendation, as he has often said, it is doubtful whether he would have missed out on the chance to share in the £31,500 of prize money on offer at The Curragh.

ROCK OF GIBRALTAR

The fact is that Ferguson certainly did not have much input, if any, into the decision to run the horse in the Railway Stakes or where it would make its next appearance after The Curragh, not least because he did not 'own' Rocky until August.

Much later on, the public were told that John Magnier obviously didn't know what a good horse he had in the stables or he would not have given it to Ferguson. It's insulting to a man of his expertise and reputation to think that he did not know that Rock Of Gibraltar was potentially a very excellent horse indeed. 'Some people in the media tried to make out that the horse wasn't worth any money when Ferguson was given a share,' said an Irish breeding expert. 'That's a gross insult to Magnier. The horse's breeding alone meant that he was worth plenty. He had also won the Railway Stakes, which is a Group 3 race, beating Hawk Wing in the process.'

Neither John Magnier nor anyone other than the Oracle of Delphi could possibly have known, however, that Rocky would turn out to be a world-record breaker. By mid-2001, they did know at Coolmore–Ballydoyle that he was a very speedy and tough animal, but it was never planned that Rocky would do what he did, and Magnier and Aidan O'Brien had certainly not mapped out his entire career at that juncture for the simple and glaringly obvious reason that they did not know Rock Of Gibraltar's best distance, or which ground he would cope with best. Magnier and O'Brien also had two other potential superstars in Johannesburg and Hawk Wing – both rated ahead of Rocky in their two-year-old season, don't forget – and the racing plans of all three horses varied as each developed.

As with all owners and trainers who have several good horses at the same age in their stables, Magnier and O'Brien had no wish to see their horses contest too many events together. Given O'Brien's embarrassment of juvenile riches that year, a lot of variations took place in the plans for Rocky and his fellow stars. There is ample press coverage of O'Brien changing his plans for the colts, especially later in the 2001 season, to prove that he did indeed alter the targets for Johannesburg, Hawk Wing, Landseer and, above all, Rock Of Gibraltar, who arguably had the longest and toughest season of them all as a result – he certainly had the hardest races.

THE GIMCRACK CRAIC

I have been told that the horse lined up for Ferguson was actually Landseer, and certainly he was probably more of a Gimcrack 'type' than Rocky, as he was ahead in his work. He had already won the Coventry Stakes over the same distance of six furlongs, and would certainly like York's flat course. Weatherbys in Britain, who act as the secretariat for all racing in this country, have confirmed that Landseer was entered for the 2001 Gimcrack at the initial entry stage for which the deadline was 29 June. But O'Brien had numerous colts entered in the race – in total he had 20 of the 108 initial entries, a not untypical mass entry by him – and it is certain that the trainer left the choice of horse to contest the Gimcrack until the last possible moment. The horses he eventually plumped for were Wiseman's Ferry and Rock Of Gibraltar, and with Rocky obviously going to be the first string, he would carry Ferguson's colours.

There is evidence, which this book makes fully public for the first time, to support the Gimcrack Craic version. It is a matter of public record confirmed by the Registration Department of Horse Racing Ireland, which has scrupulously maintained all records kept by its various predecessors, that Sir Alex Ferguson was first registered as Rock Of Gibraltar's co-owner by Coolmore–Ballydoyle on 17 August 2001. Furthermore, he was listed as 'first' owner, because under the rules for owners' partnerships, then as now, the name of the person whose colours will be worn by the jockey must be stated first.

That date is highly significant, as racing operates a system of prior declaration of runners at several stages before the race. The most important sign that a horse is actually going to run in a major race, especially a Group race, is the confirmation of entry stage which takes place usually five days before the race. For a race like the Gimcrack, known as an 'early closing' race, there is a first-entry stage, usually six weeks or so before the day of the race. A trainer must enter the horse by that first date and then the weights for the race are published, usually three weeks before the event. But to confirm that a horse is going to run, a trainer must actively take steps to ensure that the horse is among the stated runners at the confirmation of entry stage. The trainer can still cancel the entry at the 'final declaration' stage either 48 or 24 hours before a race, but if he does so afterwards, e.g. if he doesn't like the weather on the morning of the race and pulls out the horse, the stewards can fine the trainer if they do not think his excuse is valid.

In the card for the 2001 Gimcrack issued by Weatherbys on behalf of the BHB, Rock Of Gibraltar's name appeared as a confirmed entry for the Gimcrack, which means that his participation was declared by his trainer before noon on 17 August 2001. The horse was certainly in the Gimcrack in the card for York races issued to the media that day. Landseer and the other O'Brien entries were not on this card, although they had appeared in the list of initial entries, suggesting that an eleventh-hour decision had been made.

It is matter of public record that the form nominating Sir Alex Ferguson for the first time as the registered equal co-owner of Rock Of Gibraltar was submitted to Horse Racing Ireland *on the same day* as Rocky was declared to run in the Gimcrack. Horse Racing Ireland's registration department have confirmed that the date on the registration form was 17 August 2001, five days before the Gimcrack on 22 August. The form simply alters the name of the owner from one owner – Susan Magnier – to two, namely Sir Alex Ferguson and Mrs Magnier. Ferguson's name was first, meaning that the horse would run in his colours. As an owner who had registered before for other horses, Ferguson's colours were already known and there was no need to delay his co-ownership to allow colours to be designed.

The importance of this information is quite simple – it suggests that the decision to run Rock Of Gibraltar in the Gimcrack was indeed taken at the last minute, with Landseer being left out of the race, as recorded by Weatherbys at Wellingborough in Northamptonshire. Almost simultaneously, an alteration was made in the ownership registration of Rock Of Gibraltar in Ireland to ensure that it ran in Ferguson's colours. The forms certainly call into question Sir Alex Ferguson's memory of how he acquired his share in Rock Of Gibraltar. The timing of the beginning of his involvement as co-owner of the horse is certainly open to question. It would appear that the written documentation – a matter of public record – gainsays Sir Alex Ferguson's recollection of events.

Coolmore–Ballydoyle subsequently let it be known that Ferguson

THE GIMCRACK CRAIC

was registered as Rocky's owner on 17 August 2001. They might not be impartial, you could say, as the time and manner of Ferguson's first involvement with the horse is key to the issue of his ownership, but the public records show that they made the change on that day, just five days before Rocky won his Group 2 race.

There is one record which could show exactly what Sir Alex Ferguson gained or did not gain from his 'ownership' of Rocky, which is the Weatherbys financial account which all owners must institute when they come into British racing. It is this account through which they are paid prize money, and from which debits are made to pay items like jockey fees. It goes without saying that Weatherbys will never release the details of any account held with them.

The only man who could verify the United manager's account that he 'bought' the horse after the Coventry Stakes is Mike Dillon. Had the ownership case gone to court, Dillon would probably have been called as a witness. But by which side? This writer has learned – not from Mike Dillon, who would not speak to me – that the Ladbrokes man has consistently stated that he would refuse to give evidence on oath on Ferguson's behalf. Is that the real reason that he and Ferguson fell out so badly and are still not speaking? With neither man talking, that issue must remain one for informed speculation rather than definite verification.

This Gimcrack Craic story has been pooh-poohed by some people supportive of Ferguson. It is just Coolmore's spin on things, they say, a good yarn to explain away why Magnier may have had other reasons for his association with the United manager – those motives are usually meant to be the false allegation that Ferguson, Magnier and McManus were forming a consortium to take over United. That is also a fallacy which is easily disproved by the twin facts that Cubic Expression bought into United long before Ferguson was gifted his half-share in Rock Of Gibraltar and only started to acquire serious chunks of the club after the manager had fallen out with the two Irishmen. If this was their way of forming a group to take control of United, then the trio went about it in a fashion that defies logic, to say the least.

The issue of whose colours Rock Of Gibraltar carried during his career has been something of a red herring in this story. As in

Britain, the Irish racing authorities' rule is that in a partnership, where a horse is owned by two to four people, rather than a single person or a club, the horse can run in the colours of anyone who is in the partnership. Syndicates often draw lots or use a member's spare set of racing colours – they are not cheap to register – to indicate the identity of the owners. That rule was already in place in August 2001, so you could be either the majority shareholder or equal co-owner, i.e. 50 per cent owner of a horse, for it to run in your colours – as long as your name was first on the form and you had delegated authority to act on your behalf to the trainer.

The fact is that Magnier wanted Ferguson to give the Gimcrack Speech, so he took care of every last detail and left nothing to chance. Rocky would run in Ferguson's colours, and as equal owner. The manager would have the unquestionable right to give the speech.

No matter how it came about, on 17 August 2001, Ferguson was registered as equal-shares owner of Rock Of Gibraltar and the horse would run in his colours from then until the day Rocky retired more than a year later. The forms do not say that Ferguson was the majority owner or how much he paid. Nor do they need to – Weatherbys in this country, the BHB and Horse Racing Ireland have confirmed that the ownership forms which are submitted to them are not legally binding documents with the status of affidavits and no one needs to swear to the truth of their contents. They also have no status in court. In Britain, wherever syndication is involved, the group of owners usually give full details of the percentages of a particular horse that each member within the partnership owns. They are definitely required to state who is involved in the ownership but this can merely be the name of a syndicate or club such as the well-managed Elite Racing Club – and for obvious reasons the syndicate must nominate whose colours will be worn. Again, all such documents have no legal standing.

On that Gimcrack day, Ferguson could not attend York as he was with his team preparing for that evening's match against Blackburn Rovers. He delayed the team's departure in order to watch the race on television, and was glad he had done so.

THE GIMCRACK CRAIC

YORK, 22 AUGUST 2001, AT 3.45 P.M. (OFF 3.46 P.M.).

The Scottish Equitable Gimcrack Stakes, a Group 2 race for two-year-old colts and geldings.

Distance: six furlongs. Going: good. Nine ran.

Prizes: 1. £72,500; 2. £27,500; 3. £13,750; 4. £6,250; 5. £3,125; 6. £1,875.

1. Rock Of Gibraltar, 9-0, M.J. Kinane, 11-4, A.P. O'Brien.
2. Ho Choi, 8-11, J. Carroll, 33-1, 3 l, Miss L.A. Perratt.
3. Twilight Blues, 8-11, B. Doyle, 33-1, ½ l, B.J. Meehan.
4. Waldenburg, 8-11, L. Dettori, 13-8 fav, hd, J.H. Gosden.
5. Saddad, 8-11, R. Hills, 6-1, 1 l, Sir Michael Stoute.
6. Anna Walhaan, 8-11, S. Drowne, 12-1, 3½ l, M. Channon.

Also ran: Kulachi, Prince Dayjur, Mister Cosmi.

Winner's time: 1 min 11.23 secs (slower than standard by 0.23 secs).

Winning owners: Sir Alex Ferguson and Mrs Sue Magnier.

This was when Rocky really came to the attention of the British racing public, and his performance marked him out to the experts as a high-class colt who would be worth following in future. As always with the horse, though, there were plenty of detractors who were quick to point out that it was a disappointing race because the other highly fancied colts in the race didn't live up to expectations . . . as if Rocky could do anything about that. And in any case, hindsight is the vision of those who lack perception, and it suited some commentators to rubbish the race afterwards rather than admit they were wrong beforehand about Rocky.

Not that anyone decried the Gimcrack prior to the race, because the field contained some animals which had already shown they were capable of challenging for major honours. Sir Michael Stoute's Saddad, for instance, had hacked up in a decent maiden at Yarmouth, and any well-bred juvenile colt owned by Sheikh Hamdan Al Maktoum has to be considered a future champion, at least until it proves otherwise. The same goes for any young colt that John Gosden trains and Frankie Dettori rides, and Gosden did indeed have high hopes for Waldenburg, who had triumphed over

ROCK OF GIBRALTAR

Godolphin's big hope Dubai Destination in a hot maiden at Newbury two months previously.

The field also featured the first three home – Mister Cosmi, Prince Dayjur and Anna Walhaan – in the prestigious Gerrard Richmond Stakes at Glorious Goodwood three weeks prior to the Gimcrack. Linda Perratt had also brought Ho Choi down from her Cree Lodge stables beside Ayr racecourse for owner Alan Guthrie, who most pundits thought was tilting at windmills with his horse. There were one or two whispers for the Scottish raider but he went off at 33-1 while Rocky was sent off 11-4 second favourite behind the much fancied Waldenburg, who was getting a 3 lb weight advantage because he had not yet won a Group race.

Rock Of Gibraltar wasn't behind the favourite at all in the actual race. He was cruising from the off and Kinane had him perfectly positioned, up with the pace throughout and getting a lead from Mister Cosmi through the first quarter mile. Two furlongs out, Kinane pressed the metaphorical button and that smooth acceleration saw Rocky go powerfully into a lead he would not surrender.

Behind him, the fancied horses were toiling, with the horses who had competed in the Richmond Stakes being the first to crack. Perhaps the Gimcrack had come too soon after their exertions at Goodwood, or more likely they were not that good in the first place, as Anna Walhaan eventually went over hurdles, Mister Cosmi won a couple of minor races and Prince Dayjur finished last in his next three races.

Waldenburg and Saddad had been held up for a late run, but it never really materialised, the former simply downing tools early when Frankie Dettori asked him to do some work. Saddad threw away his chance by pulling hard for his head early on, and after a flattering burst of speed he tired quickly. Surprisingly, it was outsiders Ho Choi and Twilight Blues who posed the only challenge from inside the furlong marker. Ho Choi had appeared to be struggling but he stayed on well under pressure, while fellow 33-1 shot Twilight Blues did nothing wrong and at least showed some promise. But up ahead, Rocky was home and hosed and could have won by five or six lengths instead of the official distance of three lengths, Kinane merely keeping him going rather

THE GIMCRACK CRAIC

than needlessly thrashing him to get more speed, as his trainer recognised.

'He finished on the bit in the Coventry,' said O'Brien. 'He couldn't get out and Michael Kinane never even shook the reins at him. Michael sat on the pace all the way today and let him go, and he wasn't at his end going to the line. Michael felt in the last half furlong he was only beginning to get going, and that is a great sign.'

Of the first few finishers, Ho Choi never really showed much in Britain, but when transferred to Ivan Allan's stable in Hong Kong he won a Group 2 handicap and eventually won more money than any of the rest of the Gimcrack field – except for Rocky, of course. Twilight Blues won the Victor Chandler European Free Handicap at three and the Duke of York Hearthstead Homes Stakes at four, and while Waldenburg was disappointing afterwards, Saddad franked the Gimcrack form decisively next time out by romping away with the Group 2 Flying Childers Stakes at Doncaster.

Shortly after the race, Aidan O'Brien gave a strong clue as to his thinking about Rocky's future, nominating the first colts' Classic of 2003 as his target. 'He's a big, solid horse. The 2,000 Guineas is a long way off, but you have to be thinking that way at the minute. He's in all the top two-year-old races and we will get them out of the way first.'

The die was cast. For Rock Of Gibraltar, the only way now would be up – up in class, and up in distance. Would he cope?

Sir Alex Ferguson's new semi-acquisition may have won the Gimcrack, but it wasn't an entirely successful day for him. A David Beckham own goal meant that United only drew 2–2 with Blackburn Rovers, and their poor start to the season continued.

His later memory of events leading up to the Gimcrack can be vague. Ferguson wrote a 'first person' piece for *The Observer* newspaper in 2002:

> My first real memory of Rock Of Gibraltar was at the Gimcrack Stakes at York in August of last year. I had bought him a couple of months earlier, and he had already won once. But it was exciting to watch him there, and the way he won it I didn't expect, though John Magnier had said he had a good chance. So when it won I was excited. But I

don't think any of us, including John, expected it to turn out the way it has.

Of course, as events would later show, Ferguson had not outrightly bought the horse, and the registration documents prove he was certainly not listed as owner, 'a couple of months earlier'. He was also vague about details, writing:

> John [Magnier] knew that I'd had one or two successes with the horses, and he said, 'We'll try and get you a Group 1 winner.' And I said, how's that? and he said, 'Well, we'll offer you the chance to buy one of our horses.'

Perhaps Magnier did say that, or words to that effect, but the fact is that Ferguson never did buy a Coolmore horse outright.

Ferguson was certainly not treated as a full owner of the horse, or at least he didn't act like one. Most owners demand to be at least consulted on where and when their horses race. That did not happen with Ferguson and Rock Of Gibraltar. The evidence which runs contrary to the impression that was sometimes given by Ferguson's use of language that he had some say in Rock Of Gibraltar's running plans was given to me in October 2001. In the interview, he told me categorically that he left such matters to Aidan O'Brien, and that assertion was printed in *Scotland on Sunday* and picked up by other newspapers, especially Irish dailies.

But such ambiguity was all in the future. At that time, everyone loved the story of Ferguson and his horse and certainly Ferguson's Irish friends were doing well. The Gimcrack and the Ebor Handicap, which was won that afternoon by Kinane aboard Mediterranean, had put O'Brien well into the lead over Sir Michael Stoute in the British trainers' championship. The Maestro of Ballydoyle was hoovering up Group 1 races around this time, Milan lifting the St Leger, while his juveniles were sweeping all before them, with Hawk Wing breaking the course record at The Curragh in the National Stakes. On the day before the St Leger, Rocky ran in the Champagne Stakes at Doncaster. It would be the last time he would taste defeat in Europe.

THE GIMCRACK CRAIC

DONCASTER, 14 SEPTEMBER 2001, AT 3.05 P.M. (OFF 3.08 P.M.).

The Rothmans Royals Champagne Stakes, a Group 2 race for two-year-old colts and geldings.

Distance: seven furlongs. Going: good to soft. Eight ran.

Prizes: 1. £60,000; 2. £23,000; 3. £11,500; 4. £5,500.

1. Dubai Destination, 8–10, L. Dettori, 3–1, D.R. Loder.
2. Rock Of Gibraltar, 9–0, M.J. Kinane, 11–10 fav, 1 l, A.P. O'Brien.
3. Leo's Luckyman, 8–10, K. Darley, 9–1, 4 l, M. Johnston.
4. Wiseman's Ferry, 8–10, J.P. Spencer, 8–1, ½ l, A.P. O'Brien.
5. Sohaib, 8–10, R. Hills, 8–1, 3 l, B.W. Hills.
6. Amour Sans Fin, 8–10, B. Doyle, 50–1, 2 l, B.J. Meehan.

Also ran: Great View, Ice And Fire.

Winner's time: 1 min 26.45 secs (slower than standard by 1.35 secs).

Winning owner: Sheikh Mohammed.

I have written extensively about this race in Chapter One, as it was the first time I ever saw Rocky race in the flesh, but other details are worth recounting. This was a setback for Rock Of Gibraltar, though not much of one, and it contained one element which indeed would later help his march to glory.

Stable confidence had been high in his ability to last the extra furlong on good to soft ground, and the punters latched on to this and made him hot favourite, despite the impressive claims of Dubai Destination, Godolphin's strongest hope for Classic honours the following year. Indeed, Frankie Dettori's mount drifted in the market to an almost generous 3–1. This was presumably because Waldenburg, who had finished well behind Rocky in the Gimcrack, had narrowly beaten Dubai Destination in his maiden race – the Scottish Life Maiden at Newbury in June.

After this debut race, however, Dubai Destination had greatly improved. In his next race, the Strutt & Parker Maiden at Newmarket in July, Dubai Destination had gone off 1–3 favourite and had won like a long odds-on shot, slaughtering a field of potentially high-class juveniles on softish ground. By the time of the Champagne Stakes, that maiden race had already produced winners, so Dubai Destination's drift in the market was unexpected. The bookmakers, who pushed everything else out to 8-1 or bigger, though, would prove to be spot on about there being only two in the race, except for the identity of the winner.

After hacking up on his debut at Ayr, there had been some confidence early in the season in Leo's Luckyman. Hailing from Mark Johnston's superb stable at Middleham in North Yorkshire, it was felt in the summer of 2001 that Leo's Luckyman would be that trainer's best hope for a 2,000 Guineas winner since Mister Baileys gave him his first Classic victory in 1994. But he had flopped behind Hawk Wing in the Futurity Stakes at The Curragh on his previous outing and he could not be seen as a real threat to the big two.

By far the most interesting runner in the rest of the field was O'Brien's other entrant, Wiseman's Ferry. The reason for the interest, frankly, was to see how close he would finish to Rocky after finishing six lengths and four lengths in two previous outings behind the stable's top-ranked two year old, Johannesburg.

There was a sizeable crowd at Doncaster that day, though of course there would be many more on the following day when the St Leger would be run, and as with all juveniles, the question was whether they could handle the attention without being distracted.

This may well be one of the keys to understanding Rocky's surprising defeat. The field broke well, but Dubai Destination was immediately reined back by Frankie Dettori, while up ahead stable companion Ice And Fire went to the front under the vastly experienced Willie Ryan to act as pacemaker, with Sohaib's rider Richard Hills trying to match him. Kinane settled Rocky in behind the leaders, and he kept up with the stout pace along with Leo's Luckyman.

Once again, Rock Of Gibraltar seemed to be cruising effortlessly to victory, even if Dettori had not moved a muscle on Dubai Destination in last place and Sheikh Mohammed's colt was clearly racing well within himself. If anything, Kinane took Rocky to the front too soon – more than two furlongs out, in fact – but he could hardly be blamed as all around him other horses were tiring. Leo's Luckyman tried to follow him as the leaders faded, Sohaib in particular fading fast and hanging to his right. It was all over, some

TOP: The race that showed Rock Of Gibraltar's promise – wearing Sir Alex Ferguson's distinctive colours, Rocky wins the Scottish Equitable Gimcrack Stakes at York in August 2001. (© Mirrorpix)

ABOVE: Sir Alex Ferguson in sunny mood at Manchester United's Carrington training ground. (Robert Perry, © Scotsman Publications)

TOP: John Magnier. (© Empics)

ABOVE: Rock Of Gibraltar wins the Grand Criterium at Longchamp, Paris, in October 2001. (© Mirrorpix)

ABOVE: A tranquil early morning view of Ballydoyle stables in Co. Tipperary.

LEFT: As close as I got to Coolmore's main gate.

TOP: The author pictured beside the statue of Be My Guest outside Coolmore.

ABOVE: Rock Of Gibraltar wins the Sagitta 2,000 Guineas. (© Mirrorpix)

TOP: The distinctive features of Guineas-winning jockey Johnny Murtagh.

ABOVE: J.P. McManus. (© John Grossick)

TOP: Rock Of Gibraltar wins the St James's Palace Stakes. (© Empics)

ABOVE LEFT: Mick Kinane and Sir Alex Ferguson
confer after the Ascot victory. (© Empics)

ABOVE RIGHT: McCarthy's Hotel in Fethard, Co. Tipperary.

TOP AND ABOVE: Two faces of Sir Alex Ferguson.
(© Scotsman Publications)

RIGHT: Aidan O'Brien in typical racecourse pose. (© Empics)

An example of Coolmore's largesse – a sponsored rugby club's prize jersey, signed by the 2003 Ireland Rugby World Cup squad, in McCarthy's Hotel.

A face in the crowd – Mike Dillon of Ladbrokes at Aintree on Grand National day, 2004.

people thought, as Rock Of Gibraltar's usual acceleration took him clear, but behind Rocky, the race had been set up perfectly for the finishing burst of Dubai Destination and Dettori is an all-time master at making a winning run at exactly the right moment.

Dettori's colt was something special that day, and given the perfect timing of the run, once he hit the front Dubai Destination was never going to lose. Rock Of Gibraltar and Kinane seemed to have been caught on the hop, perhaps thinking the race was won, or maybe the horse was merely soaking up the cheers and had his attention diverted from his job. Hard though Rocky tried to respond, there was no time or distance in which to do so, and in a trademark piece of pure theatrical chutzpah, like a boxer showboating, Dettori took his foot off the gas in the shadow of the pole as if to say 'That was easy-peasy'. It only looked that way – Dubai Destination had the benefit of a pacemaker and was receiving 4 lbs from Rocky, equivalent in distance to more than a length. Yes, Dubai Destination could have won by two lengths, but no more than that, which meant that at level weights Rock Of Gibraltar would have run to within less than a length of a horse with a pacemaker to aid it, and a colt who, for that matter, was immediately made 6-1 favourite for the following year's 2,000 Guineas by Ladbrokes, with the other big chains offering 7s or 8s. Coral disagreed, retaining Johannesburg as their 5-1 favourite with Rocky pushed out by everyone to 12s or 16s.

The *Racing Post*'s form expert reported that Rocky 'clearly stays seven furlongs well, and although his dam was a sprinter he may well prove at home over a mile next season'. He got that bang on the button. It was also a learning experience for the colt, and a lesson he obviously never forgot, as Rocky never surrendered a lead in the rest of his career and would never be beaten in Europe again. But the real significance of the race is the way it changed Kinane's way of riding Rock Of Gibraltar.

In 2001, Michael Kinane was, by common consent, the finest big-race jockey in Europe, rivalled only by Godolphin's star Frankie Dettori. Indeed, the title of the fine authorised biography of Kinane by Michael Clower is *Big Race King*. He had become stable jockey to Ballydoyle in 1998, after 15 years with top Irish trainer Dermot Weld. Five years previously, he had refused to leave

Weld to become Sheikh Mohammed's retained jockey, but by the time the offer came from Coolmore-Ballydoyle, Kinane was coming up for 40 and realised that he would probably only ever get one chance to ride the kind of horses that Magnier and Aidan O'Brien could provide.

Kinane's family of jockeys includes his father, Tommy, who won the 1978 Champion Hurdle at Cheltenham aboard Monksfield, while three of his brothers are also jockeys. He is married with two daughters, and though he is no socialite, he is one of the more pleasant people to talk to immediately after a big race – he's won so many of them that he rarely gets fazed. He rode his first winner in 1975 at Leopardstown, apprenticed to Liam Browne. Basing himself in Ireland but with frequent stints in Hong Kong, he soon became renowned for his consistent performances in big events. At the end of the 2003 season, Kinane parted company with Ballydoyle and for the 2004 season he signed to ride for trainer John Oxx, replacing Johnny Murtagh who went freelance, while Jamie Spencer stepped up to be stable jockey for O'Brien.

By 2004, Kinane had won the Irish jockeys' championship 13 times, and he holds the Irish seasonal record with 115 in 1993. In all, he had ridden 58 Group 1 victories for O'Brien and he has won almost every top race in Europe, including the Prix de l'Arc de Triomphe on Carroll House in 1989 and Montjeu in 1999. He is the only jockey to have won the Breeders' Cup, the Arc, the Epsom Derby, the Belmont Stakes, the Melbourne Cup – aboard Vintage Crop in 1993 – and the Japan Cup, in which he rode the great Pilsudski to victory in 1997. In 2000, he rode Giant's Causeway in his run of Group 1 successes, though he was blamed for the Iron Horse's defeat in the Breeders' Cup.

By the Doncaster meeting of September 2001, he had already won the Irish 1,000 Guineas and Epsom Oaks with Imagine, the Epsom and Irish Derbys and King George VI and Queen Elizabeth Stakes on Galileo, and the July Cup on Mozart. The day after Rocky's defeat, he would win the St Leger aboard Milan and later in the year he would ride Johannesburg to a memorable victory in the Breeders' Cup Juvenile at Belmont Park.

Rock Of Gibraltar was not the only one to learn a lesson that day. In an exclusive interview for this book, Frankie Dettori pinpointed the Champagne Stakes as the race in which Mick Kinane realised how much of a horse he had under him and how he would ride him in the future. Dettori admitted: 'Yes, we rode the race to suit us that day, and that's because we realised what a good horse we were up against.

'I had a good horse that day, too, and the race worked out perfectly for us. Once we passed them they were never going to catch us.

'But after that race, Michael changed the way he rode Rock Of Gibraltar, and he would hold him up to make use of his speed, and that worked out really well for them, so maybe it was a good thing for them in the long run.'

Aidan O'Brien was the first to point out that Rock Of Gibraltar had conceded 4 lb to the winner and had run him pretty close. 'He's run a really solid race considering he would have preferred faster ground,' he said, 'and although the winner came past, I don't think you can say he didn't stay.' Though it was not commented on by others, it was hard to believe that O'Brien failed to notice that his second string, Wiseman's Ferry, had finished almost five lengths behind Rocky. The performance by the stable companion was on a par with his placings behind Johannesburg. Perhaps it was then that the Maestro of Ballydoyle realised that Rocky was right alongside Johannesburg as a prospect, but more likely he knew some time before that day at Doncaster.

For O'Brien promptly hinted that the Dewhurst Stakes would provide the stage to boost Rocky's claims to be a Classic contender. With David Loder suggesting the Newmarket race as his horse's next target, and Hawk Wing and Johannesburg also in the picture, the pundits were drooling over the prospect of a battle royal on Champions' Day at Headquarters. First up, however, was a trip to Paris in all its autumnal splendour.

> LONGCHAMP, 7 OCTOBER 2001, AT 3.45 P.M.
> (OFF 3.43 P.M.).
> Grand Criterium, a Group 1 race for two-year-old colts and geldings.
> Distance: seven furlongs. Going: holding. Five ran.
> Prizes: 1. £121,242; 2. £48,497; 3. £24,248; 4. £12,124; 5. £6,062.

ROCK OF GIBRALTAR

1. Rock Of Gibraltar, 9-0, M.J. Kinane, 4-5 jfav, A.P. O'Brien.
2. Bernebeu, 9-0, O. Peslier, 21-10, 3 l, A. Fabre.
3. Dobby Road, 9-0, A. Junk, 15-2, 1½ l, Mlle V. Dissaux.
4. Shah Jehan, 9-0, J.P. Spencer, 4-5 jfav, 2½ l, A.P. O'Brien.
5. Imtiyaz, 9-0, L. Dettori, 37-10, 4 l, D.R. Loder.

Winner's time: 1 min 22.9 secs (slower than standard by 2.9 secs).

Winning owners: Sir Alex Ferguson and Mrs Sue Magnier.

This was the race which made every serious punter and pundit in Britain sit up and notice that Rock Of Gibraltar was not just a rich football manager's plaything. So comprehensive was the manner of Rocky's victory in his first-ever Group 1 race that he was immediately elevated to the rank of potential star in his own right, rather than a probable supporting actor to the stable's likely male leads, Johannesburg and Hawk Wing.

The going was officially described as 'holding' but that's presumably because the French don't have a word for quagmire. It had rained heavily in the morning and some punters and pundits wondered if O'Brien might pull Rocky out of the race at the last moment, given that he had expressed public concern about the going becoming too soft.

Due probably to the wet conditions and rain-threatening weather, the crowd was perhaps not as numerous as that which normally attends Longchamp on Arc day, but it was still large and noisy. Rock Of Gibraltar behaved like an angel in the parade ring and as he cantered down to the start, there was no obvious sign that the ground was affecting him. David Loder had sent over Imtiyaz from Newmarket to oppose Rocky, and the trainer positively relished the prospect of meeting O'Brien's horses on soft ground. The home brigade was led by André Fabre's colt Bernebeu, who had finished second to Guys And Dolls, trained by Paul Cole, in the Prix la Rochette over the Longchamp course.

This being France, where they are not so precious about such things, the race actually went off two minutes early, but even if the other horses had started then and Rocky had started at the proper post time he would probably still have won. For this was his most commanding performance up to that point in his career, and from the off there was no doubt about the eventual winner. Rock Of Gibraltar broke away fast but Kinane settled him down and allowed Bernebeu to cut out the running, though after 300 yards Frankie Dettori sussed that the pace was playing into Kinane's hands and he moved Imtiyaz into the lead, which he held from there until inside the two-furlong pole. Then something quite extraordinary happened – a real 'whoosh' moment.

Rocky had been bowling along in fourth as if he were a Parisian gentleman out for a stroll in the Bois de Boulogne. As he motored up to Imtiyaz, Kinane didn't even seem to twitch as he asked his colt to go and win the race, and with a smooth and powerful movement like a Rolls-Royce going up through the gears, Rock Of Gibraltar just catapulted by the leader and within the space of 100 yards or less he was almost 12 lengths clear of the field, and the race had been reduced to a processionary triumph for a horse that was simply in a different league to its rivals.

Infamously at Longchamp, there are two winning posts to cater for different distances, and it looked to some as if Kinane had mistaken the first post for the winning line, but he had merely been looking round to see the distance between himself and the rest of the toiling colts and had decided to let Rocky saunter home.

Even in neutral, he still coasted home by an official margin of three lengths. In all seriousness, it could have been 13 lengths, such was the superiority of Rock Of Gibraltar on that day in Paris. The superlatives flowed after the race, and the bookmakers reacted accordingly. Some had pushed Rocky out as far as 25–1 for the following year's 2,000 Guineas but almost as soon as an emotional Sir Alex Ferguson appeared to lead in his winner, the odds had been slashed to as low as 6s with Coral or 12s with Ladbrokes. Not the least of the controversies stirred by the colt in his career was his ability to elicit such a divergence of opinion among the turf accountancies, who frequently chalked up entirely different ante-post odds on Rocky.

In truth, Rock Of Gibraltar had beaten horses who were not of the calibre normally encountered in the very top Group 1 contests, and none went on to achieve anything like their consummate conqueror. Bernebeu did win the Group 3 Prix Daphnis the following year, and Imtiyaz won the Listed Glasgow Stakes at York and the Foundation Stakes at Goodwood, though his best performance was finishing a short head second to L'Oiseau D'Argent in the Group 1 Prix Jean Prat at Chantilly.

While some pundits and many punters raved about what they had seen, the expert opinion was a bit more subdued, but even the most grudging critics acknowledged that Rocky had won the race in the manner of an improving colt and had coped with the heaviest ground he had yet encountered in the manner of a true professional – that word was being used more and more to describe Rock Of Gibraltar.

When he eventually managed to get a word in edgeways alongside a hugely excited Ferguson, Kinane was equally professional in his verdict on the performance, saying, 'I was a shade disappointed with him at Doncaster, but he was much better behaved in the preliminaries today.

'He has handled every ground we have put at him, but it was a slight concern. There is always a question at the back of your mind about seven furlongs on heavy ground with such a fast horse, but he answered any stamina doubts. He still has scope for improvement and I have got no worries about him training on at three – we will see a lot more of him.'

As we shall see, come the following May, Kinane would wish he had seen rather more of Rocky and possibly a bit less of the stewards' room.

Ferguson was ecstatic after the easy victory, saying, 'It is a special moment when you get a result like that and you didn't expect it. I looked at Michael and he was sitting well, but I couldn't believe the way he accelerated. This is a fantastic thrill for me. It is easy to get trapped in racing and it is easy to see why there is such a love of it.'

One amazed observer at Longchamp was pop superstar Mick Hucknall of Simply Red, who lived in Paris. A diehard United fan, Hucknall had met Ferguson before and now asked to join the party at Longchamp, as Ferguson described to me a few days later: 'John Magnier said to me before the race that I wasn't to get too disappointed if he didn't win because the ground was very heavy, and Aidan O'Brien said the same thing, and then Micky Joe

THE GIMCRACK CRAIC

[Kinane] said the same thing, that the ground was bottomless. So I didn't bother to bet on the horse and of course it sluiced up.

'The surprise of it caught me out. I was standing watching the race with Mick Hucknall and when the horse started to canter away to win I just ran away in the excitement, and left Mick standing there screaming, "Where are you going?"'

Ferguson would later reminisce in *The Observer* that Paris supplied the victory which made him think that he had half a superstar on his hands:

> The moment I realised he was a lot better than we had all thought was when he won the Grand Criterium in Paris. No one expected it. Not even Aidan. He won so well, we were puzzled really. We didn't think he would like ground like that, but he showed us that, with the quality he has, the toughness, he can win on any ground.

It was a remarkable day at Longchamp for the Godolphin–Coolmore rivals – Sakhee won the Prix de l'Arc de Triomphe in storming style under a superb ride from Frankie Dettori, while John Magnier and Michael Tabor added to their haul of Group 1 races with Imperial Beauty in the famous sprint, the Prix de L'Abbaye. Such has been the dominance of these two rivals in European racing in recent years it's a wonder they have not been given a nickname borrowed from two great rivals in football – the Old Firm.

When Rocky was examined back at Ballydoyle, he was found to be fine, and having proved in the Grand Criterium at Longchamp that soft ground was not a concern for him, it was clear he could run again as long as the autumnal ground did not turn too squelchy. Even if the weather did turn foul, there were no doubt times in late 2001 that Alex Ferguson must have wished that he could just stay at the racetrack. By the time Rocky was looking good for Group 1 honours, Ferguson had already announced that he would not seek a new contract and would retire at the age of 60 from the managership of United at the end of the 2001–02 season. As many experts had predicted, though, by a third of the way though the season, United's usually smooth machine had begun to misfire. Aidan O'Brien and Rock Of Gibraltar's year only got better, however, as they approached the small matter of the biggest race for two year olds in Britain.

Just prior to Newmarket's big Champions' Day meeting, Dubai Destination pulled out of the Dewhurst Stakes with injury, leaving the path clear for Rocky to win his second Group 1 race, albeit after a tremendous scramble with stablemates Landseer and Tendulkar. 'I thought we were beat,' was Kinane's verdict, but for once the great jockey was wrong.

> NEWMARKET, 20 OCTOBER 2001, AT 3.30 P.M.
> (OFF 3.36 P.M.).
> The Darley Dewhurst Stakes, a Group 1 race for two year olds.
> Distance: seven furlongs. Going: good to soft. Eight ran.
> Prizes: 1. £116,000; 2. £44,000; 3. £22,000; 4. £10,000; 5. £5,000; 6. £3,000.
> 1. Rock Of Gibraltar, 9-0, M.J. Kinane, 4-6 fav, A.P. O'Brien.
> 2. Landseer, 9-0, J.P. Spencer, 13-2, sh hd, A.P. O'Brien.
> 3. Tendulkar, 9-0, J.P. Murtagh, 8-1, hd, A.P. O'Brien.
> 4. Where Or When, 9-0, T. Quinn, 14-1, 1¼ l, T.G. Mills.
> 5. Comfy, 9-0, K. Fallon, 5-1, 1½ l, Sir Michael Stoute.
> 6. Parasol, 9-0, S. Drowne, 20-1, hd, M.R. Channon.
> Also ran: Shah Jehan, Prince Tulum.
> Winner's time: 1 min 28.7 secs (slower than standard by 4.3 secs).
> Winning owners: Sir Alex Ferguson and Mrs Sue Magnier.

There was now no denying Aidan O'Brien's determination to capture the record number of Group 1 races in a season after he declared four runners for the Dewhurst, traditionally the 'championship' race for two year olds. If landed, it would be a first Dewhurst for the trainer and would be the 20th Group 1 race of the season for O'Brien, which would leave him just two short of the annual record held by America's leading trainer Bob Baffert. The race was to prove unattractive to the purists, but very exciting for those who love their racing in the raw – it was tooth and claw stuff by the finishing line, and the punters loved it.

THE GIMCRACK CRAIC

The biggest disappointment for everyone involved at Newmarket came on the Thursday before Champions' Day when David Loder announced from his stables not too far away from the racecourse that Dubai Destination would miss the big race. The colt had suffered what was described as 'a slight setback in training' and Loder had decided that enough was enough for the two year old, who was duly packed off to Dubai for the winter along with every other Godolphin star.

Rock Of Gibraltar could hardly have been said to have taken part in a hard race in Paris, but there were many people who were sceptical of O'Brien's attempt to win a second Group 1 prize with the colt inside 13 days. Even with a field that consisted half of Ballydoyle horses and the other half of less than superstar juveniles, it was still going to be a remarkable feat at the end of a long season for Rocky if he could snatch the big prize. And despite a massive scare, he did prevail in a rough and tumble event that should only have been watched through scrunched-up eyelids.

One of the 50 per cent of the field that didn't hail from Ballydoyle did have the potential to upset the applecart. Comfy from Sir Michael Stoute's yard had won the Acomb Stakes in fine style at York in August and had enjoyed a rest before going for the Dewhurst. Where Or When from the relatively unfashionable but hard-working yard of Terry Mills at Epsom had won the Group 3 Somerville Tattersalls Stakes over the course and distance on his previous outing, and also rated as a danger. In the end, however, the only threats to the O'Brien trio were themselves.

For neither Spencer nor Murtagh had read the script marked Rocky and they almost spoiled the party, with Spencer's mount Landseer coming closest to toppling his regular jousting opponent. Jimmy Fortune aboard the rag Prince Tulum also did his best to spoil things, although to be fair he was simply trying to do his best for his horse, which also faded spectacularly.

Prince Tulum made the early running at a slow pace which seemed to unsettle Rocky, who uncharacteristically refused to settle down to his task. Stable companions Tendulkar and Landseer were going well, both being held up for a late run, while Comfy, Where Or When and Parasol also looked as if they could threaten. It took all of Kinane's strength and experience to rein in

ROCK OF GIBRALTAR

Rock Of Gibraltar, and then just as he was about to say 'go' some two furlongs or so from home, Prince Tulum began to falter and Rocky suddenly found himself having to more or less shove the tiring horse aside. Now for the first time on a racecourse we saw another of his strengths – sheer fighting spirit, and maybe that bit of badness that all great athletes in contact sports seem to have.

Parasol under Steven Drowne had made its move, but that only put him in Rocky's path. And just as Kinane switched the horse to the centre of the track, who should appear but stablemate Landseer – it was the Coventry Stakes all over again, with the second string again rushing into the lead and again moving off a straight line. And as in the Coventry it was looking as if Landseer would keep Rock Of Gibraltar behind him. Kinane was now in full driving mode, however, and unlike Doncaster's Champagne Stakes, there was still time for the leader to be caught.

Many another two-year-old colt would have chucked it in, but not Rocky. He dug deep for Kinane and went head to head with Landseer inside the final 100 yards, while Tendulkar, who had been off the track since May Day, suddenly started to fly after he, too, was hampered and had to move to virgin territory for his run. In a really rumbustious scrap, Rock Of Gibraltar got his nose in front of Landseer but seemed to tire very late on and back came Spencer and Landseer for a final lunge. An exhausted Rocky just about kept his head in front on the line, however, and it was 'one for the judge' as the two colts flashed past the post together with their stable companion Tendulkar just failing to join in. Kinane thought he had lost – it was that close.

He said: 'That was too close for comfort and I thought Landseer may have got me. You like everything to go right for you in a Group 1 and everything went wrong, but he's still overcome it. He's had a long year and it's a great testimony to the colt that he has borne up as well as he did to win two Group 1s in his last two races.

'Everybody wanted to keep things tight – as I would if I were on the outside and there was an odds-on shot in the middle. I was fair game, but he has overcome everything and quickened nicely, and just emptied in the last three strides. The manner in which he over-raced, and the tough passage I had, definitely cost him a good few lengths.'

O'Brien treated his extraordinary feat of training the first three home in a Group 1 race with his usual modesty, saying, 'They had all been working really well, and half a furlong out I knew we'd have to be very unlucky for one of them not to win. Hopefully, they'll all be back at Newmarket for the Guineas next spring.'

Rocky's winning distance over Landseer was a very short head, while Tendulkar's late run and finishing burst left him just a head behind Landseer. That performance marked him out as potentially something special. Sadly, Tendulkar was injured in the 2,000 Guineas the following May, and after one further defeat he was retired to stud. Comfy, too, has had an injury-ravaged career but in 2004 was still at Stoute's stables. Landseer's ultimately tragic history will be detailed in Chapter Seven.

The following September, Where Or When featured in one of the great fairy tales of British racing in the past decade, giving his handler Terry Mills the biggest thrill of his life by winning the Queen Elizabeth II Stakes at Ascot, beating none other than Hawk Wing in the process. It was the first Group 1 victory for the veteran Mills, after 30 years as first an owner and then a trainer. It was also further proof, as if any were needed, that the Dewhurst victory of Rock Of Gibraltar had been achieved over some very fine horses.

Nevertheless, despite successive Group 1 victories, as the year drew to a close with Johannesburg's famous victory in the Breeders' Cup Juvenile and O'Brien's record-breaking 23rd Group 1 victory of the season, gained for him in the Criterium de Saint-Cloud by Ballingarry, Rocky was still only third favourite for the following year's 2,000 Guineas behind Hawk Wing and Dubai Destination.

It had been a long and hard season for Rock Of Gibraltar but it had been truly extraordinary for Alex Ferguson and especially wonderful for Aidan O'Brien, who was crowned champion in both Ireland and Britain. The trainer had also won nine of the ten European Group 1 races for juvenile colts.

'We've had an exceptional bunch,' said O'Brien. 'It's grand for the team. Everyone has worked very hard.'

The Ferguson influence was certainly spreading at Ballydoyle – Aidan O'Brien was even beginning to talk like him. But no one really talks like Ferguson, as a bunch of diners in York were about to find out.

CHAPTER SIX

The Triumphs

Authors shouldn't appear in their own works, but then I didn't know I was going to write this book as long ago as October 2001. Back then, no one could have foreseen the events that would surround Rock Of Gibraltar, and even the man who co-owned him had not a clue that Rocky was going to do what he eventually did. But he still knew enough to tell me that the horse was the key to his future. After the Grand Criterium and the Dewhurst, Sir Alex Ferguson gave me his first lengthy interview in which he detailed his intentions to retire from football and take up a new pursuit of owning and breeding horses. He told me just how important Rock Of Gibraltar was to his future, and indeed that it all depended on the horse.

It's worth telling the story of how I gained access to Ferguson, as he rarely grants personal interviews to journalists outside a small coterie who have known him from the early days of his professional life. Amongst these are Hugh McIlvanney of the *Sunday Times*, who co-authored Ferguson's excellent memoirs *Managing My Life*, Glenn Gibbons, chief football writer of *The Scotsman*, and local writer David Meek of the *Manchester Evening News*.

THE TRIUMPHS

As a long-term admirer, I knew Ferguson's career and life story very well, and had noticed a couple of similarities between us. I also thought he would appreciate a bit of Glaswegian impudence. So I wrote to Ferguson pointing out I had been born in Govan and so had he; that his grandfather came from the Vale of Leven in Dunbartonshire, and so did mine – indeed all my family hail from there; that he had been a shop steward and so had I; and the clincher, that he and I were exogamists. I thought that detail would intrigue a man who I knew took delight in quizzes and wordplay. Sure enough, the phone went a couple of days later and Ferguson said simply, 'It's Alex.'

I almost said 'Alex who?' before he asked, 'What's an exogamist?' The trick had worked, much to my amazement. I explained that it was a person who marries outside his tribe, and in sectarian Scotland where these things still matter to a few misguided people, marriage outside the 'tribe' includes a Protestant who marries a Catholic, as Ferguson did, or the other way round as in my case.

He chuckled and as he did so, I assured Ferguson I was only interested in the horse angle and his future in racing. He demurred for an instant, then said, 'OK, come down a week on Friday and be at the training ground at 9.30 sharp. You can have an hour, no more.'

An hour alone to chew the fat with Sir Alex Ferguson? It was gold dust for any sportswriter, and certainly a coup for one whose first sport wasn't even football. No wonder there was incredulity among my colleagues when I told them that the 'cheeky letter' had worked.

Accompanying me to Manchester was Robert Perry, one of Scotland's finest newspaper photographers, whose portraits of sportspeople in particular have adorned the Scotsman Group's newspapers for years. He's also good fun to be with on assignment, and being from the West of Scotland we reckoned that the more home-town accents which confronted Ferguson, the happier he would be. The picture of Ferguson on the front cover of this book was taken by Robert on the morning of the interview.

We travelled down the evening before and stayed in one of Manchester's better hotels – a reward for gaining an exclusive with the Great Man, I supposed. Neither Robert nor I even tried to pretend that we were being blasé about the assignment. I knew that I had a good chance of a definitive interview with the manager, while Robert had always wanted the chance to try to convey Ferguson's real character – the one he frequently hides behind a stony face. We were both up early and on the road shortly after eight to Carrington, United's superb training complex to the west of the city. Just as well we left early – Carrington is stuck out at the end of a strange concrete road and isn't the easiest place to find. It also has security guards who wouldn't be out of place at Fort Knox. We still got there in plenty of time, only to walk right into a Ferguson-inspired brouhaha of monumental proportions.

While we sipped coffee upstairs in the lounging area outside his office, Ferguson was in his Stonewall mood, batting back some intense questioning in one of his regular Friday morning press conferences with the English press. His relationships with the media are always strained, but at that time the level of criticism of him and his team was vociferous, though not nearly enough to justify the rage Ferguson displayed that morning. We could hear raised voices, but put that down to the loudspeaker system. How wrong we were.

Robert had gone downstairs to 'case the joint', looking for a suitable place to take his shots of Ferguson. As he did so, a gaggle of sportswriters, news reporters and broadcasters emptied from the press room. I could hear doors slamming and Robert came upstairs, ashen-faced, to say that Ferguson had just expelled the entire press corps from Carrington indefinitely. The visions of 'exclusive' signs above our names disappeared.

Up the stairs came the creator of all the fuss, wearing T-shirt and shorts. As I watched him approach, Ferguson at first seemed full of anger, then his mood switched to one of gloom and doom. Any reporter could have been forgiven for feeling a tad nervous: Ferguson had just had a contretemps with sportswriters from English newspapers which ended with him cancelling his weekly press conference when it had barely started, and vowing that he would not give any interviews for the rest of the season.

The cause of his considerable ire was the general media

THE TRIUMPHS

contention that the announcement of his retirement had been premature and was the root cause of United's loss of form. 'This is an agenda which is becoming a bit suffocating because everyone is going to keep talking about it. It just ignores the facts,' said Ferguson in his last words on the subject.

Even Massimo Cragnotti, chief executive of Italian club Lazio, had recently ventured that United should have dropped Ferguson as soon as he said he wanted to go. Ferguson was not amused. 'What is the boss of a football club talking about any other club for anyway?' he hissed. Given Lazio's subsequent financial nightmare, perhaps Cragnotti should have been taking the beam out of his own eye at that point.

Ferguson reached us and snorted, 'Oh, forgot about you. Right. You've got an hour.' He sat down, the blue eyes flashing. Time to risk a journalistic life. 'So, Alex,' I said, 'here you are with a Group 1 winner after only a few years in the sport, and after all that success at the footie. Tell me, were you born a jammy bastard?'

It was a lame attempt at humour to break the ice, but it worked. For a split second, Ferguson scowled and then burst out laughing – a genuine laugh, that of a person who was used to laughing off his problems. He began to speak and soon held us spellbound with his obvious passion for his two sports. He was clearly a man who had things to say, and he knew exactly what he was saying. I swear that he never looked at his watch, but at 58 minutes into the interview – I taped it, so I know the timing – Ferguson looked up and said, 'Right, that's your lot.'

By that time he had told me plenty. He would retire at the end of the season, come hell or high water, and Rock Of Gibraltar, having already won two Group 1 races, would be the foundation of his new career as an owner and breeder. It was the first time that Ferguson had revealed the true extent of his ambitions in racing. He accepted that he was a novice at the pursuit, but I was impressed that he had already begun the vast amount of research necessary to succeed as a breeder. He told me: 'I had thought about doing it before, but I will have more time when I finish here. Somebody said to me recently, "I believe you are going to be a trainer." I said, "You must be bloody joking! No chance! I wouldn't even dream of it."

ROCK OF GIBRALTAR

'What I hope to do is to venture into the breeding part of racing, and hopefully Rock Of Gibraltar will be the start of it. It is something I need to learn about, and indeed I am looking at the catalogues of broodmares at the moment, especially those for the Newmarket and Goffs broodmare sales. I am trying to learn as much as I can because if you are going to get into this game you need to know what you are talking about. Otherwise, you can lose a lot of money.'

Everything was predicated on the likely income from Rock Of Gibraltar: 'It won the Gimcrack Stakes at York so impressively that we began to think it really could be a Group 1 colt. It went for the Champagne Stakes at Doncaster, but had a weight penalty for winning the Gimcrack and it just wasn't his day. Aidan and I looked at the opportunities and we thought the Grand Criterium at Longchamp on Arc day last month was the one to go for.

'I'm now going through something which many owners have experienced over the years with two year olds that have won a Group 1 race. You just spend the winter wondering how it will go. You're dreaming all the time about it.'

When I asked him about his advisers, he said: 'You must rely on people who know better than you. Aidan O'Brien is the best and his operation will make sure everything is prepared. They will make the decision about which is the best race for Rock Of Gibraltar, whether it's the 2,000 Guineas at Newmarket, or the Irish or the French Guineas, or even the Kentucky Derby. They know much more than I do, and they know best.'

Mike Dillon was still in Ferguson's camp at that time: 'After Rock Of Gibraltar won in Paris, Mike said to me, "Enjoy it because it might be the best horse you'll ever get, and you might never get anything like it in your life. But you've had a Group 1 winner and no one can take that away from you." So I'm just enjoying it while I can.'

For his part, Dillon was supportive of his friend whom he had introduced to ownership, saying to me, 'It is great relaxation for him away from all the stress of his job, and he really does enjoy the company of the people and the characters who go racing.' At that time, I asked Dillon about Ferguson's situation with the bookmakers. Dillon refused to say whether the manager was in

THE TRIUMPHS

credit or debit, adding, 'Let's just say he likes to have a flutter here and there.'

Dillon was sure that Ferguson would be a successful owner–breeder. 'I am positive he will do well. After all, he has already found a Group 1 winner after just five years of ownership, and usually nobody is that lucky.'

Rock Of Gibraltar's first win on British soil also meant that, shortly after the interview, Ferguson would make the Gimcrack Speech, and basically he was going to tell the racing world to get its act together and stop bickering. He told me: 'There are some observations I will make, but I'll keep them to the dinner. I certainly won't be making a declaration about how I would change the industry, because there are people in place to do that. The important thing is that you cannot make stands on principle without negotiating. You must always have your principles, but you must negotiate, and you can't use the press to conduct a war of words. Sometimes, the BHB and the others in the industry seem to have nothing but divisions. They spend more time arguing in the pages of the *Racing Post* than they spend talking to each other.'

Given the events of the following 30 months, his next comments were words he should have cut out of the newspaper I was writing for and stuck on his wall: 'You have always got to respect other people's opinions, and debate is never a problem as long is it's not conducted through the newspapers. The important thing is to get together, negotiate, come out with a settlement, shake hands and move on.'

At that point, I asked Ferguson if he was sure about his deal with Magnier over Rock Of Gibraltar. I don't really know why I asked it. I just had the slightest suspicion that he might not have been aware that Magnier had a reputation as a tough operator. I have a distinct recollection of Ferguson pausing for an instant, and then looking at me as if I was daft. 'It's all sorted,' he assured me.

He was also adamant that football management or administration was not to be his future. 'When I leave Manchester United, I'm finished with football forever. Full stop. So, yes, I will walk away. I've been doing this for 28 years and that is a long time. The important thing in life is to count your blessings and not to think that you can go on forever.' Some 14 weeks later, Ferguson announced that he was changing his mind, leaving me and a lot of other journalists bewildered and millions of United fans ecstatic.

Much later, when all the fun and games over Rocky's true ownership had kicked off, I wrote in my weekly racing column of my recollection that Ferguson had done the deal and seemed very sure that Rock Of Gibraltar would be the foundation stallion for his stud plans. I invited him to call me if he needed the evidence from my transcript of the tape, especially his recollection that Magnier had 'offered me a half share in it [Rock Of Gibraltar] before it even saw the track'. His lawyers called, I sent them the article and I heard nothing more.

But first came the Gimcrack Speech in December of 2001, and John Magnier was proven admirably correct in his choice of speaker. Ferguson was nervous at first, but soon warmed to his theme. I make no apologies for quoting extensively from it – the sport of racing would do well to heed his words, now more than ever.

> In spite of the unfamiliar look of Manchester United's formline recently, I trust you will not think it inappropriate if I commend the teamwork principle to British racing as a whole. I have never been interested in sending out a collection of brilliant individuals. There is no substitute for talent, but talent without unity of purpose is a hopeless, devalued currency. Togetherness is not just a nice concept that you can take or leave according to your taste. If you don't have it, you are nothing.
>
> Selfishness, factionalism, cliquishness – all are death to a football team, and their influence could be as destructive for racing. Unless the industry embraces the teamwork principle wholeheartedly, instead of merely paying lip service to it, British racing will never have the success it deserves.
>
> Racing means so much to me that I am depressed to see its future well-being jeopardised by the competing agendas of sectional interests. Government has rightly decided that it wants to have as little to do with racing as possible, so it is up to those within the sport to shape its destiny. Only

THE TRIUMPHS

teamwork will meet the challenge. Persisting with factional hostilities will be disastrous.

He went on:

> Sometimes, racing gives the impression that it is embarrassed by how glamorous and exciting it can be.
>
> We should be galvanising ourselves to reach new audiences, to make racing more appealing to women, to the young and to ethnic minorities. Above all, we need to be more realistic. The internet and the interactive age may have possibilities, but it is folly to imagine that they represent a shortcut to riches.
>
> What matters is what we do to make racing come alive in the public consciousness. There may be no individual who can do for racing what Tiger Woods did for golf, but we should make the most of star performers. And we should maximise the impact of the most thrilling events in the calendar.

Playing to the crowd, Ferguson latched on to a favourite belief of John Magnier's that the Breeders' Cup should be promoted as something akin to golf's Ryder Cup, and be staged on both sides of the Atlantic. 'York – the flattest track in Britain – would be an excellent home. The Breeders' Cup on the Knavesmire would be a perfect symbol of a forward-looking industry.'

Ferguson went out of his way to praise Aidan O'Brien and Mick Kinane, but particularly the Magniers, who were happy for Ferguson to represent them on the evening – his words perhaps seem ironic in hindsight. 'My deepest gratitude is due to two friends who are not here, to Sue and John Magnier. It is because I have been given the privilege of teaming up with them that I am standing before you this evening. Nobody could be blessed with better partners on the Turf.'

He also had the audience laughing when he said, 'Though Rock Of Gibraltar may move as gracefully as a Veron or a Beckham, it costs a lot less to keep him happy. And lately he has been more consistent than my Old Trafford thoroughbreds!'

The speech was well received by the industry and those at the dinner, though one gentleman in a dinner jacket sitting close to Ferguson was spotted applauding the Scottish shipbuilder's son with no enthusiasm whatsoever. Yet Ferguson was absolutely correct in his view. Racing as an industry is even more faction-driven now than when Ferguson made his speech – they should have listened to him.

In the early months of 2002, after he had rescinded his retirement and got United back on League-winning track, the only question for Ferguson to consider was whether Rock Of Gibraltar would be chosen from among O'Brien's stars to step up to the mark in the opening Classic of the season, the Sagitta 2,000 Guineas at Newmarket, scheduled for FA Cup final day, 4 May 2002.

United were not in that final, but Rocky did make it to Newmarket, after being entered for the Dante Stakes at York in April and not running. Perhaps more worryingly, O'Brien's stable had not yet begun to perform in its usual style, and there had also been a devastating defeat for O'Brien and a wonderful horse owned by a famous Irishman – respectively, Istabraq and J.P. McManus.

Magnier's friend for over two decades has been John Patrick McManus of Limerick. For a shy man who doesn't actively court publicity, there has been a lot written about the legendary Sundance Kid, the best-known racing gambler in Europe.

Friends and business partners they may be, but they are chalk and cheese in some respects. They are physically different, McManus being the shorter and stockier figure with jet-black hair, a ruddy complexion and bright blue eyes, as opposed to the silver-haired Magnier's permanent tan and dark, brooding eyes. McManus is also a National Hunt man through and through, and Magnier's main interest has always been the Flat. McManus has had horses that have run on the Flat, and Magnier has had several horses that have campaigned over jumps – Rhinestone Cowboy, winner of the Irish Champion Stayers' Hurdle at the 2004 Punchestown Festival when ridden by his son, John Paul, is just one example. Jumps racing is McManus's consuming passion, however, and if he sold his horses tomorrow, he would never be forgotten for his gambling exploits at the Cheltenham National Hunt Festival and for his ownership of Istabraq, the great champion hurdler trained by Aidan O'Brien.

McManus began working in his family's plant hire firm, and at one point he famously worked on Martinstown Stud farm, which he later bought and which is now his Irish home. He had developed an interest in betting on horses and dogs and was barely out of his teens when he became a bookmaker at Limerick's greyhound track. But that side of the business did not entice him and a series of spectacular gambles made his name and fortune. He was only 26 when he bought his first racehorse, Cill Dara, and in 1982, he won £250,000 backing a horse called Mister Donovan at a race at Cheltenham.

It is often said that it was because bookmakers were so afraid of him and he couldn't get a bet that he turned to the real source of his fortune – the foreign exchange markets. It is estimated that his talents in that field have made him a fortune of anywhere between £500 million and £800 million. He is known to have close links with the billionaire financier Joe Lewis, whose syndicates also involve John Magnier.

Although he now lives in Switzerland, McManus has a private jet, which takes him home frequently to Limerick where his charity work has raised millions for local projects. His annual charity golf tournament, the J.P. McManus Invitational Pro-Am, is one of the few non-tour events in which Tiger Woods regularly competes. A non-drinker, McManus is married to Noreen, and they have three children, John, Sue-Ann and Kieran.

It is difficult to see why this relatively nondescript figure can electrify a racecourse crowd simply by turning up. Yet he does – a buzz goes round the crowd if it is reported that McManus has had 'a touch' on a horse, and if he has plumped for a particular runner, its odds tumble instantly, such is his reputation for successful gambles. He is something of a national hero to the Irish because he did what that entire nation would love to do – take on the bookies and win.

McManus has pumped millions into racing. It is a standing joke in National Hunt that he has tried to buy just about every horse with a decent chance of giving him the one trophy he really wants and which still eludes him at the time of writing – the Cheltenham Gold Cup. Like all the best jokes, there is a grain of truth in it. Once known for having horses in dozens of yards in Britain and Ireland, in recent years he has tended to concentrate his wealth on a few trainers, and now supports one in particular. He has installed Jonjo O'Neill, the former champion jockey turned trainer, in Jackdaws Castle in the Cotswolds – the best-equipped training centre in these islands. It reportedly cost him £4 million to buy Jackdaws and, in early 2004, he showed his commitment to making it a centre of excellence when he pulled off arguably his most audacious coup yet by prising the extraordinary Tony McCoy, the greatest National Hunt jockey of all time, from the stable of champion trainer Martin Pipe to become his retained jockey.

McManus's famous green-and-gold stripes have been associated with the Cheltenham Festival for many years, and it is there that he struck many of his famous bets, including the occasion when he apparently lost £1 million on one day and got it back the next. Scottish bookmaker Freddie Williams acquired his nickname of 'Fearless' simply because he took several six-figure bets from the Sundance Kid. Freddie won't say who is ahead in their long-running duel.

In 1997, McManus teamed up with Celtic FC's major shareholder Dermot Desmond to buy the Sandy Lane resort hotel in Barbados for around £40 million. It has cost the two men twice that sum to develop, and it is one of the investments that McManus never talks about.

For someone who left school at 16, McManus is acutely aware of the benefits of education. He has endowed a range of scholarship schemes and has donated millions to the University of Limerick. Yet perhaps the most extraordinary story of McManus's generosity concerns the plan to build a new National Stadium for rugby and football in Dublin – McManus offered £50 million towards the project, and when his donation was questioned, he was defended in the Irish parliament, the Dáil, by Government ministers, no less.

He has had many fine horses, including the multiple champion stayer Baracouda, and steeplechasers First Gold and Mini

THE TRIUMPHS

Sensation plus Cheltenham winner Like-A-Butterfly. His best horse by a mile, however, has been Istabraq. Trained by Aidan O'Brien, Istabraq was a decent horse on the Flat who was transformed into a superstar over hurdles. He won the Champion Hurdle at Cheltenham three times from 1998 to 2000 and was robbed of a record fourth title by the foot-and-mouth outbreak of 2001. He also won the Irish Champion Hurdle and many other top hurdle races and became the first National Hunt horse to win £1 million. He was a true phenomenon of racing and, like Arkle, he became a household name in Ireland, where his exploits were avidly followed.

In March 2002, McManus watched from his box opposite the winning line at Cheltenham when his beloved Istabraq went for a record fourth Champion Hurdle. But the horse was now ten years old, and galloping down to the start, Istabraq did not look happy. I was there that day and had bet him early, but knew I had lost my money even before the race was off. Istabraq promptly hurt himself jumping the first hurdle, aggravating an arthritic condition in his back, and was pulled up. The Cheltenham crowd responded to a loser as never before, a wave of warm applause greeting the great horse as he made his way slowly back to the stables. That massive gathering knew instinctively they had just seen Istabraq's final race, and so it proved – McManus promptly retired his hero, who will live out his days in Ireland.

That day in March proved to be a devastating disappointment for everyone at Ballydoyle. Aidan O'Brien had retained his interest in jumps racing almost solely for Istabraq and the shock of his defeat did not augur well for the new season. O'Brien was now on the lookout for a new superstar, as was racing as a whole.

At the start of 2002, racing had barely recovered from the foot-and-mouth epidemic which was estimated to have cost this vital sporting industry anywhere between £12 million and £25 million. At least the Chancellor of the Exchequer, Gordon Brown, had finally woken up to the fact that the UK treasury was haemorrhaging money in lost betting duty to offshore and internet bookmakers. Brown's solution, as suggested by the bookmaking industry, was brilliant but simple – he scrapped betting tax, as punters called it, and replaced it with a 15 per cent tax on the gross profits of the bookmakers. The bookies were effectively disallowed from passing on that profits tax to their customers, and they also had to promise to stay in Britain and not go offshore, with the result – as predicted by everyone calling for the change – that a betting boom began in 2002 which shows no sign of flagging yet. The big bookmaking chains have recorded sustained rises in profits, which means that more people are betting – and losing more, too. Now if Mr Brown could just fix that problem . . .

Despite that good news, racing also suffered badly in 2002 from a series of genuine image-battering scandals. A major inquiry began in Hong Kong into alleged race fixing, with well-known British jockey John Egan arrested, though he later returned to the UK to continue riding after being acquitted. In June, the *Kenyon Confronts* programme featured allegations of race-fixing, and though some of the claims were frankly laughable, the mud stuck, and trainers Ferdy Murphy and Jamie Osborne were harshly fined £4,000 each by the Jockey Club for their talkative part in the programme. The glaur was piled even higher on racing thanks to a long-running and quite sensational money-laundering case which involved large sums of illicit cash from the drugs trade being bet on 'sure things' whose identities were allegedly passed on by people involved in racing. It ended with former jockeys Dermot Browne and Graham Bradley being booted out of racing by the Jockey Club for a cumulative total of 28 years. The drugs kingpin Brian Wright was warned off *sine die*.

There was near panic in some racing circles when it was reported that the prestigious BBC *Panorama* programme was investigating racing. The *Panorama* team suckered the head of security at the Jockey Club, Jeremy Phipps, into some bizarre off-hand but 'on-camera' remarks which cost him his job. When the programme was eventually shown in October, it led to the Jockey Club being cast as 'institutionally incompetent' and plans were made to change their role as the provider of security and integrity services for racing.

Just when racing needed good news and positive vibes, Rock Of Gibraltar and Sir Alex Ferguson turned up to become the heroes of the hour. Yet it could have been so very different. For Rock Of Gibraltar might well have raced in America or France.

THE TRIUMPHS

O'Brien had arrived unannounced in England in April with six of the best horses in his stable. He secretly took Rocky and five other stars including Hawk Wing, by then the ante-post favourite for the 2,000 Guineas and the Epsom Derby, to Lingfield for a gallop on the all-weather Polytrack surface there. They were spotted, of course, and it was presumed by the press that the trip to Surrey was to see if the horses could stand the surface and then go to America for the Triple Crown races.

In fact, it is now known that at that time Rocky was being aimed at the French 2,000 Guineas, the Poule d'Essai des Poulins. As spring wore on, however, Rocky was clearly thriving and O'Brien became determined to give the colt the chance to go for the more prestigious Newmarket Classic.

Ferguson also went to Ballydoyle to see Rocky, telling the *Racing Post* he was happy with the way the colt was shaping up. 'I have been out to see him at Aidan O'Brien's – he is pleased with him, and he's looking big and strong.'

Indeed he was. Rock Of Gibraltar had filled out over the winter and was looking in the peak of condition when he arrived at Newmarket for the Guineas. O'Brien had eschewed a pre-Guineas 'prep' for the colt and the worry was that he would not be fit enough to last the mile. That did not concern those of us who managed to get an amazing 11–1 each-way on him in the early betting. Of more concern was that some pundits were convinced he had been given the worst draw in stall 22 on the wide outside of the field – traditionally the worst place from which to start.

NEWMARKET, 4 MAY 2002, AT 3.55 P.M. (OFF 4.02 P.M.).
The Sagitta 2,000 Guineas Stakes, a Group 1 race for three
  year olds.
Distance: one mile. Going: good to firm. 22 ran.
Prizes: 1. £174,000; 2. £66,000; 3. £33,000; 4. £15,000;
  5. £7,500; 6. £4,500.
1. Rock Of Gibraltar, 9–0, J.P. Murtagh, 9–1, A.P. O'Brien.
2. Hawk Wing, 9–0, J.P. Spencer, 6–4 fav, nk, A.P. O'Brien.
3. Redback, 9–0, D. Holland, 25–1, 1¼ l, A.P. O'Brien.
4. Zipping, 9–0, D. Bonilla, 40–1, 2½ l, Robert Collet.
5. Twilight Blues, 9–0, P. Eddery, 50–1, nk, B.J. Meehan.

ROCK OF GIBRALTAR

6. Aramram, 9–0, S. Drowne, 50–1, 1 l, M.R. Channon.

Also ran: Compton Dragon, Massalani, King Of Happiness, Steenberg, Where Or When, Ho Choi, Love Regardless, Naheef, Coshocton, Parasol, Bragadino, Sholokhov, Mehsaheer, Tendulkar, Rapscallion, Sweet Band.

Winner's time: 1 min 46.5 secs (faster than standard by 0.7 secs).

Winning owners: Sir Alex Ferguson and Mrs Sue Magnier.

The 2002 running of this wonderful Classic race will still cause controversy wherever racing people meet and talk. For it threw up the supposedly great unanswered question of Rocky's career on track – how good was he in relation to his stablemate, the mighty Hawk Wing?

The answer is simple to those who prefer actual racing to mere statistics: on the day, and for the second time, Rock Of Gibraltar beat Hawk Wing. That should be all that matters, though the question of what it means for Rocky is dealt with in the final chapter.

After O'Brien's decision to aim Rocky at the English rather than the French 2,000 Guineas, in the days leading up to the first Classic of the season, the speculation revolved around which jockey would be allocated Hawk Wing, who was always going to start a hot favourite. Kinane was absent because he had been suspended by the stewards at Newmarket for a riding offence – and in any case, he would have been in America to ride Johannesburg in the Kentucky Derby. Jamie Spencer was handed the plum ride on Hawk Wing while Derby-winning Johnny Murtagh landed Rock Of Gibraltar.

The field did not contain the best of the previous year's juveniles. Dubai Destination had not recovered fully from injury, and Johannesburg was across the Pond in Louisville trying, and failing, to win the Run for the Roses, as the Kentucky Derby is also known. The main threats to the Ballydoyle bid were from the usual sources – Godolphin's Naheef was backed probably only because Frankie Dettori was aboard, but top French trainer André Fabre's Massalani was an unbeaten and improving colt, and was

THE TRIUMPHS

France's main hope for victory as he was rated above Robert Collet's Zipping, though the latter already had bold, black type next to his name indicating that he had previously won a major race, in his case, the Prix Robert Papin. Love Regardless from Mark Johnston's stable was highly regarded, but the principal danger was the unbeaten King Of Happiness, Sir Michael Stoute's son of Spinning World, who had won the Craven Stakes in fine fashion and had Kieren Fallon aboard.

The draw proved crucial. When he was handed the number 22 stall right out on the rail furthest from the stands, the experts among Rocky's growing number of fans groaned as results over the years showed it could be the 'coffin box', a name which needs no explanation. Hawk Wing was drawn 10, which meant he could choose which side of the track to come down, or even follow a group up the middle if that happened. The television pundits predicted that the field would split into two divisions, and that is more or less what happened.

There was a firmer strip of ground on Rocky's side, and that made a vital difference as the runners split immediately into two packs, five going well over to the far side at first and the rest running from near the centre of the track to the stands' rail. As the race developed, the field became three separate groups – far, near and middle. It was soon clear that the far side were in front, with Redback fairly scooting along in the lead and giving Rocky a lovely tow. Frankie Dettori had Naheef in front of the stands-side group, in which Hawk Wing could be seen moving sideways to his left to take up position almost on the rail.

The genius of O'Brien, and his will to win above all costs, was proven on Newmarket's Rowley mile right at that moment in the 2,000 Guineas when the field divided. In talking to Murtagh and Spencer before the race, and realising that there would effectively be two separate races, he had ordered the two jockeys to stay as far apart as possible. It was this instruction that would give his stable first and second places in the Classic.

As the three-furlong pole was passed, some of the jockeys who had their mounts more towards the centre of the track could see that Redback and Rock Of Gibraltar were enjoying better ground, and Where Or When, Steenberg, Love Regardless, Coshocton,

Parasol and Sholokhov all began to move to the favoured side, though the effort of doing so meant that none of them really got in a blow.

Naheef began to tire in front of the stands-side group, while Redback led his mob into the Dip. Up to this point, Hawk Wing had never been off the bridle, but Spencer pulled him out from the group to make his run. Murtagh had Rocky perfectly placed and primed, however, and as they approached the final furlong, Rock Of Gibraltar breezed past Redback and moved smoothly into the lead of the far-side group. The movement didn't make you go 'whoosh', but merely purr with delight at the sight of a consummate racing horse doing his job. The question now was would Rocky – without a 'prep' race, don't forget – stay that final furlong which was 220 yards further than he had ever raced in his young life?

Hawk Wing, meanwhile, had shot to the front of the stands-side group in which the rest were floundering. A furlong or so from home he had a deficit of seven or eight lengths on Rocky, but Spencer called on his horse for a supreme effort and, like the champion he eventually became, Hawk Wing responded with a blistering run, gobbling up the lush turf in a tremendous display of sheer power.

The two Ballydoyle horses were running almost the width of the track apart, but it was clear from some way out that the race was between only those two. Hawk Wing was supercharged as Spencer drove for the line, but on the far side, like a boxer knowing he was going to go beyond ten rounds for the first time, Rocky had held just enough in reserve and, though he did slow almost imperceptibly towards the end, he finished in front of Hawk Wing by a neck.

Rock Of Gibraltar had won a Classic and immortality beckoned. Behind him and Hawk Wing, the rest of the field were strewn about Newmarket like the remnants of a nineteenth-century cavalry charge that had just been scythed down by opposing cannon fire. Redback kept going for third, while Zipping and Twilight Blues earned the reward for their high draw by staying on at one pace for fourth and fifth.

Zipping was four lengths behind Rock Of Gibraltar and thus

THE TRIUMPHS

paid Rocky a great compliment as he had finished a length nearer to Johannesburg in the Middle Park Stakes. He reverted to sprinting and went on to enjoy mixed fortunes until his career ended with a crashing fall during the Group 1 Prix Maurice de Gheest, for which he was favourite. The major disappointment of the race for many punters was Frankie Dettori's mount Naheef, who later finished seventh in the Derby won by High Chaparral but went on to win Pattern races in Dubai and at York. Massalani never raced again, and King Of Happiness, having lost his unbeaten record, never won another race. As with other Mark Johnston horses, Love Regardless went on his travels and won two Group 3 races for jockey Keith Dalgleish in Germany.

The Classic had been won for Ferguson, Magnier, O'Brien and Ireland. Rock Of Gibraltar may have been lucky to win, but a more correct interpretation is that Hawk Wing was unlucky to lose.

The significance for racing of Britain's most famous football manager, a household name, lifting a Classic trophy on FA Cup final day was lost on nobody in the media. As usual, Brough Scott summed it up better than just about anybody, writing:

> No entry into ownership has ever paid such quick dividends for the whole racing game and it is supremely appropriate that the perfectly named Rock Of Gibraltar should embody just those qualities of courage and excellence which Ferguson instils into the teams he sends out.

O'Brien was as cool as a cucumber after the race: 'It's very hard to say whether Hawk Wing was beaten by the draw. It was probably a very good horse, rather than the draw, that has beaten him. Obviously, they are two very good colts. They were spread out and that's just the way the race panned out for them.

'Both ran huge races and both thought they had won, so, mentally, the two of them are going to be super after it. It was a big relief that they were so far apart. Being realistic, for the future of the horses, it was better that way because only one could win, but both think they won, so it was a good result.'

Ferguson was in seventh heaven: 'This beats not being in the final at Cardiff. I was a bundle of nerves. I was in and out of the box and couldn't see where my horse was – and then all of a sudden he appeared from nowhere.

'Last Saturday, I was watching Liverpool and Tottenham – we had an evening fixture – when John Magnier told me there was a change of tack and we were going for the 2,000 Guineas because the horse was going so well.

'When we got the draw on Thursday, Mike Dillon and John said we did not have a great draw, but it's turned out probably the right draw because we had the lead off Redback. Hawk Wing is certainly a horse with talent, but my horse has guts.'

Ferguson again repeated the story of how he became involved in Rock Of Gibraltar after Royal Ascot the previous June. This time he named himself as the instigator: 'It was the Coventry Stakes and I said to John he had a lovely horse. Two weeks later, he invited me into the partnership. I am very lucky. I had my first winner here with Queensland Star in 1998 and now my first Classic winner.

'Aidan is a master. He really fancied Rock Of Gibraltar. He said he would be in the first three and he was bang on. He takes such care and concentration. It's great to see him progress. When I saw Aidan three years ago and see him now, it's unbelievable the development in a young person like that. He is blessed with the great attributes of single-mindedness and determination and is able to make the right decisions.'

Johnny Murtagh would have nothing to do with the hard luck on Hawk Wing stories, saying: 'I was always travelling well and as soon as I asked him, the acceleration was very good. I saw Hawk Wing coming at the end but I knew the line would come in time. I can only ride my horse to beat my side [of the track]. My horse is a very nice colt with a good turn of foot. He was a comfortable winner in the end. OK, Hawk Wing looked a bit unlucky but take nothing away from mine – he's a pretty decent horse.'

For Rock Of Gibraltar, the next task was the small matter of trying to become the first Irish-trained horse, and the first horse from anywhere since Rodrigo De Triano a decade previously, to win the Newmarket Guineas and its Irish equivalent. It was a tough 'ask' for a young colt. There were just three weeks between the English and Irish races, but when they got Rocky home, the Ballydoyle crew were amazed at how well he was. It seemed he was

THE TRIUMPHS

one of those animals who just thrived on racing. He was even improving on the gallops at home, and stable confidence was sky high when Rocky went to The Curragh.

Before the Entenmann's Irish 2,000 Guineas, Rocky looked quite fabulous, but there was no doubting the centre of attention at The Curragh that day. Ireland's most famous footballer and Manchester United's captain, Roy Keane, had stormed out of Ireland's World Cup training camp after a blazing barney with manager Mick McCarthy. The story led the front pages in Britain and in Ireland. Keano's departure was the only topic of conversation on television, radio and in pubs and clubs across the land, as it was among the Irish diaspora around the globe.

Alastair Down summed it up with his usual humour and perspicacity:

> If they found Hitler was alive, well and running a pub with Stalin in Clonmel, it wouldn't move our Roy off the front page at the moment and Ferguson's reputation as the man who can tame the mean in Keane meant his every move was covered by the machine-gun blitz of the paparazzi's cameras' motor-drives.

The news snappers kept their lenses on Ferguson, who gave them no reaction, but everyone else had their eyes on the track as Rock Of Gibraltar ran into history.

> THE CURRAGH, 25 MAY 2002, AT 3.45 P.M.
> The Entenmann's Irish 2,000 Guineas Stakes, a Group 1 race for three year olds.
> Distance: one mile. Going: soft to heavy. Seven ran.
> Prizes: 1. £145,607; 2. £47,448; 3. £22,908; 4. £8,184; 5. £5,730; 6. £3,276; 7. £822.
> 1. Rock Of Gibraltar, 9–0, M.J. Kinane, 4–7 fav, A.P. O'Brien.
> 2. Century City, 9–0, J.A. Heffernan, 6–1, 1½ l, A.P. O'Brien.
> 3. Della Francesca, 9–0, C. O'Donoghue, 20–1, 3 l, A.P. O'Brien.

4. Foreign Accent, 9–0, J. Fortune, 11–1, 5 l, J.H. Gosden.
5. Ahsanabad, 9–0, J.P. Murtagh, 10–1, sh hd, J. Oxx.
6. Nostradamus, 9–0, P.J. Scallan, 25–1, 3½ l, M.R. Channon.

Also ran: Sights On Gold.

Winner's time: 1 min 47.3 secs (slower than standard by 9.3 secs).

Winning owners: Sir Alex Ferguson and Mrs Sue Magnier.

With Landseer having won the French 2,000 Guineas, Aidan O'Brien was going for the unprecedented treble of English, Irish and French mile Classics and he was taking no chances with his historic opportunity. Four of the seven runners hailed from Ballydoyle, and though Rock Of Gibraltar was easily the best of the quartet, both Century City and Della Francesca were rated as eminently capable of winning. Rarely can the journey up the N8 and N7 from Tipperary to The Curragh have been made with such confidence.

It is often the sign of a great horse that other owners and trainers are just plain scared to take it on because they don't want their precious possessions to look average by comparison. On this occasion, the 'fearties' were quite right to stay away. For Rock Of Gibraltar was not just brilliant in winning his second Classic, he was utterly imperious.

If the Newmarket Guineas had been a hard race for Rocky, especially as it was his seasonal debut, then you would not have known it from the condition of the horse as he pranced around the parade ring like a prince come to claim his kingdom. It was a windy day and that stirred up a few of the horses, but nothing short of a massive infusion of cocaine and steroids would allow them to catch Rocky.

The only English raider, and how appropriately named, was Foreign Accent, trained by John Gosden and ridden by Jimmy Fortune, who was expected to improve considerably from his seventh in the Greenham Stakes at Newbury. Gosden is one of the Turf's true sportsmen, and though he knew his horse was up against it, he still wanted to make 'a sporting challenge' – would there were more like him in the top echelon of racing.

THE TRIUMPHS

If you don't compete you can't win, and another man who likes to make a sporting challenge is the Aga Khan, who provided Ahsanabad from the John Oxx stable. He had finished third behind Rocky's stablemate High Chaparral in the Derrinstown Stud Derby Trial but had not stayed the ten furlongs in that race and so he dropped back to the mile, though there was some doubt that he would go on the ground. Dermot Weld's Sights On Gold had been second behind Century City at Leopardstown and his odds of 14–1 were about right for a horse expected to improve for that seasonal debut, though again the tacky ground was against him.

Of the remaining Ballydoyle runners, Century City was in the race entirely on merit, having won the Leopardstown 2,000 Guineas Trial and the Group 3 Tetrarch Stakes over seven furlongs on soft ground at The Curragh. Della Francesca had finished second behind King Of Happiness in the Craven Stakes but had flopped in the French Guineas behind Landseer. Only Nostradamus was without a chance – you didn't have to be a prophet to see that his thankless task was to act as pacemaker for Rocky and the others.

Nostradamus and Paul Scallan set a sensible pace in front of a field which tracked over to the stands side in search of shelter from the wind which was blowing into their faces from a one o'clock position. Mick Kinane tucked Rocky in behind the rest of the field and the odds-on favourite, while keen to go on, was held up at a canter while those in front took the full brunt of the wind.

From halfway, the only questions were how far was Rocky going to win by and, more pressingly, how would he make his way to the front from the rear? The latter was answered two furlongs out when Ahsanabad and Century City made their move and created space, with the latter taking the lead, a sight which persuaded Kinane to cut loose. The response from Rock Of Gibraltar was all about smooth acceleration – the turbo wasn't needed as he cruised up to second place behind Century City and as they entered the final furlong, Kinane, who hadn't moved a muscle, was already looking to either side to ensure there were no dangers. A modicum of effort – hardly a twitch, really – and Century City was relegated to second in an instant by Rocky, who was clearly enjoying himself. At the post, the distance was officially one and a half lengths, but Rock Of Gibraltar had won very easily. History had been made – he was the first Irish-trained horse to win the Newmarket and Irish 2,000 Guineas, and O'Brien had his French–English–Irish Guineas treble.

Century City took second and Della Francesca came through to make it a 1–2–3 for O'Brien, who immediately nominated Royal Ascot as Rocky's next target, saying, 'It's unusual to have a horse get a mile so well that has as much speed as this fellow. Dropping him down in distance certainly wouldn't be a problem, but the St James's Palace Stakes is the plan.'

Judged by the standards of previous runnings, that Irish Guineas was not of the highest quality and the muddy ground certainly affected some of the field, but Century City went on to lift the Group 2 Goffs International Stakes before moving to America where, as a four year old, he finished third behind brilliant French filly Six Perfections in the Breeders' Cup Mile. Della Francesca won the Group 3 Gallinule Stakes next time out before finishing sixth in the Irish Derby behind High Chaparral. He, too, went to the USA but did not prosper. Ahsanabad was later sold to race in Hong Kong, was renamed Surveyor and was still competing in Group races in 2004.

Afterwards, for the first time, people began to talk of Rocky in reverential tones. The smarter pundits noted he had improved with each race and now they asked how good could he become?

Alastair Down called it 'the quick passing the dead' and indeed it was a stunning performance by Rocky. An enthused Ferguson mentioned having a crack at the Epsom Derby, but his breeding dictated that Rocky could never run as far as that, though it would have been interesting if he had tried. Anyway, as O'Brien quickly pointed out, Epsom was the target for Hawk Wing and High Chaparral. The obvious next race for Rocky was the St James's Palace Stakes at Royal Ascot, and at Ballydoyle, O'Brien calls the shots – all three colts went when and where he said they would.

In the days before the trip to Ascot, Rock Of Gibraltar suddenly became the focus of public attention for the meeting. Whether it was the 'Fergie Factor' or not, the horse was the biggest punt in the pre-Ascot market, and he was put in at odds-on 4–7 favourite.

THE TRIUMPHS

The St James's Palace Stakes was turning into a benefit for O'Brien. Giant's Causeway and Black Minnaloushe had won the last two runnings, but Rocky faced a stiff task. He was trying to become only the second horse in all and the first horse since Right Tack, ridden by Geoff Lewis in 1969, to lift the treble of English and Irish 2,000 Guineas and the St James's Palace Stakes.

Sir Alexander Ferguson, knight of the realm, should not have felt out of place at Royal Ascot, but the tell-tale fiddling with his morning dress betrayed a certain nervousness. He certainly looked smart in his top hat and tails, and even the aristocrats, high-rollers and multi-millionaires who inhabit the Royal meeting were a little awestruck in the presence of the man who had just guided Manchester United to yet another League title. By 4 p.m., he was the talk of that glamorous, shimmering corner of Berkshire, and by the teatime news on television, he and 'his' horse were being discussed across the UK and Ireland. Even the World Cup took a back seat for a minute.

ROYAL ASCOT, 18 JUNE 2002, AT 3.45 P.M.

The St James's Palace Stakes, a Group 1 race for three-year-old colts.

Distance: one mile. Going: good. Nine ran.

Prizes: 1. £168,200; 2. £63,800; 3. £31,900; 4. £14,500; 5. £7,250; 6. £4,350.

1. Rock Of Gibraltar, 9–0, M.J. Kinane, 4–5 fav, A.P. O'Brien.
2. Landseer, 9–0, J.P. Murtagh, 13–2, 1¾ l, A.P. O'Brien.
3. Aramram, 9–0, S. Drowne, 20–1, 4 l, M.R. Channon.
4. Dupont, 9–0, D. Holland, 14–1, nk, W.J. Haggas.
5. Where Or When, 9–0, J. Fortune, 66–1, 1 l, T.G. Mills.
6. Bowman, 9–0, L. Dettori, 4–1, hd, A. Fabre.

Also ran: Sahara Desert, King Of Happiness, Camp Commander.

Winner's time: 1 min 40.91 secs (faster than standard by 0.69 secs).

Winning owners: Sir Alex Ferguson and Mrs Sue Magnier.

With a field that included the winners of Europe's five top 2,000 Guineas or equivalent races, there was no doubt that this was truly the Continent's mile championship for three-year-old colts. In the presence of the Royal Family, Rock Of Gibraltar reigned supreme, and even his few remaining detractors could not deny the magnificent manner of his victory.

Before the race, a case could be made for four or five of the field. Bowman, winner of the Group 3 Prix de Fontainebleu at Longchamp and third behind Landseer in the French 2,000 Guineas, was strongly fancied, especially with Frankie Dettori in the saddle, and dual Classic winner Dupont from Willie Haggas's stable was also not without a chance, having won both the Premio Parioli and the Mehl-Mullens-Rennen, the 2,000 Guineas races of Italy and Germany respectively. Improving from his Newmarket Guineas run, Mick Channon's Aramram might well have won the Prix Jean Prat in his next outing, his last race before Ascot, had he not swerved violently in the straight and dumped Steven Drowne on the Chantilly turf. At least he came to Ascot with the benefit of not having had to contest a fierce finish in his previous outing.

As it turned out, Rocky's principal opponent was his stable companion Landseer, whose good win in the Gainsborough Poule d'Essai des Poulins – the French 2,000 Guineas – had alerted many punters at Royal Ascot to the each-way value on him. In the betting, Rock Of Gibraltar had been as low as 4–7 for the race, but drifted as far as evens before going off 4–5 favourite, with Bowman as second favourite at 4s and Landseer third in the market on 13–2. Everything pointed to a duel between Bowman and the Ballydoyle pair, but at the business end the race really only concerned the latter two.

Almost from the start, Sahara Desert took the lead in his role of pacemaker and, as in the Irish 2,000 Guineas, Paul Scallan did an excellent job of ensuring that the pace was steady, which played right into Kinane's hands and Rocky's hooves. Bowman and King Of Happiness were both too fractiously keen and along with Rocky were held up towards the rear, with Where Or When right out the back in last. The difference from his two-year-old days was that Rock Of Gibraltar, who had almost thrown away his chance in the Dewhurst by wanting to race too early, had matured with racing and Kinane did not have to try hard to keep his mount on an even keel.

THE TRIUMPHS

Landseer went after the leader, as did Dupont, but as the nine horses came down the straight it was plain to see that Rocky was going threateningly well. Dupont pushed his way to the front and Landseer made his effort as Sahara Desert began to fade, but Kinane had all the moves covered and switched Rock Of Gibraltar to the outside of the pack. As the others realised the danger, it was already too late. Rocky went through the gears in his usual fashion, so by the furlong pole he was in the lead, and it was clear that he was going to bag his fifth Group 1 race on the trot. And trot was the operative word – he wasn't brash or bold in making the final half-furlong look easy, he was just totally in racing mode and nothing was going to beat him.

Landseer vainly tried to pursue his stable companion, but swerved right and hampered Dupont, who possibly lost third place as a result – although the objection by Dupont's connections was overruled – while Aramram stayed on in promising fashion to snatch the bronze medal position and earn an extra £17,500 as a result. Where Or When also finished well from a long way back for fifth, but the disappointing Bowman had blown his chance with his early antics as had King Of Happiness who couldn't even beat the pacemaker. Camp Commander finished where all 150–1 shots should finish – a long way last.

The field which had looked so distinguished never really caught fire after Rocky drubbed them – horses can suffer a loss of confidence when they see another animal being so superior. Aramram continued to be a monkey on the track, throwing Drowne off again in his next race, the Prix Eugene Adam – the Grand Prix of Maisons-Lafitte. In 2003–04, he campaigned in Dubai. Of the other horses, both Dupont and Bowman did not flourish as expected but the latter came back in the autumn to have another attempt to scale The Rock.

For once, there was no dispute among the pundits. Rock Of Gibraltar had confirmed himself as the best of the three-year-old milers. His trainer said, 'He looks to be getting better and better and the Sussex Stakes will give him the chance to take on the best of the older generation.' The prospect made the mouth water.

Now the superlatives began to flow from those who had previously been unconvinced by Rocky. Wonder of wonders, such

ROCK OF GIBRALTAR

was the quality of Rocky's performance that even John Magnier emerged to say his piece. And when he did, he caused a minor sensation by suggesting that Rocky could step down, not up, in distance.

'It would be tempting to try to do something else with him,' said Magnier. 'There are two ways to go, up or down, for races like the July Cup or something over a mile and a quarter. It's not really up to me, it will all depend on what Aidan feels at the time and how the horses are going. Obviously, the Sussex Stakes will be in our thinking as well, but he could certainly try different distances.'

Aidan O'Brien went along with the idea immediately, saying, 'Rock Of Gibraltar would have no problem going down in distance, because he has plenty of pace, or going further, because he relaxed well today.' A horse that could be aimed at a six-furlong sprint championship or a ten-furlong Group 1 event like the Eclipse Stakes – what kind of wondrous animal was this?

In the end, the Sussex Stakes was the target, but his co-owner at that point was just happy to have a versatile, improving horse. Ferguson's argot may have caught on at Ballydoyle but the manager himself was learning the 'speak' of the racehorse owner with a vengeance, and remembered to say all the right things in the winner's circle.

'The Guineas form has held up against the German and the French, so I'm very pleased,' Ferguson said. 'It shows he can travel on any ground. I hoped he'd be Group class but he just gets better and better.'

Kinane, who earned a double on the day aboard Statue Of Liberty in Rocky's nemesis race, the Coventry Stakes, said, 'He's a very good colt with tremendous acceleration. He won as I hoped he would. He was a champion at two and you don't see many of those get better at three.' For the first time, the comparison was made by a Ballydoyle representative between Rocky and their Iron Horse of two years previously. 'Giant's Causeway backed up five races in a very short space of time, which would be very hard to top, but this horse is equally tough,' said Kinane.

O'Brien agreed, saying, 'This is a serious horse who can accelerate on all types of ground. It's hard to believe it's his fifth

THE TRIUMPHS

Group 1 in a row. When Giant's Causeway won this race it was only his first of five.'

One thing neither Alex Ferguson nor Mike Dillon would disclose was just how much the manager had wagered on his horse, but the bookmakers had taken a hammering at Royal Ascot – some £250,000 was taken out of the betting ring in large bets alone.

A northern bookmaker later told me that the result had not been too damaging for his chain nationwide. They had lost a packet in Manchester, but shops elsewhere in the country reported strong business in betting against the horse which ran in Manchester United's colours for the Reds manager. Apparently, this betting trend may reflect a pattern of support which is not unknown in football . . .

CHAPTER SEVEN

Those Two Impostors (Triumph in Paris and Disaster in Chicago)

As Rudyard Kipling should have written, 'If you can meet with triumph and disaster, and treat those two impostors just the same', then you should be in horse racing.

In the summer of 2002, Aidan O'Brien was hit by the devastating news that several of his finest horses had come down with a virus. For the first time in his career, the young Maestro of Ballydoyle was facing the thing which trainers fear most in their yard – that awful sight of a whole stable full of animals coughing and racking. There was nothing he could do as box after box began to contain sick animals. Millions of pounds worth of magnificent horseflesh was reduced to a shower of snifflers. The whole yard would eventually have to shut down, such was the severity of the outbreak, and the trainer had no choice but to allow the virus to run its course. It started with the older horses, spread through the three year olds and Ballydoyle was not free of the outbreak until the late autumn. It was easily the biggest crisis in the soaring career of O'Brien.

He was just 32 at the time, and he and wife Anne-Marie had four young children to cope with. Lesser men would have crumbled as they saw their dreams of glory coughed away just as their stable threatened to become completely dominant – but not O'Brien. He is an extraordinary man by any standards. Hailing from Co. Wexford where his father owned point-to-pointers and let his son train them as a teenager, O'Brien was destined for a life in the saddle even before he left school.

After a spell as a forklift truck driver for the Waterford Co-op, he twice became Ireland's champion amateur jockey before he turned to National Hunt training with his wife. His explanation, given ten years later, of his switch to training in 1993 says much about him: 'There were others who could get more out of a horse than I could. Simple as that. As I was never going to be the best I decided to go into training instead,' he told the *Mirror*.

He wanted to win, and that is what he has done ever since. He became champion National Hunt trainer of Ireland in his first year of holding a licence, and repeated the feat the following year, but O'Brien was nevertheless a totally surprising choice less than two years later when John Magnier selected him to run Ballydoyle in succession to Vincent O'Brien and his son David. But then, Vincent had made the same switch from National Hunt to Flat almost 40 years previously – could the new Maestro replace the old Master of Ballydoyle?

His first couple of seasons at Ballydoyle saw him organise the great stable to his own specifications. 'A few older lads were paid off,' said a source in Fethard, 'but they were mostly taken back on again as he realised the need for experience around the place.' Everyone around Ballydoyle and Coolmore soon appreciated that no one worked harder than the trainer, and his commitment to the task was total.

Curiously, for a supposed Flat horse trainer, it was his success with Istabraq at the Cheltenham Festival of 1997, when McManus's gelding won the Royal & SunAlliance novices hurdle, which really made his name with the racing public. He also trained his first Royal Ascot winner that year with Harbour Master. It was a sign of things to come. From 1997 onwards, the winners simply flowed out of Ballydoyle and Coolmore, with O'Brien and Magnier becoming the only real rivals to the mighty Godolphin empire of Sheikh Mohammed, and then surpassing it. Istabraq's hat-trick of Champion Hurdles under Irish champion jockey Charlie Swan, from 1998 to 2000, showed that O'Brien had lost none of his skills in the jumping sphere. In a very short space of time he had become the complete trainer, due in no small part to his total dedication to the job.

His first British Classic winner was King Of Kings in the Sagitta 2,000 Guineas of 1998, followed the next month by Shahtoush in the Vodafone Oaks, a race he won again in 2001 with Imagine, the day before Galileo's devastating 'whoosh' gave O'Brien his first Derby. By that time, it was clear that European racing had a new young genius at its helm. A season which saw the likes of Rock Of Gibraltar, Hawk Wing and Johannesburg's victories in the juvenile ranks would be memorable for most trainers, but 2001 was the unforgettable year of Galileo and Giant's Causeway, and they inspired that stunning world record of 23 Group 1 wins. O'Brien would set another world record with Rocky in 2002 and, though 2003 was quieter – no Classics in the UK, for instance – he still garnered another world record with Hawk Wing's mammoth win in the Lockinge Stakes – its 11-length victory was the biggest winning distance in a Group 1 race. O'Brien has become the name most punters rely on, but the signs in early 2004 were that the stable was still having a quiet time by its own exalted standards. The practice of training champions at Ballydoyle for stud duty at Coolmore, which was begun by Vincent O'Brien, has been perfected under his namesake. Giant's Causeway, Galileo, High Chaparral, Black Minnaloushe, Milan, Hold That Tiger and, of course, Rock Of Gibraltar are just some of the stars now standing at Coolmore's various branches after passing through Aidan O'Brien's hands.

Those who know him say that this ascetic-looking man who could pass for a novice missionary is almost an apostle for the hands-on method of training. He knows every member of staff at Ballydoyle by their first name – there can be as many as 200 of them – and knows each horse not only by its name but also by its health, state of preparation and potential. Every morning, he adjusts each horse's workout to the plan he carries in his mind for each individual in the yard. It is a prodigious feat of memory, if nothing else.

THOSE TWO IMPOSTORS...

He also emphasises teamwork. 'We are a team here,' he told journalists before the Derby of 2003, and went on to explain that his real pleasure was just to work with the horses, although he realised that the business of results was paramount.

The key to O'Brien, apart from his obsession with winning, is that he takes a holistic approach to training – he looks as much at a horse's face as he does at its hind quarters. He investigates every sign that a horse gives out to gauge the animal's possible mood and state of preparedness. He once boasted – though that is not a word you would associate with O'Brien – to a room full of racing correspondents that he could tell how they were feeling just by looking at their eyes and skin. So it is with horses for O'Brien.

In the faces of his horses in the summer of 2002, he saw only pain and misery. Except for one – Rock Of Gibraltar, the horse he had helped to breed. And it was Rocky who would get O'Brien through that hardest of times, though in truth even the Maestro of Ballydoyle was not sure that his new star had evaded the virus completely. The two year olds in the yard were already coughing in high summer, and a few days before the Sussex Stakes at Glorious Goodwood, the virus spread to the three year olds, with Hawk Wing among the first to succumb. Incredibly, Rocky was still free of the bug in the last days of July, but it was surely only a matter of time before he, too, joined those on the sick list.

With all his plans in tatters, O'Brien did the only thing he could do in the circumstances, and took Rock Of Gibraltar to the racetrack – a particularly green and pleasant one in England.

> GOODWOOD, 31 JULY 2002, AT 3.20 P.M.
> The Sussex Stakes, a Group 1 race for three year olds
>   upwards.
> Distance: one mile. Going: good to firm. Five ran.
> Prizes: 1. £157,675; 2. £58,300; 3. £29,150; 4. £13,250;
>   5. £6,625.
> 1. Rock Of Gibraltar, 3-8-13, M.J. Kinane, 8-13 fav, A.P.
>   O'Brien.
> 2. Noverre, 4-9-7, L. Dettori, 3-1, 2 l, Saeed Bin Suroor.
> 3. Reel Buddy, 4-9-7, R. Hughes, 33-1, 2 l, R. Hannon.

ROCK OF GIBRALTAR

   4. No Excuse Needed, 4–9–7, J.P. Murtagh, 11–2, 1¾ l,
      Sir Michael Stoute.
   5. Sahara Desert, 3–8–13, P.J. Scallan, 66–1, 3 l, A.P.
      O'Brien.
   Winner's time: 1 min 38.29 secs (slower than standard by
      0.59 secs).
   Winning owners: Sir Alex Ferguson and Mrs Sue Magnier.

In the career of every great colt or filly, there comes a time when it has to prove itself against older horses. That is usually the crunch time for a star's career – do it against the bigger boys and girls, and everyone accepts that you are a class act.

Even though he receives a weight allowance to make up for the fact that he is up against older and presumably more experienced horses, a three-year-old colt usually struggles against his elders. Not Rock Of Gibraltar. On the slopes of Glorious Goodwood, Rocky produced a performance of quite stunning simplicity – he cantered down to the post and more or less cantered back up again. The rest of that field, which included the best miler of the previous year, were making up the cast numbers, for this was the Rock Of Gibraltar and Michael Kinane show, the latter being unable to resist playing to the crowd by emphasising the ease with which he was winning.

Again, there was a suspicion that good horses had stayed away because their connections didn't fancy their chances against the year's champion three-year-old miler and the previous holder of that title, Godolphin's mighty Noverre who had won the Sussex Stakes of 2001. For once, Frankie Dettori was not talking up his mount too much, perhaps not wishing to test Noverre's already depleted store of luck – Noverre had tested positive for the banned substance methyprednisolone after he beat Vahorimix in the French 2,000 Guineas at Longchamp, and had lost the race two months later after an inquiry by French stewards. Now certainly drug free, Noverre had been second in his previous two outings, both of them Group 1 races, but didn't like it when he couldn't finish first – in the Lockinge Stakes at Newbury, he had tried to bite the winner Keltos as it passed him. Would he try to have a mouthful of 'Gibraltar Rock'?

THOSE TWO IMPOSTORS...

No Excuse Needed had finished second to Noverre in the previous year's Sussex Stakes, and obviously loved Goodwood as he had come back to lift the Celebration Mile in the previous August. Sir Michael Stoute's four-year-old son of Machiavellian was right at the top of his form, having won the Queen Anne Stakes over a mile at Royal Ascot on the same day as Rocky won his St James's Palace Stakes victory. He had won in a slightly faster time than Rocky, too, but his had been a hard-fought short-head victory over Tillerman, compared to Rocky's facile success. Reel Buddy was taking a big step up in class over a mile, but had Listed race wins to his credit and had run reasonably in the Group 1 July Cup over six furlongs.

This time, the bookies were taking no chances, and with no serious money for any of the others except Noverre, Rock Of Gibraltar went off the 8–13 favourite. Sahara Desert was once again the pacemaker for Rock Of Gibraltar and Paul Scallan did his job well, setting an even beat as the field made the long swoop round the Goodwood bend. No Excuse Needed gave himself an excuse for eventual failure by failing to settle in the opening quarter, while Reel Buddy also pulled hard for his head.

Rock Of Gibraltar sat serenely in the rear. Perhaps he was admiring the view of the Sussex Downs, because he and his jockey certainly displayed no concern about the supposedly ominous task ahead of them.

As they came into the straight, Reel Buddy was allowed to forge ahead round about the three-furlong pole and Noverre went with him. But Kinane was still displaying supreme confidence in his big strong colt, and while Noverre and Reel Buddy had their own private battle from the two to the one pole, the Irishman brought Rocky upsides and past them in a matter of seconds – now *that* was a 'whoosh' moment. It was followed quickly by a peal of laughter from the crowd as Kinane stood up in his irons and cheekily peered between his legs to look for any danger coming down the outside. With No Excuse Needed already toiling, the only threat was that Kinane would overbalance and fall, but he is far too good for that sort of mistake.

At the post, the distance to Noverre was two lengths, but everyone who saw that race knows that Rock Of Gibraltar won the

2002 Sussex Stakes with contemptuous ease. Authoritative, imperious and commanding were just some of the adjectives used to describe his performance in equalling Mill Reef's record of six successive Group 1 victories.

The only moment of concern in the race came after the post, when Rock Of Gibraltar almost lost his footing. 'He just lost his concentration pulling up and slipped a bit, but we got it together,' said Kinane, who then gave Rock Of Gibraltar the greatest compliment of all from his jockey.

'That was a great performance,' said Kinane. 'He is *the ultimate racehorse* [my italics]. No matter what you throw at him, he is always in charge. He really has developed into a fantastic horse.'

The name had been spoken – 'the ultimate racehorse'. What a compliment from Kinane, who had by that time ridden a list of equine princes and princesses to Group 1 success – Galileo, Giant's Causeway, Montjeu, Pilsudski, King's Theatre, Grand Lodge, Opera House, Kayf Tara, Entrepreneur, Belmez, and not forgetting his first Derby winner Commander In Chief or Melbourne Cup hero Vintage Crop.

That day, Kinane wanted to talk for Ireland, such was his enthusiasm for the horse. He spoke of how he had detected Rock Of Gibraltar's sheer happiness at being on the racetrack. Any human who has had to put up with being locked in beside convalescent patients will know the feeling of relief at being set free, but Kinane knew the horse's joy stemmed not just from getting out of sickbay but from being in a place where he knew he would be racing.

'I was amazed at him going down, he wanted to have a buck and a kick,' said Kinane. 'He was just full of himself. He was so well and so happy to be here. It is very hard to find that quality in horses.'

Much later, Alex Ferguson would look back to the Sussex Stakes and reveal that even a neophyte owner such as himself had realised on that day at Goodwood that perhaps even those closest to him were not fully aware of Rocky's potential. He wrote in *The Observer*:

> That was when we realised that we were underestimating him. It was another surprise. Because Aidan had had him

THOSE TWO IMPOSTORS...

put on 17 kilos before the race – because he had given him a rest – and had said that he should come on for the race. But I half expected that he wouldn't equal Mill Reef's record. The rest of the yard had been suffering from a cough, and we were worried about it for The Rock, but there was never any question in our mind that so long as he was fit he would race. Afterwards, I was almost bemused because of the ease with which he had won. And knowing what Aidan had told me – that he would come on for the race – I was left wondering, 'Well, what can we expect now?'

What Alex Ferguson and the growing legions of Rocky's fans expected was a world record. But the question-marks were gathering on the page headed 'record attempt' – would Rocky succumb to the bug, which, given the lateness in the season and the likelihood of his going straight to stud, could almost certainly end his career on track? Which race, which racecourse, which country, would see the bid for history? Would he stay the extra distance if he were stepped up to ten furlongs for, say, the Juddmonte International at York? If he got to the track, would he be fit enough to win?

That last question took on an increasing importance as Ballydoyle became fully ravaged by the virus. A few days after the Sussex Stakes, nearly every three year old was ill and O'Brien took the decision to 'stand down' the stable and rest all his horses from racing. It was the only thing he could do.

Ferguson, meanwhile, had his pre-season training and early matches to contend with, and things went quiet on several fronts for him. When a stable is effectively in quarantine, owners keep away, and in Ferguson's case he had other worries. The football season did not start as well as he would have liked, and the club that always threatens to be United's nemesis, Arsenal, were looking ominously powerful. But having signed a 'final' three-year contract earlier in 2002, which saw his pay rise to a reputed £80,000 per week, Ferguson's position looked impregnable, not least because of developments at Old Trafford involving his Irish friends, John Magnier and J.P. McManus.

As Magnier became increasingly wealthy throughout the 1980s

and 1990s, he became interested in taking shares in companies that he felt might pay long-term dividends. He invested on his own account through a Swiss-based firm, Acomita, but his most high-profile interests were taken jointly with McManus through Cubic Expression. From mid-2000 onwards, and perhaps before that point, Cubic Expression had begun to acquire small tranches of shares in United. The generally held conspiracy theory is that Mag and Mac did so because their pal Fergie thought that the share price would rise. That theory makes no sense – all the share tipsters of any note were rating United as overpriced in the early part of 2000, when the share prices of many clubs quoted on the stock market began to fall rapidly. So why did Cubic Expression start their buying spree then? Ferguson's son, Mark, works in the financial services sector, and is known to take a keen interest in United plc, but it is doubtful if he would have advised his father to tell his friends to buy overpriced stock. Nor did the manager himself have the financial expertise to understand the minutiae of the stock market. If he did, he would surely have advised waiting to see if the share price showed some hints of recovery – but the Irishmen did not wait at all. McManus is, after all, a gambler by nature, and he and Magnier ploughed into buying United shares.

Anyone wanting to buy United shares simply had to call a stockbroker as there were plenty of shares for sale following the Government's decision in 1999 to block the takeover of United by BSkyB. On the back of United's European Cup victory and the BSkyB deal, the shares reached a peak of around £4 each, valuing the club at more than £1 billion, but began to fall during 2000, so it would have made good sense for a long-term investor to buy into the club. Anybody who could read the company's annual report would see printed there a list of every individual and company holding more than 3 per cent of the stock. And it was serious shareholdings which Mag and Mac were after.

In the summer of 2000, there was virtual panic in the boardroom at Old Trafford after a flurry of buying by 'mystery investors'. It should be explained at this point that, since the company floated on the Stock Exchange in 1991, the directors and executives of United plc have lived in fear of a new owner waltzing in and kicking all of them out.

THOSE TWO IMPOSTORS...

As Manchester United's former Head of Security Ned Kelly revealed in his book *Manchester United: The Untold Story*, the paranoia among directors and officers of the club was such that he was ordered to sweep the boardroom and its surroundings for hidden microphones. He and some former colleagues from the SAS duly found the bugs in the roof space above the room where nearly every important deal involving the club had been struck.

The paranoia was justified, then, but a clearout could only have happened if the club's former owner and then chief executive, Martin Edwards, sold out. In 1998, he had tried to do just that with the abortive sale of his entire shareholding to broadcasters BSkyB, who originally bid £635 million for the entire stock. Barely on speaking terms with Ferguson after his behind-the-scenes role in opposing the takeover which would have made him indecently wealthy, Edwards systematically began to dispose of his shareholding, which went from 14 per cent in 1998 to less than 1 per cent 4 years later – some of his stock went to Cubic Expression. From 1999 onwards, the board increasingly realised their future depended on keeping the shareholders happy. And guess which club official – no lover of directors – had powerful friends willing to invest in United?

Furthermore, their initial investments were hardly done in a furtive fashion. In 2000, Cubic Expression's name had surfaced as the owner of 3.3 per cent of United plc – anyone with a holding of more than 3 per cent of a plc has a legal duty to declare it to the company, which in turn must inform the Stock Exchange. 'They [the board] were shitting themselves,' said a United employee of that period who has since left the club. 'Most of them thought Fergie was already too powerful and here were his pals coming along and buying up shares.' That is an interesting assertion, given that some executives later denied even knowing who was behind Cubic Expression. Indeed, United's present chief executive and then managing director David Gill, along with company secretary David Beswitherick, apparently admitted that they did not know who was behind Cubic Expression. If that was true, then Gill must have ignored all the gossip at Old Trafford.

'Everyone knew it was the Irish lot who were buying up the shares,' said the ex-employee quoted earlier. 'Most people at the club were pleased for Fergie, because they knew that he really ran United and the directors didn't appreciate him. The boss didn't really discuss his friends with anyone, but everybody knew he owned horses with them – it had been in all the papers, for God's sake!'

In July 2001, even before Rock Of Gibraltar was given to Ferguson, panic turned to nightmare when Cubic Expression paid more than £15 million to almost double their shareholding. The plc's share price soared, and the 6.77 per cent stake meant that Magnier and McManus had become the second largest shareholders behind BSkyB, which at that time still owned 9.9 per cent of United as a remnant of their abortive takeover. Cubic Expression issued a statement to try to allay boardroom fears. There would be no takeover, it was purely an investment, etc., etc. 'Mr McManus and Mr Magnier have been investors for some time in Manchester United and took advantage of the recent weakness in the share price to increase their joint holding,' said the statement issued by Coolmore's PR firm. Note those words: 'for some time'.

During the summer of 2001, the most commonly held theory was that Mag and Mac had bought into United to shore up the occasionally shaky position of their good friend, the club's manager. They might even launch a takeover with him, ventured some pundits, and as Michael Crick devastatingly revealed in his biography of Ferguson, the manager had indeed harboured ambitions to buy United at the time of the BSkyB deal. But the glib assertion that the Cubic Expression investment was all about helping Fergie does not hold up to a few moments of serious consideration.

For, by then, everyone knew that Ferguson would retire at the end of the 2001–02 season when his contract expired. He had been adamant about going at 60, had repeated his assertion continually in public, and the fresh contract he had signed with the club in early July 2001 even included a generous post-retirement deal.

By the time of their major purchase in 2001, United's shares had begun to look attractive again. They were sitting at less than half of their value of March 2000, so investment in clearly undervalued stock was sensible. And whether it was the Irishmen's intention or not, the move was seen as boosting Ferguson's position. Though Coolmore's various spokespeople always say the share investments and the horse ownership deals were entirely separate matters, if they and Ferguson were to be entirely honest they would have to admit that it was, at the very least, a mutually beneficial relationship for both parties.

For if it had not been so, John Magnier would have had no compunction in ending Ferguson's co-ownership of Rock Of Gibraltar as soon as the Gimcrack Speech had finished. Everyone who knows his business operations says he is ruthless, especially at cutting out 'dead wood'. That he kept Rocky running in Ferguson's colours suggests that Magnier was enjoying having the Manchester United legend as a friend and was in full support of the manager, even if he did not go to Old Trafford to see a match (by the end of the 2003-04 season, despite co-owning nearly a third of the club, Magnier still had not seen United play in the Theatre of Dreams).

Magnier also knew that if he split up the partnership between Ferguson and his horse, he would face massive public opprobrium throughout racing and beyond. More importantly, he was keeping secret what only a handful of people knew – that Ferguson had been embellishing the tale of his 'ownership' and certainly had never paid a penny towards it. As he and McManus went about buying into United, the Coolmore supremo probably had the United manager just where he wanted him – acting as a 'front man' for Rock Of Gibraltar, and beholden to Magnier for his reputation. For one word to the press at that point would have exposed the commonly held myth that Ferguson had paid for his share of Rocky.

Ironically, in view of later events, the main group that represented thousands of smaller investors, Shareholders United, welcomed Cubic Expression's buying spree. Their spokesman Oliver Houston said, 'We are always pleased to see United fans buying stakes in the club, rather than faceless City institutions. We would be surprised if this was the end of it. We look forward to talking with them as soon as possible.'

The fact is that Cubic Expression already owned a sizeable

chunk of United, and showed no signs of selling it, long before the manager changed his mind about retiring and signed a new three-year contract in February 2002. Mag and Mac were also willing to buy more stock, but not at crazy prices. By July 2002, they had made no massive purchases but, with Ferguson playing the 'grateful co-owner' role to perfection, Cubic Expression's partners owned 8.65 per cent of United, second only to BSkyB's 9.99 per cent which they had retained after being ordered by the Monopolies and Mergers Commission to reduce their stake to under 10 per cent.

Everything was going swimmingly for Ferguson, Magnier and McManus, and to the amazement of Aidan O'Brien, Rock Of Gibraltar stayed healthy – the only three year old in the stable to do so.

O'Brien decided that the record attempt would be made, and the hype began to build as the trainer announced that Rocky's target would be the Prix du Moulin at Longchamp. In the days before the race, the sports pages were filled with accounts of Rocky's life and his beaming co-owner was ubiquitous in telling of his ambitions for the colt. But O'Brien was genuinely worried. As with every horse at Ballydoyle, Rock Of Gibraltar had been forced to take a break from his work because of the coughing outbreak.

O'Brien warned a few days before the race that his stars could all need the run as they emerged from their spell on the sidelines. He knew Rocky was tough and ready to race, so maybe he was just making excuses before the event in case things went wrong; not that anything did go wrong.

The BBC didn't take up their option to show the race live, broadcasting a recording more than an hour later, while Radio Five lost their 'feed' to Longchamp and J.A. McGrath had to shout down a telephone to commentate for that part of the nation which wasn't glued to the race on satellite television.

The most disappointing aspect of the day was the paucity of the Parisian crowd. Fewer than 2,000 turned up to witness history – which I bet would have been a different story if the horse had been French. And to be fair to the French racegoers, they cheered like crazy shortly before 3 p.m. on that Sunday afternoon.

THOSE TWO IMPOSTORS...

LONGCHAMP, 8 SEPTEMBER 2002, AT 2.50 P.M.
NetJets Prix du Moulin, a Group 1 race for three year olds upwards.
Distance: one mile. Going: good. Seven ran.
Prizes: 1. £105,166; 2. £42,074; 3. £21,037; 4. £10,509; 5. £5,264.

1. Rock Of Gibraltar, 3-8-11, M.J. Kinane, 3-5 jfav, A.P. O'Brien.
2. Banks Hill, 4-8-12, R. Hughes, 24-10, ½ l, A. Fabre.
3. Gossamer, 3-8-8, J.P. Spencer, 184-10, ½ l, L.M. Cumani.
4. Proudwings, 6-8-12, Y. Take, 174-10, nk, J.E. Hammond.
5. Sahara Desert, 3-8-11, P.J. Scallan, 3-5 jfav, ¾ l, A.P. O'Brien.
6. Bowman, 3-8-11, O. Placais, 31-2, sh nk, A. Fabre.
Also ran: Execute.
Winner's time: 1 min 39.3 secs (slower than standard by 1.9 secs).
Winning owners: Sir Alex Ferguson and Mrs Sue Magnier.

The enforced rest might have done Rocky good, some pundits theorised, though conversely plenty of others thought it might have rendered him unfit for duty. Certainly, his stable companion Hawk Wing had not appeared his usual self when losing the Irish Champion Stakes at Leopardstown the day before.

As far as the public knew, there was real doubt at one point that Rocky would take part in the race. Three days prior to the race, it was speculated that Aidan O'Brien would risk the considerable wrath of the French stewards by declaring Rock Of Gibraltar and then pulling him out at the last minute. 'I will tell the stewards the truth,' he said, 'that I am trying to be fair to the public and be as open as I can. The public know what the position is with our horses and I don't want to risk running a horse who is not 100 per cent.'

He was going to need to be fully fit, too, as the field contained Banks Hill, winner of the previous year's Coronation Stakes at Royal Ascot and the Breeders' Cup Filly and Mares Turf. Her most recent outing had been in the Prix du Haras de Fresnay-Le-Buffard-Jacques

Le Marois at Deauville – the race in which she had been controversially disqualified and placed second after finishing first in 2001. In her second Jacques Le Marois, however, Prince Khalid Abdullah's darling had comfortably beaten France's best milers, including Pascal Bary's Domedriver, plus Godolphin's Best Of The Bests. Along with Noverre, she was probably the best horse to be faced by Rock Of Gibraltar at three, and was also a close relative of his – she was his half-sister as Danehill at Coolmore was also her sire.

Bowman had come back for another tilt at Rock Of Gibraltar, and a very interesting contestant was Gossamer, the winner of the Entenmann's Irish 2,000 Guineas, whose trainer Luca Cumani was a little bit in love with his charge, as he is with all the horses who bring him glory. The much-travelled Proudwings from John Hammond's yard was a winner all over the Continent. She had won races in Germany, Italy and France, and had lifted the Falmouth Stakes at Newmarket and the Capital Stakes in Tokyo as a five year old, and now at six the mare took her place in the field alongside stablemate Execute who had won the Group 2 Prix d'Harcourt at Longchamp at the start of the season.

In France's pari-mutuel totalisator system, horses in the same ownership or stable are coupled together in the betting, which is a Gallic way of recognising that teamwork often happens in races, so pacemaker Sahara Desert was sent off 3–5 joint favourite alongside Rocky, though its real chances were about 500–1. Anticipation among the crowd rose as the runners cantered down. Rock Of Gibraltar was just glad to be back on the racecourse – he was bucking and kicking and looked in the pink.

Unfortunately, for the first time when using a pacemaker for Rocky, the Ballydoyle teamwork did not go exactly according to plan. The usually excellent Paul Scallan drove Sahara Desert into the lead as expected and set the normal steady pace. He was soon ten lengths clear, however, as the others chose to run much slower, almost at a snail's pace. Perhaps the other jockeys thought they could make it a late sprint which Rocky couldn't match – they had not done their homework. Proudwings ran second, while Banks Hill, Gossamer and Rock Of Gibraltar followed him in that order.

Coming round the bend into the straight, Sahara Desert came

under pressure and both Proudwings and Banks Hill made their move. Kinane was watching them, however, and began to move to the outside. Two furlongs out, Banks Hill showed why she had previously been called a flying filly, with a marvellous burst of acceleration, which Proudwings briefly matched. Rocky went after them, speeding up noticeably then kicking again as they approached the final furlong.

It was a real battle now, and the whips were flying inside that seemingly too-long final 200 yards. Richard Hughes accidentally struck Rocky in the face with his whip but the colt barely flinched and Kinane merely had to release some rein just less than 100 yards from home for the ultimate racehorse to go and do what he was doing better than any other member of his species at that time – race and win.

He went by Banks Hill and pulled a head, a neck and then a full half-length clear. With Kinane pushing Rocky out hands and heels, by the line it looked as though he had again won a shade cosily. The record was his, and this time, without question, so was all the glory.

Banks Hill lost nothing in defeat and afterwards her jockey Richard Hughes paid Rocky the ultimate compliment: 'We were beaten by a wonder horse – the best horse in the world.' She would frank the form by finishing second in the Breeders' Cup Fillies and Mares Turf. Gossamer came late to grab third almost two lengths away, and she, too, would show in that Breeders' Cup race that she had run up to her form at Longchamp as she finished even closer to Banks Hill and ahead of Epsom Oaks winner Kazzia. Like Rock Of Gibraltar, both Banks Hill and Gossamer retired to stud at the end of that season. Who knows, perhaps they'll meet again on more pleasurable duties.

For Kinane, it had been a marvellous journey to the record, and he revealed that his French colleagues had paid Rocky their own quite remarkable compliment. 'What gave me even more pleasure was the way all the other jockeys came up to congratulate me on riding such a great horse. The French riders call him "The Monster".'

Mill Reef's record had been broken and not every pundit was pleased that the legend had been overtaken by Rocky – the arguments still rage on. That noted judge of horseflesh, James Willoughby of the *Racing Post*, praised Rocky to the heavens but appeared almost prescient with his one cautionary note: 'It appears that only bad luck stands between him and the Breeders' Cup Mile at Arlington, Chicago, next month.' James, how did you know?

It really did seem as if the whole of Britain was delighted for the horse and Sir Alex Ferguson. The hype kicked in – Rocky was worth £30 million, no, make that £100 million. Two days after the race was the National Day of Gibraltar, and the governor, David Durie, issued a statement, saying:

> The people of Gibraltar certainly know all about Rock Of Gibraltar and what a great racehorse he is, and by association I am sure they take great pride in his achievement. Firstly, there is the name, which means The Rock gets media coverage, and then there is the connection through Sir Alex Ferguson to Manchester United, which is famous around the world.

The congratulations flooded in to Old Trafford, Coolmore and Ballydoyle, many from people who knew nothing about racing. A world record is something that everyone can understand, no matter the sport in which it is achieved.

In the days that followed, one generous tribute to Rocky gave everyone at Ballydoyle and Coolmore particular delight. In the *Racing Post*, Ian Balding, trainer of Mill Reef and father of BBC racing presenter Clare, was quoted as saying:

> I'm thrilled that it has taken such a great horse to beat Mill Reef's total and nobody can deny that Rock Of Gibraltar is a true champion.
>
> It was an outstanding performance by an exceptional horse and, as records are there to be broken, I'm delighted that Mill Reef's has been beaten by such a brilliant colt.

Lester Piggott gave his approval – briefly, as usual – saying, 'I think Rock Of Gibraltar has been a joy to watch. He knows how to race. Most of his wins have been easy and Sir Alex Ferguson is very lucky to have a horse like him.'

The manager himself was delirious with joy, telling Cornelius

THOSE TWO IMPOSTORS...

Lysaght on Radio Five: 'It was fantastic, a really marvellous performance. It's difficult for me to know when a horse is travelling well because I'm used to seeing footballers travelling well. It was a bit nerve-racking today but everyone assured me he would win well.

'He was hit by a whip in the last furlong and I think he would have won more convincingly if he hadn't been. It was an accident, of course, but it just stopped the horse for a stride or two, but fortunately he got there.'

Even O'Brien became atypically gushy: 'He's a super horse and has so much speed. We were a little worried before the race and it would have been very hard on Rock Of Gibraltar if he'd been beaten. It's so easy for him in his races – he settles so well and it doesn't matter what pace is set, as he quickens and stays.

'What more can you say about him? It would have taken four horses to do what he has done already. He's amazing – I think he could stay a mile and a quarter without any problem.'

But with probably only one or two suitable races left for the horse in 2002, where would O'Brien send him next for an eighth Group 1 that would probably ensure his world record would stand for a very long time? 'Rock Of Gibraltar will be aimed at the Breeders' Cup Mile, and if he comes out of this race well, he could take in the Queen Elizabeth II Stakes at Ascot,' said O'Brien.

On returning to Ballydoyle, O'Brien decided to let Rock Of Gibraltar put on a bit of weight, which is always necessary when a horse is going on a long trip as they lose lumps of weight in transit. The Breeders' Cup Mile at Arlington racetrack in Chicago would be the destination for Rocky and though no final decision had been made, it was looking very likely that John Magnier would call a halt to his career on the racecourse at that point. Why risk a world record holder? Sadly, at Arlington he would see all too graphically the evidence that racing is indeed a risky business for horses.

His friends tried everything to try to get Alex Ferguson to Chicago – it was even suggested that United's home match against Aston Villa on that Breeders' Cup weekend might be rearranged. But football came first, and like just about every other Rocky fan in Britain, Ferguson watched the big race on satellite television.

ROCK OF GIBRALTAR

ARLINGTON, CHICAGO, 26 OCTOBER 2002,
    AT 7.35 P.M. (OFF 7.37 P.M.).
NetJets Breeders' Cup Mile, a Grade 1 race for three year
    olds upwards.
Distance: one mile. Going: yielding. 14 ran.
Prizes: 1. £381,096; 2. £146,575; 3. £87,945; 4. £41,041;
    5. £14,658.
1. Domedriver, 4–9–0, T. Thulliez, 26–1, P. Bary.
2. Rock Of Gibraltar, 3–8–10, M.J. Kinane, 4–5 fav, ¾ l,
    A.P. O'Brien.
3. Good Journey, 6–9–0, P. Day, 54–10, nose, W. Dollase.
4. Forbidden Apple, 7–9–0, C. Nakatani, 151–10, 1¼ l, C.
    Clement.
5. Green Fee, 6–9–0, J.R. Velazquez, 45–1, 1¼ l, D. Peitz.
6. Beat Hollow, 5–9–0, J. Bailey, 13–2, 1¾ l, R.J. Frankel.
Also ran: Del Mar Show, Dress To Thrill, Medecis, Touch
    Of The Blues, Aldebaran, Nuclear Debate, Boston
    Common, Landseer.
Winner's time: 1 min 36.88 secs.
Winning owners: the Niarchos Family.

The details of this race are distressing to fans of Rocky, but also to all who love the racehorse as a species.

All horses need luck to stay healthy enough to get to the track, and they need the luck of the draw and luck in running, too. Apart from the Coventry and Dewhurst Stakes, Rocky had enjoyed a run of good fortune without which no world record can be set. Even the normal coffin-box draw at Newmarket had turned out to be in his favour in the 2,000 Guineas. His naturally strong constitution had helped him withstand the coughing epidemic at Ballydoyle, but perhaps he also just got lucky and avoided the microscopic spores of virus floating around the stables.

Rock Of Gibraltar's luck began to run out on the Wednesday of the week before the Breeders' Cup meeting. He was handed stall 10, wide on the track, and Aidan O'Brien was immediately concerned that the pace of the race would leave him stranded and unable to get to his normal position sitting behind the leaders. He was opposed in the race by some very fine horses, including

THOSE TWO IMPOSTERS...

French hope Domedriver, who had run close to Banks Hill in the Prix Jacques Le Marois and had been aimed at Chicago ever since. Rock Of Gibraltar's own stablemate Landseer was the only horse in the field to have beaten Rocky but that victory in the Coventry Stakes of 2001 had been reversed in the Dewhurst and St James's Palace Stakes, though as French 2,000 Guineas winner, he was perhaps the best three-year-old miler in the field other than Rock Of Gibraltar. Dress To Thrill from Dermot Weld's stable was a Group 2 winner and she completed the Irish raiding trio.

The home contingent hadn't exactly set the earth on fire, though Good Journey had won the Grade 1 Atto Mile at Woodbine in fine style and was a tough and consistent six year old with the inestimable advantage of having the brilliant Pat Day in the saddle. Good Journey and Domedriver were drawn next to each other in stalls 5 and 4 respectively, and that looked to be a useful advantage. Another home-trained horse who was familiar to British racegoers was Beat Hollow, formerly trained at Newmarket by Henry Cecil, as had been Aldebaran. Beat Hollow had finished third behind Sinndar in the Derby of 2000 and later won the Group 1 Grand Prix de Paris at Longchamp before switching to America where his greatest success had been victory in the Arlington Million a little over two months prior to Breeders' Cup Day, though Landseer had beaten him in the Keeneland Turf Mile on 6 October. Third to Beat Hollow in the Million had been Grade 1 winner Forbidden Apple, who had finished third behind Fantastic Light in the previous December's Hong Kong Cup.

Only a few American stars to beat, therefore, and the betting showed that the bookmakers on both sides of the Atlantic, as well as the racing public, had eyes only for one horse. In the week leading up to the Mile, Rock Of Gibraltar's odds hardened from 7–4 in places to evens on the morning of the race and by post time the best odds available were 4–5. He was hot favourite, with Good Journey second in the market but five points and more behind.

Before the race, Rocky played up a bit. Perhaps he was just too keen to get racing again, but he was soon settled down by Kinane and his usage of vital energy at that point cannot be blamed for what happened in the race. From the off, Boston Common raced hard for the bend just 125 yards from the start, and perhaps discomfited Rocky in the stall immediately outside him who was noticeably slow away. So, too, was Domedriver. Kinane seemed determined to race Rocky in the same manner which had made him King of Europe, and he dropped Rock Of Gibraltar behind the field as Boston Common took them along at a pace that slowed rapidly. Del Mar Show was prominent behind Boston Common in the van of the field, and as they swept round the Arlington oval, the home crowd could see that Good Journey was placed best of all in third, and he was going well. Indeed, Pat Day moved his horse into the lead three furlongs from home and looked as if he might have stolen the race as he began the final bend that would lead them into the straight. Landseer had always been up with the pace and his jockey Edgar Prado made an early move to try to win the race.

Some eight or nine lengths behind the leader, Kinane decided to take Rock Of Gibraltar, lying in twelfth or thirteenth on the bend, to the outside of the pack to deliver his run, but ahead of him at that point was Thierry Thulliez, who was about to produce the race of his life on Domedriver, and it started with the gamble of remaining on the inside and waiting for those ahead to tire. It looked as if Good Journey would see out the final two furlongs, but now Kinane had Rocky in full and seemingly irresistible flow as he made the smooth forward move which had become so familiar over the summer. Landseer had by then moved into third and looked a sure bet for a place when suddenly he jinked to the outside, right in front of the charging Rock Of Gibraltar. Landseer was clearly in distress, and Prado quickly pulled him up.

The damage had been done to Rock Of Gibraltar's run. Kinane was almost on top of Landseer when he was forced to pull Rocky to the left. His momentum had been checked, albeit slightly, and he took three or four strides to adjust his angle, losing his position in the process. But now he was flying as they passed the furlong pole and the only question was would the post come too soon? It looked that way as Pat Day went for the wire, throwing everything at Good Journey.

Behind the leaders to the inside, Thulliez had held up Domedriver until the last possible second but as Rock Of Gibraltar swooped down the outside, the jockey gave his colt the equivalent of a motorist's third-gear start and Domedriver hit top velocity in a matter of strides. Blasting along the inside, gaps opened up miraculously and Domedriver suddenly had enough space and definitely had enough speed to overhaul Good Journey.

With Rocky also catching Day's horse, Domedriver hit the front just 50 or 60 yards from the finishing line, and just like Frankie Dettori in the Champagne Stakes at Doncaster the year before, Thulliez had timed his run to perfection. Kinane's run would also have been perfect and everyone would have hailed a wondrous performance had he only had Good Journey to catch, which he did in the shadow of the wire, beating the home hope by a nose. Sadly for Rocky's fans, Thulliez and Domedriver were a little over half a length further on. Forbidden Apple stayed on grimly for fourth while Green Fee came from behind in Domedriver's slipstream to snatch fifth inside the final half-furlong, Beat Hollow staying on at one pace for sixth.

In all honesty, even given another 100 yards, Rock Of Gibraltar would probably not have caught Domedriver, as the French horse's powerful surge was a sustained and winning one. Kinane took all the criticism immediately afterwards, much of it unfair, though thanks to America's enlightened policy of providing sectional timings on its courses, it could be seen that Rocky had run the final quarter-mile in 22.46 secs, more than three seconds faster than the opening quarter. One expert viewed the race several times before pronouncing that Rock Of Gibraltar had made up an incredible seven lengths on the leader in that final quarter, which was all the more remarkable given the interference he suffered at the start of his run. Still, Rock Of Gibraltar had lost, and though Kinane's riding of the horse had not been perfect on this occasion, the torrent of abuse he took was not necessary. Most experts agree that the injury to Landseer and the need to avoid the stricken horse cost Rocky as much as a length. At the line, he was officially beaten by three-quarters of a length.

Back on the track, Edgar Prado lay prone for a while after his fall from Landseer, who was clearly beyond help. Prado got up, thankfully only winded, and walked away.

'I'm fine, thank God,' he said. 'I heard a crack. I tried to pull him up, but he was full of run.'

The collapse happened just as Kinane asked Rock Of Gibraltar for his greatest effort. 'He just ran into the back of Landseer,' said O'Brien. 'It stopped him at a bad time in the race. I think it's great

ROCK OF GIBRALTAR

testimony to the horse, the ground he made up in the stretch. He did come close, but the post came too quick for him.'

Like Rock Of Gibraltar, Beat Hollow ran his last race in Chicago. He, too, went off to stud, and further retirements included Forbidden Apple and Green Fee. Good Journey raced once more before retiring. Domedriver's campaign in 2003 saw him run fourth, some 20 lengths behind Hawk Wing in the Lockinge, and he later finished second to the wonderful Six Perfections in the Prix Jacques Le Marois before going off to stud.

Of the horses who finished down the field, Aldebaran later went on to win a clutch of Grade 1 and Grade 2 races, though not of the very highest quality. Dress To Thrill came out and won the Grade 1 Matriarch Stakes in her very next race, though she did not hit the heights at four. Touch Of The Blues improved considerably in 2003, winning the Atto Mile and finishing just under a length second to Six Perfections in the Breeders' Cup Mile at Santa Anita, which was a lot closer than he got to Rocky.

Whether it was bad luck or bad judgement, or both, the race had not worked out well for the world record holder. Rock Of Gibraltar's career ended disappointingly, but his reputation was assured with the racing public. His fame, however, was really only just beginning.

I have a theory about sport, and about racing. Momentum is everything. I call it the Big Mo. The best football clubs at their peak – Arsenal and Celtic of season 2003–04 for example – have an irresistible flow to their work, their confidence and willingness to fight to the last second to avoid defeat carrying them on and on to new heights. Momentum is everything for a horse, too, and never more so than when they are starting that winning run to glory. But if something interrupts the Big Mo, it can be very hard to get it back. That is what happened to Rock Of Gibraltar when Landseer broke down in front of him. It was a small deviation in his path, but it cost Rocky victory, because he was just too late in getting his Big Mo back on track.

Not that anyone at Ballydoyle and Coolmore cared about the defeat in the hours after the race.

On an afternoon of celebration of the finest horses in the world, the event was marred irretrievably by the tragedy which befell Landseer. In breaking down just after the crown of the bend,

Landseer had fractured the cannon bone in his near-foreleg. When that happens to a horse in full flight, the adrenalin coursing through its veins allows it to carry on stumbling forward. Edgar Prado knew immediately that the injury was massive, even as he was being thrown from the saddle. All decent jockeys know instantly when something goes seriously wrong with the animal underneath them and Prado realised in milliseconds that he was dealing with a moribund horse.

For Landseer, the end came swiftly, and it was merciful. He had some of the best veterinarian care in the world at his side within seconds, but nothing could be done. The extent of his injury made his survival impossible and the only humane thing to do in such a situation is to put the animal out of the suffering – it is not capable of understanding or dealing with the pain. The rituals of equine death on the track are unfortunately familiar to regular racegoers – the animal lying prone, the canvas shields going up, then the headshakes and tears of the grief-stricken grooms and trainer as they walk away from the dead animal in which they have invested so much emotion.

Earlier that year, as Hawk Wing and High Chaparral fought out their mighty duel in the Epsom Derby, behind them Paul Cole's Coshocton broke its leg in the final furlong and had to be put down. It all happened in front of Her Majesty the Queen and the thousands of spectators on the course. The millions watching on television were spared the sight.

I can recall vividly even now the tears in the eyes of Coshocton's devoted groom, Colin Dalton, as he was led away crying from the scene of that Epsom fatality. A kindly police inspector put an arm around his shoulders as Dalton, a veteran of the racing game, grieved for the colt he loved and which he no doubt hoped would be a champion.

That Saturday night in Chicago, it was the turn of Irish eyes to cry. As with Colin Dalton, there could be no consolation for everyone associated with Landseer. In Flat racing, equine fatalities on the track are actually quite rare – accidents in training kill more horses – but such public deaths at a course have a greater resonance.

For John Magnier, the death of Landseer robbed him of a proven Classic winner and potential star at stud in whose success he could have revelled for years, not to mention earning millions of pounds from stud fees. But I'm pretty sure the loss of money didn't bother Magnier at Arlington – it was the loss of a brilliant animal which hurt.

For on Derby Day, I had watched as Magnier stood mute and seemingly almost at prayer, as he and Michael Tabor were presented with the Vodafone Derby trophy just a few dozen yards from where Coshocton lay. There were no smiles and both men acted with great dignity, quickly removing themselves from the arena in recognition of the tragic events being played out nearby.

Now the situation was reversed, and it was Magnier's horse who died. Again, Magnier conducted himself with dignity and a kind of serene equanimity – treating those two impostors just the same.

Owners who have lost horses on the track are invariably upset, but strangely they are often the most philosophical about their loss. The people who really grieve are the trainer, who may have lavished many hours of attention on the animal, and especially the groom who has probably cared for the horse from the moment it entered the stable. O'Brien and all his staff were devastated by the loss of Landseer. A little over two hours later at Arlington, High Chaparral and Mick Kinane secured the Breeders' Cup Turf for the stable, but no one from Ballydoyle really felt like celebrating. Rock Of Gibraltar's second was in many ways an irrelevance.

Death on the racecourse is, sadly, an occupational hazard for horses. Yet they can roll in the hay in their box and twist a gut and die in agony, or break a leg just galloping round a paddock, and nobody hears about their death. But dying in full public glare on a track appears to matter more, and when a fatal accident happens in such a high-profile event as the Breeders' Cup, it gives a boost to the case made by various animal rights groups that racing is cruel.

The only defence for racing in the face of such criticism is not much of one – Landseer, Coshocton and so many more horses died doing quite literally what they were born to do, for the thoroughbred racehorse species was created to race and has no other reason for existence.

This chapter started with a quotation from Rudyard Kipling. It will end with something close to one. To paraphrase the poet, on the racetrack, Rock Of Gibraltar had filled every unforgiving minute with sixty seconds' worth of distance run. And now the earth was his.

Or the next best thing – every good-looking mare on the planet.

CHAPTER EIGHT

The Final Furlong

By the time Rock Of Gibraltar and the O'Brien camp pitched back at Ballydoyle, John Magnier had already decided to retire Rocky at the end of his three-year-old season. The only question was whether Rocky would be risked one more time on the racetrack, but nobody around Ballydoyle really had the heart for it. The death of Landseer had raised the awful spectre of a similar calamity befalling Rocky. It was time to call it a day.

Normally, such a premature end to a career would have pundits and public alike railing against the loss of a champion who would surely have taken to a higher level at four what we had already seen of him at three, for the horse was still improving with every race. Landseer's demise, however, rendered such arguments conspicuous by their absence – how could anyone really say to Magnier that he should risk his fabulous colt on the track when he had already suffered the loss of a great one?

Coolmore let it be known in early November that there was still some consideration that Rocky might stay in training at four, such was their regard for the sheer toughness of the colt. But it was that very quality of perseverance and the ability to withstand hard races which became the deciding factor – he had been so busy both as

ROCK OF GIBRALTAR

a juvenile and in his Classic season that there was a fear of a reaction on his part in the following season. Far better to get him off to stud where his durability would be tested in a different way.

In the fortnight after the Breeders' Cup, there was some talk of sending him to Asia for its big event, the Hong Kong Mile, but it came to nil. Shortly afterwards, the name of Rock Of Gibraltar appeared on the likely list of stallions for Coolmore Stud's 2003 roster. There was no surprise, therefore, when the news came from Ballydoyle on 11 November that Rock Of Gibraltar had been retired to Coolmore Stud.

He had raced thirteen times, winning ten, finishing second twice and his only unplaced finish had been in the botched Coventry Stakes. He had won a total of £1,269,800, of which £1,100,230 was earned by his victories. And, of course, he retired as a world record holder, which he still is in 2004.

The Press Association's racing desk reported the decision in the sombre terms it usually adopts for the death of the sport's great ones:

> Manchester United manager Alex Ferguson today led tributes to Rock Of Gibraltar, the horse who has given him so much enjoyment over the last two seasons. Rock Of Gibraltar carried Ferguson's red and white colours to a record-breaking seven successive Group 1 races.
> In a statement to PA Sport, Ferguson said:
>
> *As a relative newcomer into ownership, I cannot adequately express the pleasure I have derived from the association with such a great horse.*
>
> *I owe an eternal debt of thanks to everyone associated with Ballydoyle. Whilst I will be saddened not to see Rock Of Gibraltar in action on the racecourse, I look forward to the future with keen anticipation and I have every confidence that he will transmit his amazing talent and courage to his offspring.*

The media were still unaware of the true nature of Rocky's ownership. One of several generous valedictory stories reported that 'owners Mr and Mrs John Magnier sold a share in the colt to

THE FINAL FURLONG

Ferguson', and the writer added, 'the Ferguson silks were to prove lucky from the start'.

The announcement from Tipperary was a stark one-liner: 'Rock Of Gibraltar will stand the 2003 season alongside his sire Danehill at Coolmore.' It was almost as if they were ashamed of depriving the sport of its greatest star of the day.

Which he most certainly was. It took Rocky's retirement to bring forth a torrent of praise for the horse and its connections, with many commentators pointing out that the horse's finest hour had arguably come in the defeat in Chicago.

Aidan O'Brien led the tributes, saying: 'He always showed an exceptional, natural talent from the start. He was a top-class two year old and improved with every run at three. It is never fair to compare, but he was an unbelievable horse and was unique in that he was the only older one who didn't get the virus this year. All his wins were highlights to me. He was great for everybody who had anything to do with him and will be very hard to replace.'

Mick Kinane had just clinched his 12th Irish jockeys' championship, beating Johnny Murtagh with a last-day treble for O'Brien. He had called Rocky 'the ultimate racehorse', and now added a further level of praise: 'I haven't ridden better – it was a pleasure to be associated with him. He had fantastic acceleration and I haven't had a horse I've enjoyed being involved with on the racecourse so much.'

Murtagh, Rocky's only other jockey, chimed in: 'He was a wonderful horse and he kept improving all through the year. To win seven Group 1s in a row is amazing and he was a truly great horse. I was lucky enough to ride him in the Guineas and it was a great thrill to win for Sir Alex Ferguson.

'I can't speak highly enough of the horse – he really was The Rock. If you tried to sit behind him he would outsprint you, if you sat in front of him you just gave him a lead – he didn't lack in any department.'

The words from O'Brien's fellow trainers showed how those within racing really rated Rock Of Gibraltar, and many more experts said their piece. 'He is one of the greats in my lifetime,' said trainer Luca Cumani. 'He had tremendous acceleration and was unlucky not to complete his career with a resounding victory in the Breeders' Cup.' Journalists combed through the thesaurus for superlatives, Tony Morris of the *Racing Post* penning one of the best of the tributes:

> Forget the mathematics, think aesthetics, and ponder on which horse most stirred the emotions, gave most pleasure in 2002. The answer has to be Rock Of Gibraltar. It was said he was lucky when he beat his stable companion – that big girl's blouse Hawk Wing – in the 2,000 Guineas. You could say he was lucky over and over again – at The Curragh, at Ascot, at Goodwood and at Longchamp – lucky to meet adversaries who were always inferior.
>
> Stretch the point a little, and he was lucky at Arlington – lucky to be hailed the moral victor of the one race he did not win. It's easy to be cynical, easier sometimes than to give credit where credit is due. OK, he never beat a Brigadier Gerard or an El Gran Senor, and where he ranks in the pantheon of milers is anybody's guess. But he kept winning, and winning with ease, against the best who took him on.

After the initial tributes came the awards, which piled up the trophies in the Ferguson, O'Brien and Magnier cabinets. The Animal Health Trust gave their annual award in the racing category to Rocky, Ferguson collecting it in front of nearly 500 guests, including the Trust's President, Princess Anne – the Princess Royal. The other nominees were Cheltenham Gold Cup-winner Best Mate, Tony McCoy and Sir Michael Stoute.

The most prestigious prizes of all, the Cartier Racing Awards, saw Rocky win both the top award as Horse of the Year and also top three-year-old colt. Ferguson was on Champions League duty with United, but sent in this statement:

> Thank you to Cartier for presenting this prestigious award. It has been a truly fantastic year for us and I've so many people to thank, starting at Ballydoyle with Aidan and all his team, who have done a fantastic job with a tremendous horse.

THE FINAL FURLONG

He praised Kinane and Johnny Murtagh, John and Sue Magnier, and singled out Mike Dillon, 'who has been a great comfort to me, given me proper advice at the right time and really guided me throughout the year'.

Ironically, Ferguson himself came in for high praise for his advice and assistance to O'Brien and Kinane. The trainer spoke to Michael Clower, one of Ireland's foremost racing journalists, at the Bisquit Cognac/Irish Independent racing awards lunch in Dublin, where he was presented with the Racing Personality of the Year award on his own account and also accepted on behalf of Ferguson the Unique Racing Achievement award for Rocky's world record run of Group 1 races.

O'Brien told Clower:

> Alex has a great knowledge of life and of people and he often gives me little bits of advice. The best advice he ever gave me was in the summer of 2000 when Mick was under the weather because his back was giving him all sorts of problems.
>
> When he did not ride Ciro in that year's Irish Derby, people were wondering whether we would have a jockey for the following year.
>
> We arranged for Mick to go over to Manchester United for a few days and we got Alex to have a look at him to see how long his body was going to last. We had to decide whether we were going to retain him in 2001. Word came back from Alex that we should retain him, but only play him on the big days.

That account ties in with what Kinane himself had said earlier – that Ferguson had arranged physiotherapy for him, and had personally picked up the jockey and driven him to and from Old Trafford.

O'Brien added:

> We have been delighted to have Alex as an owner. He comes over to watch the work and he gets a great buzz out of it.
>
> After having a horse like Rock Of Gibraltar, though, the

only way he can go as an owner is down. So hopefully he will get a mare or two and then he can watch the little Rocks running.

The International Classifications for 2002 were published early in 2003 and rated Rocky as the best horse in the world on a mark of 128, which only served to get the statistics junkies frothing at the mouth – too high, was their general verdict. As had happened during his career, there were plenty of people prepared to knock Rock Of Gibraltar down many places in the list of racing greats. The acerbic Paul Haigh unleashed fury when he wrote in the *Racing Post* that Rocky was not 'anything like the colossus he's been cracked up to be'.

Warming to his theme, Haigh added:

> In all the time I've been following racing, I don't think there's ever been a horse so mightily hyped, or one who's been so consistently and unquestioningly granted a status he simply did not deserve. The guys with the slide-rules have been conned by public opinion.

He added memorably that his fans – people like me – were 'Rock groupies so in love they can't think straight'. By 2004, Haigh had still not altered his view that Rocky 'beat nothing much, did he?'. Write on, Paul.

There were more articles on that theme, but many times more letters and comments defending Rock Of Gibraltar. But the best award of all had already been bestowed by the public who take their racing seriously – the people who read the *Racing Post*. For the first time, the Bible of racing had teamed up with the Racehorse Owners Association (ROA) in a poll to decide the ROA's top award for Horse of the Year. The result proved to be a staggering endorsement by racing fans of 'their' Rock Of Gibraltar.

Chris Smith, now editor of the *Racing Post*, summed up that result succinctly and brilliantly, writing that 2002 had been 'The Year of The Rock' and putting Rocky's achievements in the context of the bewildering events that had afflicted racing. The four nominees for the award were High Chaparral, Florida Pearl, Best

THE FINAL FURLONG

Mate and Rock Of Gibraltar, and Rocky was chosen by almost half of the voters. He won by a mile.

'We thought the voting might be close,' wrote Smith. 'It wasn't: Rock Of Gibraltar first, the rest some way behind.'

Rocky had polled just less than 48 per cent of the vote, 'which came as a bit of a shock at the *Post*,' admitted Smith. He went on:

> Surely the Aidan O'Brien-trained colt would struggle to beat Best Mate and Florida Pearl now they were back in action. Surely the traditionally passionate jumping fraternity would refuse to believe that a mere three-year-old miler could have achieved something worthier than either of their great heroes.
>
> But Rock Of Gibraltar was more than just an outstanding racehorse. He was one of the finest advertisements for the sport for years. His exhilarating performances and Premier League ownership sent an ocean liner of positive public interest surging through the season that will have left *Kenyon Confronts*, *Panorama* and various political squabblings floundering irrelevantly in the wash.
>
> Make no mistake, Rock Of Gibraltar was that old cliché – the talk of the pubs and clubs. He transcended racing into household namedom. People with little or no interest in horse racing switched on their tellies to see how Sir Alex's horse would get on. Now he ranks right up there with Red Rum, Shergar, Frankie Dettori and Jenny Pitman.
>
> Obviously, much of this is because of his famous owner. But by no means all. Rock Of Gibraltar was a sensational racehorse. Don't let the ratings boys tell you he was no better than Keltos, or Observatory or Mark Of Esteem or even Dancing Brave or Mill Reef. They don't know for sure. None of us knows.
>
> To the traditionalists, it will be heresy, but you can mention Rock Of Gibraltar in the same breath as Mill Reef and Brigadier Gerard. There's no collateral formline that shows they were better. They may have been, but how does anyone know? And can't you just imagine Mick Kinane sitting motionless astride The Rock with a couple of

furlongs to go with Geoff Lewis already beginning to get to work on The Reef?

The thing about Kinane and Rock Of Gibraltar was that they did everything with such imperious ease, such shameless extravagance. A glorious sight, and we don't get to see it very often.

The awards would continue to roll in, but the main question, to which every breeder wanted an answer, was where Rocky would stand at stud and how much his services would cost. Coolmore announced to general surprise that he would stand in Ireland *and* Australia, despite intense pressure from breeders in the USA who were desperate for Rock Of Gibraltar to stand at Coolmore's Ashford Stud in Kentucky. After the Breeders' Cup loss, while the British press lamented Rocky's bad luck and more than a few blamed Kinane, the more sanguine American owners, trainers and breeders who were at Arlington were virtually unanimous in their wonder at Rock Of Gibraltar's speed in the finish. One owner said he had never seen a horse come from so far back in a big race at Arlington and finish so close. 'They were buzzing about the horse,' said one journalist who spoke to several of the home contingent after the meeting, 'and with that reaction he could have gone to stud in America.'

The stud fee was steep. It had been set at €90,000, or just less than £60,000 in Ireland, and Aus$132,000 – again just under £60,000 – at Coolmore's stud down under. It was the inevitable law of supply and demand, the price reflecting the clamour by breeders to grab a piece of The Rock.

And the lucky young stallion was about to get the cream of the crop – the dams of champions on three continents were lined up for his first year at stud. The new young kid on the block was certainly out to prove he could be a hit with the 'older ladies'. Among the mares that he would see in his first session at stud were Irish 1,000 Guineas winners of yesteryear Marling and Tarascon. In all, he would cover six Group 1 winners, as well as the dams of eight Group 1 race winners, including the mothers of Desert Prince, Lady Of Chad and the late, great Persian Punch. The 2,000 Guineas winner of 2001, Golan, was already at Coolmore – one wonders if he saw his mummy, Highland Gift, sneaking in for her tryst with Rocky.

Making a serious point, Coolmore manager Christy Grassick said, 'We're very fortunate to have the last two 2,000 Guineas winners at Coolmore for 2003. They both have the looks, pedigrees and race records to make outstanding sires and both are proving very popular with breeders.' Indeed, that was the case with Rocky, who in his first sessions in Ireland and Australia was visited by around 200 mares, the majority of whom were later found to be in foal. This meant that in his first year alone, Rock Of Gibraltar earned his owners £10 million – nice work for him, and for them. Rocky certainly took to the new life like a duck to water, putting on weight and displaying that perfect temperament which he had developed late in his career on track.

Almost every journalist at that time also wrote how lucky Ferguson had been – how were they to know that everything behind the scenes was not as straightforward as it had been portrayed? Such was the hype about Ferguson's likely tax-free earnings from Rocky that he came in for a lambasting from an unlikely source – the Catholic Church.

The well-known Irish priest Father Sean Healy, renowned for his campaign work against poverty, said Ferguson should not be allowed to walk away with tax-free proceeds from Rocky's efforts.

Father Healy told the *Mirror*, 'That horse will make a ten million euro profit a year and he will get half of that, but Ferguson will not pay a cent of tax in Ireland. I believe five million euro is a bit too much to go untaxed. Even a modest levy would bring money into the Exchequer and still leave him with an enormous amount of money in his pocket.' In view of later events, perhaps Father Healy should now take up his case with John Magnier.

Yet already there had been a couple of minor stories suggesting that Ferguson's ownership of half the breeding rights was not secure. Even before Rocky had run his last race, the *Daily Telegraph*'s 'Peterborough' column had reported a rumour circulating in racing circles that Ferguson had not done the deal properly and that Magnier was disputing the arrangement. The story was picked up and used elsewhere by other papers, but it was given no credibility because Ferguson's friends and 'insiders' had let it be known that he had paid his £120,000 share and that meant he was surely entitled to half the horse in law.

I had heard the same story from a senior figure in the racing world who has been consistently correct in his briefings to me about this whole saga. He is not an owner or administrator, but knows both Ferguson and O'Brien, and everything he has told me from day one has ultimately proved correct – which is why Manchester United fans may be pleased by the end of this book.

'That rumour might be true,' my source told me, 'but the key to it is whether Ferguson will go public or even go to court, and before then it would be unwise to say anything, as you don't want to make enemies of either man.' So I didn't write anything. And in any case Michael Clower had reported in September 2001 that Mike Dillon had told him that Ferguson owned 50 per cent of the horse and that included the breeding rights.

More pertinently from my viewpoint, Ferguson himself had told me the deal was done. 'It's all sorted,' were his exact words the previous October. At that point, I did not know that he had not paid a penny up front or in arrears for the horse. His talk to me of training fees and 'soon going through the money' was also later proved unsound, for he had not paid those fees for Rocky and his other Coolmore–Ballydoyle horses.

I knew enough about the law of contract to be sure that payment of an agreed sum validates an arrangement, so I believed that Ferguson was due his half of the stud fees. I also could not believe that Ferguson would have allowed the stories about his approaching wealth to circulate widely without at least tacit approval from himself. My conclusion, and most other people's in January 2003, was that Alex Ferguson was going to be a very, very rich man thanks to his 50 per cent ownership of Rock Of Gibraltar.

Yet in retrospect, there were two curious developments in February 2003 which should have set the alarm bells ringing off the wall. It has been reported by the *Daily Mail*'s Colin MacKenzie – whose coverage of this story throughout has been nothing short of excellent – that in that month, Ferguson first called Coolmore to ask about the money he would earn from Rock Of Gibraltar. I have checked on this call. I was told that Ferguson's call was met with a bemused employee's answer that, in effect, amounted to the question, 'What money?'

Weatherbys Ireland, holders of the stud book for that country, have confirmed to me that they also received a call in February 2003 asking about the names in which Rocky's ownership had been registered. The name was a matter of public record. It was 'Rock Of Gibraltar Syndicate' and not Mrs John Magnier and Sir Alex Ferguson as in Horse Racing Ireland's form for registration of ownership. Weatherbys, circumspect as always, could not or would not say who made the call.

I learned that more phone calls on the subject of Ferguson's 'entitlement' were made to Coolmore and elsewhere. The sources say he was bemusing people, because he was 'rattling on about money due to him from the horse, when anyone who knows anything about breeding knows that you only get paid on a date several months after the mare is found to be in foal'. In Rock Of Gibraltar's case, that date had been set at 1 October 2003. Indeed, in February of that year, the stallion had hardly begun covering mares. One can only imagine Ferguson's incandescent response when he found out that his 'ownership' had been cancelled. Indeed, we do not have to imagine it at all – we may have seen it. For the 'response' may have been plastered all over the swoon-inducing features of David Beckham, and the front pages of every newspaper in Britain.

Sources in Ireland cannot state with certainty when Alex Ferguson made his initial contact with Coolmore on the matter. Several calls were made, and the best guess of those I have spoken to is that sometime in the second week of February 2003, i.e. during the week ending Friday, 14 February, Ferguson was told once and for all by John Magnier that he was not getting half of the income.

The whole footballing and celebrity-loving world knows what happened on Saturday, 15 February 2003. It was an event which would fundamentally alter the future of Sir Alex Ferguson, Manchester United, Real Madrid, the England football team and David and Victoria Beckham and their family. On that Saturday, Ferguson was in a dour mood all day, but was there a more-than-normal bitterness about him after United lost their FA Cup match

2–0 to their greatest enemies, Arsenal? Ferguson was visibly full of barely suppressed anger, and his comments about Arsenal players' conduct showed that he was upset to the point of losing control. As soon as he was in a supposedly private place, he could not keep himself in check and let rip at his players in the dressing-room – the infamous 'hairdryer' treatment. But this time it was not just hot air and swear-words he was casting around.

In a fit of extreme temper, the manager lashed out at a football boot lying on the floor and it took off at a rate of knots to land with nearly extreme prejudice directly above the left eyebrow of the captain of England, David Beckham. The player, by his own admission in his bestselling memoirs, had to be physically restrained from retaliating against the sexagenarian manager. The resultant furore remained secret for all of a day or so – the threat of death or worse for leaking the story clearly did not bother someone in that room.

The story of Becks and the Fergie Boot exploded into the supertrooper lights of high-profile publicity. *The Sun*'s headline was up with the very best in their considerable canon – 'FERGIE DECKS BECKS' – telling the whole tale in three words, which is tabloid journalism as it should be. Beckham's tactic of turning up for training wearing a sticking plaster on his cut eyebrow was a master stroke of PR and seemingly turned the whole nation against Ferguson.

It was generally agreed that the manager had gone too far, and most commentators – including those who knew him – effectively said that Ferguson must have been under extraordinary pressure, that something had caused him more than the usual strain. Some pundits pointed out that it was even more strange as Ferguson had only recently been relieved of the worry that had niggled him all his life – he was finally and absolutely 'in the money'. No one could put a finger on why a man who was about to be catapulted into the ranks of the mega-rich by a randy racehorse should have reacted like a husband reading the Visa bill after he had loaned the card to a spendthrift wife.

Since no one can remember with precision when calls were made to Coolmore and elsewhere, it cannot be stated with certainty that Sir Alex Ferguson's reactions were coloured by his

THE FINAL FURLONG

nascent troubles with Rocky. At the very least, there is a clear suggestion that the titanic tantrum of Ferguson may not have been entirely due to Beckham's poor play 'causing' the victory of Arsene Wenger's men.

There is, however, absolute proof that his relationship with Coolmore had fundamentally altered around that time. The 'divorce' might even have been finalised by that third weekend in February which proved so disastrous for Ferguson. For within three days of the boot being biffed at Beckham, Ferguson was definitely signalling to the racing world that he and Coolmore were not entirely full and exclusive partners any more.

The proof was in fairly innocuous stories reporting that Ferguson had got together with former footballing hero turned racehorse trainer Mick Channon to race a two year old named Gatwick.

Colin MacKenzie in the *Daily Mail* reported, 'Surprisingly, it appears that Fergie is not reinvesting in another horse with the Coolmore team this year, reasoning that lightning is unlikely to strike twice. Rock Of Gibraltar is now earning him around £6 million a year from stud fees.'

On 19 February, just two days after the tale of the Boot hit the front pages, a curious story appeared in the *Racing Post* under the by-line of Graham Green. I have the editor's permission to reprint it in full. It read:

> Mick Channon will have to be wary of flying horseshoes if the juvenile in which Sir Alex Ferguson owns a share fails to live up to expectations this season. However, the two soccer legends, who are teaming up for the first time, have got off on the right foot, having already scored a significant success before Gatwick even sees the racecourse.
>
> Although Weatherbys had reservations about granting the name chosen for the colt, who is out of the mare Airport, the registration was recently approved by the Jockey Club despite the potential for confusion with the year-older Gatwick. Ferguson, named Owner of the Year in 2002 following the exploits of Rock Of Gibraltar, whom he owned in partnership with Sue Magnier, has long been an

admirer of Channon and was among the contributors when the West Ilsley trainer appeared on *This Is Your Life* [in 2001].

The pair have now been brought together by syndicate manager Henry Ponsonby, who ran the ill-fated MURC and introduced Ferguson to syndicate racing through the Tim Easterby-trained Roman Mistress.

Ponsonby said, 'After Roman Mistress, Alex said he would come into another horse with me provided it was trained by Mick Channon because he admires Mick immensely. So we looked at several horses and Gatwick is the one we decided on.'

Ferguson's fellow shareholders in the son of Sussex Stakes winner Ali-Royal, sire of last season's Dewhurst winner Tout Seul, include Weatherbys chairman Johnny Weatherby, who was a director of the MURC, Stephen Crown, treasurer of the ROA, and Chris and Jenny Powell, who had Goggles with Henry Candy.

Channon said yesterday, 'I've known Alex a long time, obviously through football, and he was the manager at Aberdeen when we first came across each other.'

So just a few days after he 'bootwhacked' Beckham, and possibly a week or less after Coolmore had told him the bad news, Ferguson permitted his new racing partners to show his hand – and Channon's and Ponsonby's comments in this story would not have appeared had Ferguson not agreed they could talk to the *Daily Mail* and *Racing Post*.

Why would he do that? Why, if he was so 'in' with Coolmore and Ballydoyle, did he not stay only with them? He was supposedly going to be a rich man, so why not maintain links with the people who had got him there? After all, he had received an open invitation from Aidan O'Brien to carry on their association, so why sever his links with Ballydoyle – he has not been back to Tipperary since – and fetch up in a syndicate which, despite its wealth, could not hope to match the long-term supply of potential champion horses from Coolmore?

Why is it that in February of 2003, Alex Ferguson walked away from his supposed friends and partners, the greatest names in European racing, and went to the manager of the racing club he had presided over and which had had no significant success? Mick Channon is a fine trainer, and I am sure he will become one of the greats, but with all due respect to him, why did Ferguson abandon Ballydoyle and O'Brien and fetch up at West Ilsley? Most importantly, why did that story about Ferguson's new horse appear when it did? It takes time to set up syndicates and buy horses – but why did the story about Ponsonby's new arrangement with Ferguson only surface a few days after the decisive calls to Coolmore? Perhaps crucially, Colin MacKenzie had reported that Gatwick had been acquired by Henry Ponsonby for around £25,000 and that Fergie had bought a one-twelfth share – that's a little over £2,000 of an outlay from a man who, as the world had been led to believe, was awaiting millions from the efforts of 'his' Rock Of Gibraltar.

Of course, it could all just be coincidence, but the split with Coolmore and the resultant repudiation of millions of pounds may also be a plausible explanation for why Ferguson reacted so uncontrollably that February day. With all the ramifications his misconduct caused for his club and David Beckham, there *needs* to be an explanation of why Sir Alex Ferguson was so utterly bellicose that Saturday.

It can be stated with certainty that by early March of 2003, the great game was finally on: Sir Alex Ferguson versus John Magnier in a no-holds-barred contest to the finish. And at first, nobody had a clue it was coming outside a few people close to both soon-to-be duellists.

It is perhaps appropriate at this point to let Alex Ferguson have his final say about Rock Of Gibraltar – words which he had written himself in *The Observer* a short time before Rocky's retirement:

> As for how good he really is – I've read some pretty amazing stuff in the papers. One guy said he wouldn't be in the top 100 of racehorses. Well, I can't answer for every horse, because I can't remember every horse. I can certainly remember Brigadier Gerard, and Mill Reef. I remember the

Brigadier very well, because I was a young player and had a big interest in horses at that time. You can't forget Brigadier Gerard.

But I've watched Rock Of Gibraltar's progress over the last six months, and all I've seen is a horse improve every time, and Mick Kinane guiding him past horses with the minimum of effort. How do you judge a horse if it's winning its races so easily? Is it work, or are the rest all hopeless? What do they want it to do? To win by ten lengths and beat the arse off someone to prove it's the best horse ever? Is the jockey's job not to win with the minimum of effort in order to save the horse?

Intriguingly for a man who, less than a year previously, had been telling me he would build a breeding career round Rocky, Ferguson added this strange farewell: 'Rock's success, and his likely success at stud, will have no effect on my football plans. Once you make a decision in life you stick by it. I'm going to stay for another three years at Old Trafford; I'm going to enjoy it. There's still a great challenge here with this football team of mine.'

It was a challenge he would face with his usual drive and commitment, not to mention his disdain for the press. Once again, Ferguson circled the wagons round Old Trafford as the team began to fight its way back to the top of the Premiership. More than a few pundits had written in late 2002 that Ferguson's team were having problems because he had been sidetracked by Rocky's success, but he was presumably far more distracted by the serious – and seriously ludicrous – allegations of sexual misconduct towards a young South African woman, Nadia Abrahams, which followed a trip to that country by the United manager, where one of his activities had been the presentation of a trophy for a 'Rock Of Gibraltar Stakes' at one of the country's racecourses. That whole nasty incident ended with Alex Ferguson being completely exonerated by the South African authorities in early October, but he would have been less than human if he had not been affected by that bizarre allegation against a man who was then, after all, a 61-year-old grandfather.

At the time of the Beckham boot incident, Arsenal were out in

THE FINAL FURLONG

front and looking good for the title, and the FA Cup loss may just have piled even more frustration on Ferguson's head, which was compounded when they drew away to Bolton the following weekend. At that point, United were five points behind Arsenal, and only three ahead of Newcastle, who had a game in hand.

Yet after the poor start to the season, the team had begun to play well. They were going strong in the Champions League, and after that draw at Bolton they romped unbeaten through the remainder of their League fixtures and clinched the title, the League Cup loss to Liverpool being the only blemish. They were playing some good stuff in early 2003, but that still didn't make them likeable as an outfit.

Manchester United are a very successful club but the arrogance of some of the people who run it often knows no bounds. Ask any journalist on the United beat who is not one of the favoured few – the very few – and he or she will tell you that while some people at the club try to be helpful, the overall corporate approach is that United are bigger than anybody, therefore the media needs the club much more than the club needs the media. Sadly, there is considerable truth in that assertion.

On a personal level, Ferguson and his players can be fine to talk to, and in their off-duty moments some of them can be good company, but there is a 'character set' to them, and they exude a combination of paranoia and arrogance which is never better displayed than when Roy Keane leads a posse to the referee to protest about a dubious decision. They are used to getting their own way, and since a team takes on the image of its leader, its manager, United often reflect the many sides of Ferguson's character.

One former employee of United describes him as 'a bully', but one who genuinely prefers people to stand up to him rather than sulk, so that the matter can be thrashed out – Ferguson nearly always wins those kind of close encounters. Now Ferguson was about to be 'stood up to' by a man who also did not know the meaning of the words 'back down'.

At the outset, and contrary to some reports, it should be emphasised that John Magnier was indeed the driving force behind Cubic Expression's foray into Manchester United. The duel with his former friend took place almost totally between him and

Ferguson, with J.P. McManus playing only a supporting, and supportive, role as a friend as well as a business partner.

McManus is the only one of the three principals involved in the row to speak to this author about it, and he politely referred me to a public relations practitioner in Ireland, who in turn wouldn't say a thing. Approached at Kelso racecourse during a golfing trip to Scotland, McManus said only two sentences: he confirmed that he had not been a defendant in Ferguson's case against Coolmore, and that he had not signed any confidentiality agreement at the conclusion of the case, for the simple reason that he was not involved. He could have said plenty, and he was invited to do so, and at one point looked as if he would, but he confined his remarks to saying, 'John Magnier has been my friend for 20 years.' And that was that.

I have subsequently discovered that J.P. McManus very much played a secondary role in the whole affair, and that John Magnier took most if not all of the substantive decisions in the events that followed Rocky's retirement. It is definitely unfair to align McManus with Magnier, though his loyalty to his friend is total and he backed him all the way.

Someone in Ireland who knows McManus and knows the intricacies of the case very well did speak to me on condition of anonymity, because they felt that McManus had been given a bit of a raw deal and yet had not spoken out because of his friendship with Magnier. The source said: 'J.P. McManus never fell out with Alex Ferguson over this case or anything else for that matter. It was very hard for him to read in the papers that he personally had fallen out with Ferguson when he had not done so. It's a very important point, especially to him, that people realise the true situation, but it all seems to have been forgotten as he is continually bracketed with John Magnier because of their joint interest in Cubic Expression.'

McManus has even been described as co-owner of Coolmore, which he isn't, and though his Irish home address is listed as care of Martinstown Stud in Co. Limerick, he has no vast breeding interests. His entry in the Directory of the Turf states he owns 11 broodmares. By comparison, Sheikh Mohammed and his Al Maktoum brothers between them own nearly 1,000.

THE FINAL FURLONG

'He has not previously had any interest in standing stallions at stud, that's John's thing. He sees himself as an owner, and that's all,' said the source, who emphasised that Magnier was the man who decided that Ferguson would be confronted.

With the fabulous prize already safely ensconced at Coolmore and making whoopee, the two contestants were circling each other, and all that was required was the choice of battleground. By accident or design, the fight took place against a background that no one anticipated. The world's biggest football club and its Theatre of Dreams, Old Trafford, became the arena for a duel which would engulf and all but jeopardise Manchester United.

The first sign of the conflict – and remember, no one even knew at this stage, in late February 2003, that there had been a fallout between Ferguson and Magnier – came when shares in United began to be traded on a comparatively heavy basis. One of the first investors to buy more shares was Dermot Desmond, the largest shareholder and a director of Celtic FC. Under internationally accepted football rules, as a director he was banned from acquiring any more than 3 per cent of another club.

Desmond is the third member of the so-called Coolmore Mafia. The brains behind Dublin's International Financial Services Centre, he is reputed to be a billionaire thanks to investments ranging from property to the high-tech companies which have powered the growth of the Celtic Tiger economy in Ireland. His rise to prominence began in 1981 when he founded his own stockbroking company, which he later sold to Ulster Bank. Since then, his most high-profile investments have been in football at Celtic and United, though, like Magnier, he has come under scrutiny for his role in Ireland's several political brouhahas which have kept a raft of lawyers and politicians busy during long and tedious investigations. Like Magnier, he has never been charged with any offence, far less found guilty, nor has any wrongdoing been revealed, and during 2004 many people in Ireland agreed with him when he rounded on one inquiry effectively for costing the country too much time and money.

There is no evidence that Desmond ever acted 'in concert' with his two friends during their time investing in United – they could not have done so without informing the company and the Stock

Exchange – but Desmond's role in the saga would eventually prove crucial. Cubic Expression also adopted curiously Desmond-like tactics. The owner of London City Airport whose main company is International Investment & Underwriting, Gibraltar-based Desmond often invests in companies which are undervalued and builds up a key stake without necessarily taking over the business. He long ago learned that control of a company's future does not necessarily mean you have to own it – Celtic plc is a case in point.

Desmond shares a love of golf and horse racing with McManus and Magnier, though he owns only a few horses, but he is easily the most knowledgeable of the three about football. Sometime in early 2003, Desmond bought between 1.5 and 2.5 per cent of Manchester United. Though he did not have to divulge his interest to the stock market because his stake was less than 3 per cent, Desmond's name was listed on the United plc share register. His closeness to Mag and Mac was well known, while at the same time it was emphasised that another mutual acquaintance of the three men, reclusive Scottish mining millionaire Harry Dobson, had already amassed 6.5 per cent of a shareholding – Dobson, too, owns racehorses in Ireland.

Desmond had already been responsible for one astonishing tilt at the United board – off his own bat, in 2002, he had commissioned the investment bank Goldman Sachs to examine the possibility of turning Manchester United into a 'people's club' owned by its fans. That idea went nowhere, and instead Desmond bought almost as much as he legally could of United, while Goldman Sachs were known to be buying shares for other investors.

Again, there was nothing sinister in Desmond's purchase – the shares had fallen to a five-year low in November as the club looked like losing the league. But perhaps it was Desmond's entry into the fray which kicked off the 2003 splurges by his friends. For his purchase seemed to spark a spending spree – Dutchman John de Mol, the creator of television's *Big Brother* and other entertainment shows, spent £8.6 million to acquire 3 per cent of the club. A bizarre entrant into the field was American shopping mall billionaire Malcolm Glazer, who had no links to United or

THE FINAL FURLONG

Britain but at least had connections to football – the American kind, as he owned the Tampa Bay Buccaneers. He bought a small share of less than 3 per cent, but the jungle drums were beating loudest about his intervention.

Rumours of a potential bid to capture United began to circulate in the City and on 7 March, United's directors and fans awoke to find out that their club was apparently 'in play' for a massive takeover bid. Or so it was reported.

It was learned that in a frantic day's trading on the stock market, Cubic Expression had spent £14 million to increase the two men's shareholding by more than 50 per cent – up from 6.77 per cent to 10.37. That figure valued their total investment in the club at around £40 million, and made them the largest individual shareholders. The rumour mill went into overdrive, and the most general conclusion was that Mag and Mac would buy United and install Ferguson as chairman when he retired from managing the club.

The reaction of the board of the plc was actually very accurate. As a director told the Press Association, Cubic Expression did not want to buy United: 'The prevailing view has been that they are not preparing for a takeover and even though they have become the largest single stakeholders there is still no reason to change that view.'

Not only did they not want to buy the club then, at the time of writing in 2004, they *still* do not want to own United.

These conclusions will seem strange to United fans who believed back then that Magnier and McManus were trying to buy their club, and that could only be good news for their hero Sir Alex Ferguson. But as we have seen, Ferguson and Magnier had already fallen out and that split was about to widen massively.

At that time, no one believed that Cubic Expression was in the hunt simply as a 'value investor' and already it was being speculated that they would move to buy out BSkyB's 9.99 per cent shareholding. But it made perfect sense for them to augment their shareholding. The shares were rated a long-term 'buy' as the value of the club – around £350 million at that time – was a third of its previous peak, and United were continuing to rake in vast profits in comparison to every other side in Europe.

Almost every press article stressed erroneously that the Irishmen's swoop was good news for Ferguson, for what no one outside a small circle of Ferguson's family and friends realised then – or for many months afterwards – was that Ferguson had already burned his boats with Magnier, though there were discussions taking place to see if a resolution could be achieved without recourse to the court action neither man wanted.

In early 2003, Magnier was dismayed by the continuing spate of articles speculating on how much Ferguson was going to earn from Rocky's stud fees, and while not accusing Ferguson of having anything to do with the distortions, he was nevertheless miffed that the media just kept on repeating the same figures, or even exaggerating them. A report that Ferguson had shot up the *Sunday Times* Rich List and was now assessed as being worth £30 million because of his stake in the horse no doubt bemused him as much as it did the Ferguson family. A source who is an expert on Irish breeding and knows Magnier well told me: 'Even before Ferguson went to court, the idea was being put about that he could sell the horse and it would be worth £100 million or so. The most money that has ever been paid for a stallion by John Magnier and Coolmore is $70 million for Fusaichi Pegasus and he won the Kentucky Derby and was beautifully bred.

'Rock Of Gibraltar did not have the kind of breeding on his dam's side that Fusaichi Pegasus had, so it was just impossible for Rock Of Gibraltar to be worth nearly twice what Fusaichi Pegasus was worth. The figure Coolmore assessed as being a realistic value for syndication purposes was closer to £30–£40 million.

'The likely income from stud-fee figures has been overstated, certainly in terms of what Ferguson thought he was entitled to. It takes five or six years for a stallion to really show what he is worth, and then he has perhaps the same number of years again at his maximum earning. Only a very small percentage of stallions reach that stage, and obviously there is no guarantee that any stallion will be fertile or live to a ripe old age – look at what happened to Danehill, after all.'

It seems that Ferguson and Magnier's relationship was definitely over at the point of Cubic's acquisition of the shares which made them the largest individual shareholder. Ferguson was still holding out for what he believed was his entitlement, i.e. 50 per cent of all income from the horse. But Magnier refused to budge from his position, and it was apparently he who first saw that his growing quarrel with the United manager could get very nasty. His position was not totally adamant and he was prepared to concede some largesse to Ferguson – but only a little by comparison with the millions Ferguson presumed were his.

The basis of Ferguson's presumption appears to have been a conversation he had with Magnier when he first got involved with Rock Of Gibraltar. Obviously, the two versions of that conversation now differ, but Ferguson has often said he was offered 50 per cent of the horse, no strings attached, while Magnier is adamant that Ferguson was offered 5 per cent of the winnings during Rocky's racing career *or* a single nomination to the horse when it went to stud. Nomination rights allow you to send a mare of your choice to the stallion. At that time, the likely value of a nomination to Rocky would have been £10,000 to £20,000 for one such nomination each year. Given Rocky's age, it would probably have been an annual gift for up to two decades. And if the horse went on to be a proven winner, as, of course, Rocky did, the nomination value would keep on rising.

One of Britain's leading owners confirmed that it was at that point, right at the start of his supposed ownership, that Ferguson should have made arrangements for all the long-term possibilities for the horse, 'because ownership and owning the breeding rights tend to mean different things to different people in partnerships and syndicates', said the owner.

'As always, you know who ends up getting involved and pocketing plenty – there is a growing practice for lawyers specialising in these matters,' added the owner, ruefully.

The original Magnier offer is stated in Coolmore's case papers lodged at the High Court in Dublin and has been well documented in the public prints. Perhaps significantly, it has never been denied outright by Ferguson or his supporters.

On the face of it, this was not a generous offer. Later, at the time the details of the Coolmore offer were leaked to the media, some commentators in the press said the offer was derisory. But was it? Normal Coolmore practice with a champion racehorse going off to stud, as confirmed by several sources, is to offer Aidan O'Brien one nomination per year to the stallions he had trained. The stable jockey gets even less – he gets to choose one horse he has ridden and is granted one nomination. It is custom and practice at the top end of racing not to deal as much in hard cash as in stud nominations and other forms of emolument. Lester Piggott was a major beneficiary of this practice back in the 1970s and 1980s, as his infamous income tax case disclosed.

Ferguson was already ahead of O'Brien and Kinane. The original offer, as Coolmore portrayed it, was for a nomination each year to Rock Of Gibraltar no matter where he stood in the Northern hemisphere, and in an attempt to 'buy off' Ferguson, Magnier agreed the United manager would also be eligible for a second nomination in the Southern hemisphere, should the horse go on the 'shuttle' to Australia.

This is perhaps one of the most crucial issues that points up the basic difference in approach to the racing industry which remains the underlying reason for Magnier's split with Ferguson. The latter, as we have seen, had no qualms about getting rid of a horse for hard cash if he could make a profit. The same is true, to an extent, of Magnier, but Magnier will always look at the long-term prospects of a stallion. His *raison d'être* in the stud business is to make a value judgement on whether a horse is worth investing in over a long period, and he is quite content to take profits from stud fees much further down the line.

The nub of the issue is this – Ferguson wanted half the value of the horse in 2003, and Magnier was determined that he would not get it. He had made Ferguson an offer and was going to stand by it, and in his breeding-orientated view it was a good offer.

To other breeders and owners, it was certainly a very good offer, since with any nomination it is always possible that the product, i.e. the foal, will turn out to be a stunning yearling which you can sell for a massive profit just less than two years after the stallion has performed its duties. Or you can retain the young horse and it may become a champion and win you millions – like Smarty Jones, 2004's wonder horse in America, whose owner–breeder Pat Chapman kept the colt as a yearling when he sold almost all the rest of his stable.

THE FINAL FURLONG

Breeding is a gamble, but having a nomination is like walking into a casino with the chips bought for you and the blackjack deck stacked in your favour. Nomination rights have value in themselves and can be traded, while the very DNA of Rock Of Gibraltar meant that any foal he produced would be unlikely to be sold for less than a high five- or even six-figure sum – Danehill's genes would have seen to that.

Sir Alex Ferguson just did not appear to appreciate what he was being offered – two chances at winning the Lottery with a couple of winning numbers already on his ticket. He wanted cash, just as when he parted company with much lesser animals such as Queensland Star. You do not need to be an expert on breeding or be a racing person to your soul to conclude that Ferguson wanted sure money rather than the gamble of waiting to see how Rocky performed at stud.

Sometime in the late spring of 2003, possibly in May, Magnier moved to try to nip the developing crisis in the bud, by effectively trying to settle the matter out of court, though at that time no one seriously thought the issue would ever go in front of a judge.

Though admitting no liability, Magnier saw the problem as one of a possible lack of communication and accepted that he perhaps should be prepared to compromise. He doubled his offer to Ferguson to a further two nominations each year, two each in Ireland and Australia, bringing the total to four – effectively a £240,000 per year offer at 2003 prices. It was a far cry from half of the breeding income, but it was still a superb offer from a breeder's perspective.

From Coolmore's viewpoint, that was as far as Magnier was prepared to go. The feeling among those who knew of the dispute at that time was that somehow Alex Ferguson felt he had contributed even more to the success of the horse than Aidan O'Brien and Mick Kinane. That upset people at Coolmore who just felt it proved that Ferguson did not really know about the business of owning and breeding racehorses. 'Could you imagine John Magnier going to Aidan O'Brien,' said one source in Ireland, 'and saying, by the way Aidan, you may have bred the horse, you may have trained it, but we are giving Alex Ferguson half of it for nothing? It is a ludicrous proposition.'

ROCK OF GIBRALTAR

Yet Ferguson rejected that offer, and this time held out for a settlement that would be equal to 20 per cent of the horse's worth at stud. At that point, Magnier sensed that Ferguson appeared to have surrendered on his claim to own 50 per cent of the horse. Magnier felt that the United manager had shot himself through the feet with both barrels of a Purdey 12-bore. For he now realised that Ferguson was not totally committed to his cause, and for a tough and battle-hardened businessman like him, such a chink in the armour of an opponent is all that is needed.

Magnier learned his trade going up against some of Ireland's wiliest horse traders who could lecture foxes in the art of cunning. His early experience in the business had stood him in good stead when it came to dealing in millions with men and women who would look you in the eye and stab you in the back at the same time. Magnier has done literally thousands of deals with some of the world's richest people. There is no record of him losing too many.

In the game of stud poker with Ferguson, Magnier had just acquired an advantage – he had seen his opponent blink. From then on, Magnier was determined to win, and knew he would.

Magnier had to remain steely eyed at that time, because according to someone who knows him well, the Coolmore owner was absolutely incensed that Ferguson was questioning his word. That Magnier supporter said: 'See it from Magnier's point of view. He has been in this business for 30 years. He does business all over the world. His word is his bond. He has been involved in literally thousands of commercial deals as a breeder, such as foal shares, stallion syndications and everything else, and had never reneged on his word.

'And now it's as if somebody is saying John Magnier is welching on his deals. He could not have that said about him – and this is the only deal where there has been such a falling out.'

That's not exactly so, as the dispute with Arrowfield in Australia over Danehill had been very messy and nearly went to court. Along with Vincent O'Brien, Magnier had also gone to court in London in 1994 against the insurers of Shergar as they and every other member of the syndicate holding nomination rights to the ill-fated stallion were refused the compensation they felt they were due. Interestingly, the company they sued was the British Bloodstock Agency (Ireland) with whom Coolmore had enjoyed a long relationship. But Coolmore claimed that the company had failed in its duty to insure Shergar properly as cover had only been taken out for death, not theft. Magnier and company lost that case, and perhaps it was that loss or his normal reticence which has seen him stay out of court ever since.

There was also further public evidence in the spring of 2003 that Ferguson and Magnier were not talking. On 8 May, Alan Lee in *The Times* reported that Ferguson was 'reviewing his racing options' and that he would not be having a horse with Coolmore–Ballydoyle for the 'forseeable future'. The source was Mike Dillon, who was quoted as saying, 'It's best Alex takes a step back for a while and there are no plans for a successor just yet. In a sense, he's been spoilt by what happened.'

No one picked up on it – Ferguson and his close associates were not going to be doing business for a while. No one asked why. Dillon clearly knew what was going on behind the scenes, and superb PR practitioner that he is, the Ladbrokes man managed to say nothing and everything at the same time. 'Spoilt by what happened' – now *that* was saying something.

The stakes were getting higher. A new batch of United shares had been made available at a sensible price and Mag and Mac were ready to jump in. But first would come the curious episode of David Beckham's sale to Real Madrid and the first serious indication that all was not well between Ferguson and his Irish friends.

CHAPTER NINE

The Finishing Post

There is only one thing as blindly fierce as Scottish stubbornness and that is Irish pride. The two men were now set on a collision course, and while all around them friends, if not family, issued warnings to the pair, they insisted on sailing to meet their destiny. 'Iceberg dead ahead' called the sirens, but these titanic captains were battling something just as dangerously large and not so submerged – their own pride and self-belief.

There were many people watching the Rock Of Gibraltar affair develop at Manchester United who asked why there was so much fuss about a horse. That racing expert I quoted earlier told me why at the time, and his succinct explanation has never been bettered: 'Let's put it this way – if Rocky lives to old age he could sire horses for 20 years, and if his progeny become champions and his stud fee increases in line with the inflation in his father Danehill's fees over the past decade, then he could make as much as £200 million for Coolmore, and maybe a lot more. And don't forget – the money earned from stallion stud fees in Ireland is all tax free. No wonder Fergie wants his cut.'

As Rock Of Gibraltar got on with the happy and lucrative business of, well, the business, Cubic Expression bought more shares in United in early March to firm up their position as the largest individual shareholders. The press still hailed this as good news for Ferguson – before events for both John Magnier and Sir Alex Ferguson suddenly took a depressing turn.

Almost as soon as the sticking plaster was removed from the Beckham physiognomy, rumours surfaced which linked the England captain with a move to Barcelona, one of the few clubs in the world able to afford him. There had been reports that the player would move at the end of the season in any case, as his relationship with the manager – who had made no secret of his ambivalence towards the player's choice of Victoria Adams, a.k.a. Posh Spice, as his spouse – had been deteriorating long before he became the studded star. In that same month of March, reports became confirmation – Barcelona *and* Real Madrid were more than interested in Beckham, and at a price that would allow Ferguson to say that he had done good business, even if large numbers of fans would never forgive him. Real Madrid denied that they were interested, but they always say that. It was still a surprise, however, when Beckham was sold to Madrid in a £25 million deal that was apparently done behind his back. It appeared at one time that he actually had wanted to stay at United, but events had rendered that impossible. His move has not been totally fulfilling, football-wise, but his problems off the field have been well documented. He also looked very jaded in the European Championships of 2004 after his first season away from United. How different his life might now be, had Ferguson not been so angry that day in February.

In May 2003, Ferguson's United won the Premiership at the expense of Wenger's Arsenal, who faltered in the closing weeks. Ferguson was rightly ecstatic, calling the win 'our greatest-ever achievement'. In that month, as far as the world knew, Ferguson became potentially even richer due to the sad death of Danehill, who was put down after sustaining a massive injury in a freak paddock accident. The stallion broke a hip and severed an artery, and nothing could be done to save him. John Magnier's major earner after Sadler's Wells was dead at seventeen, and the loss of potentially another five or six years of stud fees was estimated to have cost Coolmore anywhere between £60 million and £100 million in potential income, even though he was insured.

ROCK OF GIBRALTAR

During his career at stud, Danehill covered 1,479 mares in Australia and more than 1,600 mares in Ireland. The number of his live foals was in excess of 2,200 – a very acceptable fertility rate. His record for siring champions was second only to Sadler's Wells.

Thanks to that tragic and expensive loss, Rocky's own value soared as the best-known champion keeper of Danehill's bloodline. Despite the high price set by Magnier, owners and breeders had queued up for Rocky's services, and continue to do so, no doubt reckoning that the toughness he showed on track will be replicated in his children, while everyone wants a piece of that precious Danehill bloodline.

With Sadler's Wells on the point of retirement just as the news broke of Danehill's death, pundits came to the obvious conclusion that Ferguson's horse, Rock Of Gibraltar, as the world-record holder produced by Danehill, would now assume the mantle of number one stallion at Coolmore, earning even more money for the United manager – and wasn't he lucky to have such good friends as John Magnier and J.P. McManus? It was a logical conclusion, but only a very few people knew the truth at that time – that Magnier and Ferguson had been at daggers-drawn for months over Rock Of Gibraltar.

Since that call to Magnier in February which finally confirmed to Ferguson that he was not going to receive his five-million-pounds-a-year old-age pension courtesy of Rock Of Gibraltar, there had been some attempts at resolving the situation, with Magnier at first conciliatory. The last thing that either man wanted at that time was for the row to become public, but after Ferguson rejected a 'final' offer, worth as much as £300,000 a year during the life of Rocky, or up to £7 million if taken at once, Magnier decreed that enough was enough. He was fed up being held to ransom, in his view, and now events would have to take their course. Having rejected Magnier's last offer, Ferguson was now declared *persona non grata* at Coolmore and Ballydoyle – not that he had visited either place in months. But in retrospect, ending direct person-to-person negotiations so soon was also a mistake by Magnier. It left Ferguson with only one real recourse to pursue his side of the argument, which was to go to law, even though court action involving two of the biggest names in sport was always going to be very messy and very public.

THE FINISHING POST

That 'final' offer was made in either May or June, and in July, Cubic Expression made another purchase of Manchester United shares, paying nearly £5 million to take their holding to 11.4 per cent – and this just a few days after widespread reports that they were considering selling up and getting out of Old Trafford with a fat profit. It was not the finest hour of the City pages of certain newspapers. Or perhaps, like many other people in this story, they were being used to spin a tale that was ultimately false.

The position of Cubic Expression's two partners throughout their ownership of shares in United plc has been that their investment in United is an entirely separate matter from the dispute between Magnier and Ferguson. Apart from occasionally suspicious timing of purchases, there is no evidence that they were acting in any way other than as investors in what they thought was a gilt-edged opportunity. It cannot be denied, however, that their increasing ownership of United's stock was helpful in putting pressure on Ferguson to settle, though anyone who thinks the duo spent £200 million to protect Coolmore's interest in a horse worth, in their view, a fraction of that sum, clearly doesn't understand arithmetic, or is unaware of the fact that Magnier and McManus have always been able to separate the personal from the business.

Until August 2003, the majority of press commentators and almost all of the United fans still thought Magnier and McManus were on Ferguson's side. In retrospect, it is remarkable that the irrevocable split between the two key men did not become public knowledge until six months after it happened. There were signs that were ignored – in June, carefully leaked stories about the Irishmen's unhappiness over the price United had paid for players such as Rio Ferdinand and the money going to agents indicated their displeasure. But that was seen to be a tilt against the board as much as Ferguson, though there was no denial from either side of stories suggesting that Ferguson and Magnier were having a 'professional rift' over the matters.

At Coolmore and Ballydoyle, secrecy is a stock-in-trade and their isolation in Co. Tipperary ensures that much can be kept 'in-house'. On the other side, the only people who knew of the issue in Ferguson's circle were immediate close family. It was members of Ferguson's innermost circle who pushed him towards taking court action – including possibly his two sons, Mark and Jason.

'I don't think Alex really appreciated what he was getting into,' said one journalist who knows Ferguson well. 'If it were his sons who were pushing him to get more money, well, what did they know about racing?'

The family certainly all backed Ferguson when he decided to call in the lawyers. And it was Ferguson's decision to involve the legal process which brought the row to public attention, though who first 'went public' is still a matter of debate.

He had also kept the board informed of the issue prior to the publicity which erupted in August, starting with a highly accurate story in the *Sunday Telegraph* which outlined Ferguson's basic argument that he thought Magnier was going back on a verbal agreement that the horse's ownership was split 50–50 between the two of them.

The report quoted a source close to Coolmore Stud as saying:

> There is a major fight going on between Magnier and Ferguson . . . they have fallen out over the breeding rights to The Rock.
>
> I understand that Ferguson believes he is entitled to 50 per cent, but Magnier is adamant that it should be much less – if anything at all.

This was the first public quote revealing accurately in two sentences the extent of the disagreement. It emerged within days that the manager had already consulted his lawyers. The initial reactions were largely sympathetic to Ferguson – he had been described as owning half of Rock Of Gibraltar, and no one from Coolmore had previously contradicted that position, so surely that meant he owned half the breeding rights? It seemed an open and shut case for most pundits, who were mystified by this turn of events. But within days, the doubts began to surface about Ferguson's recollections.

From a position of silence, the two camps began to put their arguments into the public domain. It cannot be denied that both sides rehearsed their case in the media – and in the battle of the 'leaks', Coolmore won hands down. It is difficult to recall any incidence of a 'private matter' in sport which was so totally exposed in public – in the latter part of 2003 and in early 2004, almost every development in the story was widely and usually accurately covered in the press and was also thoroughly dissected by pundits who knew what they were talking about because they had been told 'off the record' what was going on. Considering that one of the principals has an avowed dislike of the press, and the other shuns publicity, it is quite amazing that almost every aspect of this matter made the public prints . . . I said almost.

Coolmore's feeling was that John Magnier had nothing to hide, and that they had truth on their side. Ferguson was strangely reticent on his own part. That may be because he had been warned by the club and his lawyers that speaking out might damage his case – judges don't like that sort of thing. Yet plenty of people were prepared to talk on behalf of Magnier and Ferguson.

Perhaps the most extraordinary quote came from the man now described as Ferguson's racing manager, Henry Ponsonby. He was quoted in the *Daily Mail* as saying that Ferguson 'is very disappointed at the behaviour of John Magnier and the Coolmore team'. I can assure you that remark *still* rankles with Coolmore.

At the outset, the *News of the World* also carried some interesting quotes that probably came directly from the Ferguson camp. Contrary to popular belief, tabloid newspapers don't need to make up quotes – there are always people prepared to talk, and sometimes they do not even need to see a cheque to do so. A friend of Ferguson's told the *News*, 'He doesn't want to say anything at this stage as this is all likely to be settled in court. The Magniers have offered him a one-off settlement of £10 million if he walks away. But compared to Rock Of Gibraltar's stud earning potential it's a pittance. All Sir Alex wants is a fair deal. He is half-owner of the horse and should at least get half the stud fees.' Ferguson turning down £10 million? He has to be seriously confident of winning in court, was the general surmise.

The fact that Ferguson's opponent also happened to be one of United's biggest shareholders just added fuel to the media's bonfire, and there were several warnings to Ferguson that his job at Old Trafford might even be on the line, while virtually every story pointed out that Magnier was not someone to be trifled with.

ROCK OF GIBRALTAR

It proved particularly interesting to the media that Ferguson appeared to be the first person to stand up to Magnier, though that was not actually the case – as we have seen, there had been the Danehill dispute with Arrowfield in Australia. But it did look as though Ferguson was going to be the first person to fully challenge Magnier in a British or Irish court, and more than a few Irish commentators in particular were salivating at the prospect of 'revelations' about the Coolmore Mafia's inner workings. They are not universally popular in their homeland, and since Coolmore's rise to wealthy pre-eminence in the breeding world there have been constant calls by politicians and others for the tax break on stud fees to be removed.

Ferguson, as we have seen, had certainly been registered as co-owner of Rocky while the horse raced, and now it was revealed to the public that his name had not figured in the 'Rock Of Gibraltar Syndicate' registered with Weatherbys Ireland in January 2003.

This seemed to suggest evidence of bad faith on Coolmore's part, and might be a vital and even conclusive piece of evidence. Or was it? For not the least of the mysteries of this case is that the documentation at Weatherbys and Horse Racing Ireland, with the latter holding records formerly amassed by the Turf Club, is *not* evidence that can be 'founded upon' by a court, as we have already seen in Britain. You can say you 'own' part of a horse and can even declare your percentage on forms, but the fact is that you are not legally bound by these declarations. No one need ever know how much you *really* own, even if you are bound to declare the extent of your ownership by racing's rules. Most people do declare their share in an ownership or partnership, so we know for instance that Alex Ferguson is one of twelve in the syndicate which owns Gatwick, though the horse's main owner is registered as syndicate manager Henry Ponsonby. Ferguson has also been registered as owning horses with the likes of major owners Robert Ogden and Ivan Allan, but nobody knows from the registration forms how much he really owned of each horse. Ownership registrations indicate percentages, but that doesn't mean to say they are true – and they do not need to be. You will be paid your prize money according to the percentages stated on the registration documents, but even then, if you choose to have a behind-the-scenes deal and transfer money to other people in the ownership, there's nothing anyone can do to stop you.

It will probably amaze most non-owners that any such document in the care of the racing authorities has no legal standing – it might be a useful piece of evidence in a court case, but it is not like the deeds of a house or the registration documents of a motor vehicle. Even though a horse might be worth the price of a mansion in Surrey or half-a-dozen Bentleys, there is no compunction on the owners to tell the truth about who owns what. What Coolmore did was entirely acceptable practice in racing – thousands of horses are stated to be owned by syndicates or partnerships, and nobody needs to know who actually owns what part of the horse, especially when a horse goes to stud and syndicates might have 40 or more names attached. There are penalties for making false declarations, but enforcement is rare.

(This is clearly a piece of laissez-faire nonsense that racing needs to address, and quickly – how can the authorities cast aspersions on the integrity of, say, betting exchanges, or hold inquiries into allegations of fixing when nobody really knows for certain that a person actually owns the percentage of a horse he or she is credited with owning?)

The issue of breeding rights, as opposed to ownership of the horse while racing, is also far from clear cut. I have spoken to many owners in the preparation of this book. Every one of them who is in, or has been in, a partnership or syndicate with co-owners maintained that breeding income or expenditure was a separate issue from prize money, and should either be negotiated when the partnership is established or before the horse has gone to stud. Such matters should also be clarified to everyone involved, and everyone should understand their rights. Of course, horsey people are a law-abiding breed apart, as every Dick Francis fan knows . . .

There really is a perception that people in this expanding industry do not need any of that 'legal stuff'. Yet candour and the certitude of documentation doesn't always happen and certainly no paperwork between the owners ever surfaced in the case of Rock Of Gibraltar. Everything was done by word of mouth or on a nod and wink basis – never a sure form of communication.

Alex Ferguson and John Magnier have stoutly maintained two

different versions of their 'verbal agreement'. Unless they misunderstood each other's accents, one or other of them got the wrong message.

From that fundamental disagreement about the ownership arrangements, all the subsequent problems flowed. Given that one of the participants was new to the game, it might well be that simple confusion led to a 'misunderstanding'. Certainly, in the latter half of 2003, Ferguson seemed to many racing pundits to be naive about certain aspects of racing.

Whatever caused the rumpus, Manchester United's top brass were deeply worried about the sensational revelations – for once, that much-abused phrase was apt. They had every reason to be disturbed, for they already knew the deep-seated nature of the problem between their greatest asset and their largest shareholder. So concerned was United's chief executive Peter Kenyon about the initial information he had received from Ferguson some weeks previously that he went to meet Magnier in mid-August and was left in no doubt about the extent of his feelings on the issue. Kenyon also knew that Ferguson was entrenched in his view and, as an ally and supporter of the manager, he was sure that Ferguson would not back down. Some three weeks after the story broke, Peter Kenyon gave his personal reaction to the crisis – he resigned and went to Chelsea FC. The arguments raging between the club's biggest shareholder and its manager were cited as the 'last straw' for Kenyon, and while the move to London was appealing in itself because his salary would vastly increase, the row over Rock Of Gibraltar came just as he was making up his mind to leave for Stamford Bridge. Another departure from Old Trafford for London had already occurred: Paddy Harverson, the club's public relations chief, had moved to Buckingham Palace's press office, which was probably just as well as he had antagonised Magnier with some ill-chosen 'off-the-record' remarks about the apparent lack of footballing knowledge of the two Irishmen threatening to take over United. Peter Kenyon's departure, however, was the more important of the two.

David Gill, the club's finance director, was immediately appointed chief executive by the shocked board, with chairman Sir Roy Gardner anxious to maintain continuity at a time when the plc was seemingly vulnerable to takeover.

THE FINISHING POST

Even before Kenyon departed (the board having immediately put him on 'garden leave' to see out his notice period) there was a development which augured badly for Ferguson. On 23 August 2003, the manager had described the modern media as 'a monster'. He then found out the size of its teeth. For newspaper after newspaper piled their best reporters onto the story, and the worst revelations were that, contrary to all the public statements he had made since August 2001, Ferguson had not paid anything for Rocky. Ferguson and people close to him had let it be known that he had paid 120,000 guineas to buy into the horse. One newspaper quoted a higher figure of £173,000. On the contrary, it was revealed that the manager had not paid anything to co-own the horse, and certainly not 'half' or anything like it. Ferguson himself may not have lied, but he did say that he had 'bought the horse', and that fuelled the confusion.

The plain fact is that Ferguson did not pay a penny for his 'share' of Rock Of Gibraltar. This non-payment was admitted to the board by Ferguson, after questions were posed as to why the manager was accepting valuable gifts such as half of a racehorse from shareholders. But it wasn't just half a horse – in early September, the *Sunday Times* revealed that Ferguson had not paid anything for any of the four horses he had been involved with at Coolmore–Ballydoyle. At a conservative estimate, based on Ballydoyle charging £800 per week for training fees, Ferguson thus avoided paying nearly £80,000 in fees. Had he paid half the actual cost of his horses at Ballydoyle he would have been at least £500,000 poorer, and possibly a lot more.

It was pointed out by Michael Crick, among others, that the manager, effectively the chief operating officer of United plc, had taken a substantial gift from shareholders at a time when they were increasing their investment in the club. But Ferguson's allies insisted that he had told the board of the arrangements, and they had not forced him to cancel or suspend his activities. At that time, there was also no evidence that Cubic Expression or Ferguson had benefited financially from any joint arrangement between the manager and Magnier – obviously, Ferguson has done so now, but not by anything like as much as he wanted.

In the early summer of 2003, Ferguson had also informed the directors of his determination to pursue his case in court if necessary. The manager was warned that going to law against the biggest single shareholders, and possible future owners, might place his position with the club in jeopardy. Ferguson was adamant, however, that his case should be brought before a judge. The problem for him was that the only appropriate courts to hear the matter were those of Dublin, and a firm of solicitors, L.K. Shields, was employed in the Irish capital to start work on the case.

From that moment on, Magnier, despite his distaste for courts and publicity, decided that he would fight Ferguson all the way, and instructed his own Dublin lawyer, William Fry, to start preparing his case, while Coolmore's formidable PR machine cranked into 'all-out war' mode. Magnier and McManus then made their most significant move in the campaign to acquire as large a shareholding in United as they could obtain without triggering a takeover bid – under Stock Exchange rules, if they came to own 30 per cent of the plc they would be required to offer to buy out every shareholder, and even Magnier and McManus did not have the estimated £700 million for such a bid lying around spare. They could raise that money if they wanted to, but, as I've said, they did not want to buy United (and still don't).

In any case, time had beaten them. For in late September and early October, United plc was the subject of takeover rumour frenzy. Bid fever began to go sky high when Malcolm Glazer's family trust increased its shareholding to 6 per cent. The American tycoon was now certain to mount a takeover for the club, said numerous reports. Glazer is a determined individual, as his ownership of Tampa Bay Buccaneers showed. He took them from also-rans to Superbowl champions, and he was known to be on the lookout for more sporting organisations to snap up, but nobody knew why Manchester United suddenly appeared on his horizon. The only justification seemed to be that his sons liked soccer.

Cubic Expression's response to that American threat was stunning. They promptly did the single biggest deal for United shares in five years. Cubic Expression bought the entire 9.9 per cent stake of BSkyB, then added a further 1.75 per cent bought from other sources to take their total holding to over 23 per cent. In all, they had spent over £70 million in a few hours, acting quickly after Malcolm Glazer raised his shareholding to just under 9 per cent.

THE FINISHING POST

The plc shares soared 13.75p to 248.75p, which meant that the share price – and thus the value of Magnier and McManus's initial stake – had doubled in a year. The share price had also now risen 50 per cent in a month and 25 per cent in a week. The view of every expert was that the world's biggest football club was surely set to be under new ownership. The board reacted by asking Cubic Expression about their intentions, receiving the reply that Magnier and McManus had not changed their mind – they were building up their stock but were not going to take over United. The *Daily Telegraph* was told by one source, 'Magnier and McManus are not about to make a bid for United. They are in this for the turn. They believe Manchester United is going to receive a takeover offer from someone else.'

The shares had shot up despite a massive blow to the club when arguably their biggest asset on the field, England defender Rio Ferdinand, went AWOL instead of attending a drugs test. He would later be given an eight-month ban from football but only after the patronising attitude of Ferguson and the club – summed up as 'the boy's innocent and anyway, what harm did he do?' – had angered non-United fans everywhere as well as football's administrators all the way up to FIFA President Sepp Blatter.

As events steamrollered on, the fans of United, as represented by such organisations as Shareholders United, the Independent Manchester United Shareholders Association (IMUSA) and the impressively committed groups which have coalesced around fan publications such as the excellent *Red Issue*, were now totally at a loss to understand what was happening to their beloved club. Most observers thought that the United fans, who were infamously and inaccurately described as being from everywhere except Manchester, would not be able to repeat the successful campaign to block the BSkyB takeover in 1998. There would be no competition matters for the Government to rule on, and the club was thus effectively up for purchase by the highest bidder.

The fans' groups did not think they were powerless. What they needed was an issue to focus on, something which could be portrayed as a genuine threat to the club, and which could be used to inspire the supporters to man the barricades. Such an issue arrived when it was reported in early October that John Magnier was going to use his ownership of nearly a quarter of the club to block Alex Ferguson's new contract which was then under negotiation, and whose existence, unusually, had been revealed by the manager himself.

Not long after the club announced record profits of £39.9 million and Cubic Expression had expressed their confidence in David Gill, Ferguson was offered a new four-year deal worth £12 million which would take him to retirement at 65. He was so confident that the deal was his that he later talked of reviewing the situation when he reached the state retirement age – his tone suggested both that the new contract was a fait accompli and that he didn't really intend to retire at 65 either. These statements came just as Rock Of Gibraltar's jockey, Mick Kinane, announced he was leaving Ballydoyle to join John Oxx, the Aga Khan's trainer in Ireland, as stable jockey. Kinane again thanked Ferguson for helping his recovery and named Rock Of Gibraltar as one of the best he had ever ridden.

Ferguson's smile of pleasure at his new contract was barely off his face when Cubic Expression bought BSkyB's shares. The Irish camp then leaked the news that they might seek a seat or two on the board. The only possible conclusion for the loyal fans was that that would see an Irish takeover followed by the departure from Old Trafford of the then 61-year-old Scot who had brought them such glory.

'We had already been talking about this a lot, and that was when we really began to get worried,' said a senior figure in one of the fans' groups. 'Most of us didn't know what to make of Magnier and McManus. We didn't know where they were coming from, but we knew they were out to get Fergie, and our instinctive loyalty was to him, no matter what he may or may not have done about a stupid horse.'

This blind support of the manager was something which baffled the manager's opponents. Magnier and McManus had by this time embarked upon a steep leaning curve to find out everything they could about the way to run a football plc, but perhaps they should have studied the psychology of a fan first of all.

Magnier had already begun to try to find out about Ferguson's monetary activities and his involvement in transfers. I was told by that senior racing figure I mentioned earlier that Magnier's reasoning was simple: 'They had paid out a nine-figure sum and wanted to ensure that their money was being used correctly, that the club was being run properly.'

No one has suggested that Dermot Desmond in any way advised them, but their fellow Irishman's way of controlling Celtic plc, where he holds a similar size of shareholding, must have been instructive – he has had no hesitation in asking awkward questions when necessary at Parkhead. Magnier was also preparing for Ferguson's impending legal action, and his attitude had hardened after Ferguson rejected through his lawyers a 'final, final' chance of a settlement, which was much the same as before – two stud nominations per year to Rocky in Australia and Ireland, four in all. With an anticipated ten years of stud income from the stallion, plus the tax-free status, plus likely inflation in the figures as Rocky's stud career progressed, this package equated to a cash settlement of around £7 million.

In early November 2003, Sir Alex Ferguson began formal legal proceedings in the High Court of Dublin against Magnier and Coolmore. In the words of one person close to the legal teams involved, 'all hell then broke loose'. It was as if Coolmore couldn't really believe that Ferguson had crossed the Rubicon.

Irish law is different in several respects from the civil law of England and Wales, and also Scots law. The process involves 'pleadings', the most important of which is the Statement of Claim in which the plaintiff, i.e. Ferguson, sets out his case, and states the damages being sought in Ireland's High Court – the amount of monetary damages being sought meant that the case went automatically to the top civil court.

The Statement of Claim was notified to Coolmore, whose immediate reaction, I have been told, was one of sheer disbelief, not least because of the variations between the Statement of Claim and earlier assertions from Ferguson's lawyers. In effect, Ferguson was seeking half the horse's value, and even at Coolmore's minimal estimate, this was still around £20 million. The grounds for this claim were also a source of some incredulity. One source who knows the details of the claim said: 'What he was asking for was crazy money. A lot of his case seemed to hinge around the assertion that his name had added value to the horse. That made no sense and would have been laughed out of court – has there ever been a breeder who has paid more for the services of a stallion because of who owned the horse? It's really rather insulting to professional breeders to suggest that.

'There was no way he could have made that claim stand up in court. Coolmore is not in the business of selling souvenir T-shirts or CDs – it's about selling expensive nominations to a stallion. This outlay is by professional people who only look at the pedigree and what the horse has done on the track – whoever owned the horse didn't make it run one second faster.

'Ferguson had also shot himself through the foot with remarks that had been broadcast on television to the effect that the publicity had been great for Coolmore and himself and for the horse but the horse didn't need him to do it, he would have made the front pages himself.'

One Scottish owner who knows Ferguson disagrees. 'There are always people who will buy a horse which has had a famous owner, possibly because they get a kick out of being associated with the celebrity. I know plenty of people who might buy a horse just for the kudos that comes with the Ferguson name, or the chance to meet him at the racecourse.'

Magnier was having none of it. He had already used the world's biggest corporate investigative agency, the New York-based Kroll, on other matters and, though no one knows exactly who commissioned them or how much they were paid, this remarkable company was brought into the Rock Of Gibraltar Affair with a clear remit: 'Find out everything about Ferguson.' Magnier had been advised that the courts would base much on the truthfulness of himself and Ferguson, and he was now convinced that his opponent could lose if it came to a test on that issue. Certainty was needed, however, so in came Kroll, whose accountancy skills plus investigative diligence have made them the best in the world at what they do – the Federal Government of the United States uses them on some inquiries, presumably because the FBI and CIA are busy elsewhere. Kroll's investigations into Ferguson were utterly thorough, as the world soon found out.

When news of the court case broke, which at a stroke legitimised every rumour and whiff of controversy reported by the media in the previous four months, Magnier instructed that a strongly worded press statement be issued. On 17 November 2003, the depth of Magnier's anger showed in the tone of his reply:

> Coolmore Stud has today been advised that legal proceedings have been initiated against Mr John Magnier by Sir Alex Ferguson alleging certain ownership rights to the stallion Rock Of Gibraltar. Coolmore Stud and John Magnier consider the action to be without merit and it will be vigorously defended.

Given that the basics of the case were so widely known, and these words were couched in legalese, the Coolmore owner might as well have added, 'A state of war exists between us.'

The United board were shattered, not least because of events at the club's Annual General Meeting. A team of new and unknown shareholders, one of them an actress, turned up at the AGM and started asking detailed questions about the conduct of transfers. They were spotted by legitimate members of Shareholders United, among them Michael Crick, whose journalistic inquiries revealed the 'shareholders' to be plants put there to speak out in a bid to embarrass Ferguson. 'They asked some excellent questions,' Crick told me, 'but they were too obvious.' The tactic backfired as it drew people to Ferguson's camp, and the embarrassment felt by Coolmore is such that they still will not admit that Kroll was even employed on the case. Kroll, as a matter of course, never admit anything.

Kroll and several journalists, including freelances, independently began to look at the transfers carried out during Kenyon and Ferguson's joint stewardship of the club. Since 2001, after United's star defender Jaap Stam alleged in his memoirs some grey-area behaviour over transfers by Ferguson – Stam left United for Lazio of Rome shortly afterwards, and that was no coincidence – journalists and researchers had been looking into the transfer deals at Old Trafford, particularly those involving Jason Ferguson and his agencies.

Michael Crick's insightful revelations about United transfers in his biography of Ferguson also cast 'The Boss' in a very dim light. Kroll zeroed in on these activities, and the implication was clear –

money lost in the transfer market clearly affects shareholder value in a football plc and, in any company, an employee losing their shareholders millions of pounds would be in serious trouble.

The *Sunday Times* duly broke the story of Magnier's concerns over the transfer deals. That story, and Magnier's involvement in it, appeared specifically because the board refused to answer the legitimate questions by Cubic Expression about the transfer deals.

The newspaper is owned by Rupert Murdoch, whose other company BSkyB had been thwarted in its ambition to buy Manchester United partly because Ferguson opposed the deal. There may have been a 'get Fergie' agenda, but anyone who knows that journalists are motivated by good stories and not the boss's whims, will realise that the *Sunday Times* reporters knew they were onto a terrific story, which they handled with the utmost professionalism. They may or may not have been fed information from Ireland about Cubic Expression's concerns, but knowing that they would have lawyers standing over their shoulders checking their copy, they still had to 'stand up' the story, which they most certainly did. That story would rumble on and on and shows no sign of going away at the time of writing in summer 2004.

Meanwhile, the tit-for-tat war on the Stock Exchange continued. Malcolm Glazer continued to build up his shareholding to more than 14 per cent, but didn't say if he was mounting a takeover. Cubic Expression retaliated with a small purchase – just a few million pounds or so – which took their holding to 24.2 per cent.

A much more serious personal issue faced Ferguson. In early December, the manager revealed that he had been suffering heart trouble and a pacemaker had been fitted to help his heart. Whatever you think of Ferguson, you can only marvel at a man who, with his problems apparently mounting up and his health badly affected, still managed to joke to his friend Glenn Gibbons of *The Scotsman*, 'The first thing they [the players] told me was that they'd had a real scare this morning – they discovered I had a heart.'

The health scare would be raised by Magnier when he again opposed the extension to Ferguson's contract, though the rest of the board wanted Ferguson to get the deal. 'Discussions over the terms and conditions of the new deal are progressing well and no problems are foreseen,' an official statement read.

THE FINISHING POST

The alleged 'split' in the boardroom as detailed by the *Mirror* newspaper among others provoked Ferguson into an ill-judged reaction at a club press conference. He described the stories as 'emanating from Ireland' and called them 'mischief-making'. Talk about lighting the blue touch paper – Magnier immediately instructed his lawyers to see if there was any hint of libel in the Ferguson statement, though any junior reporter could have told him that the manager had chosen his words well and no defamation had occurred.

At the end of December, Ferguson found out how far his opponents in Ireland – not necessarily just Coolmore – were prepared to go. Newspapers mysteriously raked up a four-year-old unfounded accusation that Ferguson had taken a five-figure sum to attend a function in aid of the John Durkan Leukaemia Trust – the charity named after the young Irishman who found Istabraq for J.P. McManus, but who died at 31 before the horse achieved greatness. Ferguson had attended the function – sponsored by Coolmore – in Dublin's Berkeley Court Hotel with United players Gary Neville, Ryan Giggs, Phil Neville and Dwight Yorke, and reported to be among the guests were Lester Piggott and Formula 1 team-owner Eddie Jordan. But the dinner had undoubtedly been billed as a testimonial tribute for Ferguson, and the players only attended because of that. His friends claimed he was the one who had donated half the takings to the Trust. At the very least, the timing of this renewed accusation was highly suspicious.

The pressure on Ferguson did not abate in the early weeks of 2004. Amid growing and voluble concern by the fans, Ferguson was forced into a humiliating acceptance of a one-year rolling contract, instead of the four-year extension he had sought. The money was better, and Ferguson said it was the deal he wanted, but the fans concluded that the manager had been massively slighted. Coincidentally, the only other one-year rolling contract for a manager of a major British club was that given previously to a man often touted as Ferguson's successor – Martin O'Neill, the manager of Celtic, whose most powerful director and largest shareholder is one Dermot Desmond.

The worst escalation of the war of words between Cubic Expression and Ferguson then arrived in the Old Trafford boardroom. They had previously tried to dismiss Magnier's questions on club accounts, but now those issues were raised in public – the so-called 99 questions found their way to the press.

On 21 January 2004, Cubic Expression wrote to the board with a series of detailed and searching questions – prepared by Coolmore's legal and PR advisers with information supplied by Kroll, I have been told. The personal nature of the questions was devastating. Magnier wanted answers on just about every transfer in the previous six years, and the clear implication was that United had paid too much or used Jason Ferguson's Elite agency, opening up questions of a possible conflict of interest. The transfers of Juan Sebastian Veron, Rio Ferdinand, Diego Forlan, Jonathan Greening, Mark Wilson, Jaap Stam, Tim Howard, Kleberson, Cristiano Ronaldo, Roy Carroll, Laurent Blanc, David Bellion and Massimo Taibi were suspected to have had some connection with the Elite agency, either directly or through associates.

But the stinging element was contained in the accompanying letter. 'Can you inform us whether you have complemented legal advice with medical advice, in light of the executive's [Ferguson's] recent health concerns and his age?' The letter added:

> We do not understand how the board can reach a conclusion that the executive will remain of central importance for the course of any extended contract. It is quite possible that the executive could suffer ill health during the course of any extension period, such that he would no longer be of central importance.

The board itself came in for a swipe:

> You have not yet answered our letter concerning corporate governance. In that letter, we made reference to the recent allegations made in the press. In our view, the board should investigate such matters before entering into any revised employment contract . . . What enquiries have the board made in this regard? How is this consistent with your statement that the board is determined to maintain a sound system of prudent and effective internal controls?

Also in the firing line was club solicitor and director Maurice Watkins:

> Can you advise why the company believes it is appropriate to obtain its advice on the employment contract from a firm of solicitors whose senior partner is a member of the board and which has, we understand, represented the executive in separate legal proceedings?

Ferguson's reaction was one of bewilderment and fury, which he made public at a press conference, saying that he has never abused his position in 17 years at the club and alleging that his family had been targeted – Jason's rubbish bins had been searched, he said, presumably for information.

It was no wonder that, a week later, chief executive David Gill finally admitted that the row over Rock Of Gibraltar was affecting the club. The club also published a letter on its website in late January which outlined the transfer process within United – the manager identified players to come or go but wasn't involved in financial negotiations. Finance director Nick Humby was instructed to review all transfers but initial indications were that no rules had been broken.

Ferguson was reported by friends to be at an all-time low, and seriously worried that his family were now 'in play'. But help for the beleaguered manager was at hand in the form of United's fans. Major groups such as Shareholders United formally stayed out of a new and loosely organised campaign which featured previously unknown outfits called the Manchester Education Committee (MEC) and United4Action who took the fans' frustrations at Magnier and McManus – they were already subjected to chants and slogans by the Old Trafford crowd – to a new and more personal level by targeting their racing interests. One renegade idiot, not connected to any supporters' group, daubed obscenities on the Magnier family home in Cork, probably unaware it was not even John Magnier's house. The action was decried by all legitimate fans.

United4Action became the best known of the protest groups, thanks largely to its leader, Sean Murphy. Despite attempts to make out that Sean Murphy was a pseudonym employed by a sophisticated *agent provocateur*, the facts are that Murphy is a genuine United fan of Irish extraction who works for an Irish bank in the City. Despite his strong connections to Irish racing – he once worked as a stable groom and even has links to Ballydoyle – he felt he had to organise the United4Action group's resistance. The groups such as the MEC and United4Action were unconsciously organised like Resistance cells – minutes of their meetings are impossible to come by – and they did see themselves as guerrillas mounting a campaign to save their club first, and Ferguson second, from the whims of rich men.

Leaflets were printed and distributed to match-day crowds, calling for protest against Cubic Expression. An e-mail and telephone campaign blitz on Ireland was mounted after Coolmore's numbers and addresses were distributed widely. Shareholders United urged people to sign up and buy shares to try to reach a target of 10 per cent of the stock, which would allow them to stop United being taken into private hands should a takeover come – the group was rewarded with a *doubling* of its membership in one week, and now has 10,000 shareholders under its banner.

No one remembers exactly who came up with the idea of protesting against Magnier and McManus's horses on racecourses, but it was a master stroke, and really did rattle the Irishmen. The first protest at Hereford was small, but the headlines were huge. And then it was announced that the National Hunt Festival at Cheltenham would be the next target. The sacred communion ground of Irish racing would see Murphy lead 150-odd demonstrators to picket Cheltenham, and he already had the tickets to get them in.

Cheltenham boss Edward Gillespie was aghast. So, too, was J.P. McManus, who could foresee the dangers of a packed Cheltenham being invaded by non-racing people who, to put it mildly, didn't understand the etiquette.

What had started out as a private dispute over a racehorse's semen now threatened to become a very public and potentially very nasty row involving thousands of people meeting in a state of mutual incomprehension.

CHAPTER TEN

Objections and Inquiries

It was only partially realised at the time, but Manchester United were just days away from complete disaster. For I have been told that, had the protest gone ahead and had trouble occurred at Cheltenham, Magnier and McManus would have acted to try to remove Ferguson, or perhaps themselves, from Old Trafford. If they had sold out at that point they would have made a profit of perhaps as much as £40 million, but more importantly they would undoubtedly have sparked a race for the takeover of the club, to be won possibly by Malcolm Glazer. But a course of action involving Ferguson was much more probable. Either the board would have been forced to act against Ferguson or an Extraordinary General Meeting would have been requisitioned to make public certain accusations against the manager and directors. Coolmore's owner had become convinced by then that 'sources close to' Ferguson were either tacitly aware, or complicit in, the protests against the club's major shareholders. He was also suspicious that leaks against Cubic Expression had emanated from Old Trafford.

One of the leading figures in the protests, speaking on condition of anonymity, told me that he was invited to a meeting

ROCK OF GIBRALTAR

at which an emissary of Coolmore–Ballydoyle made it plain that they knew that 'certain people' at the club had been helping or advising the anti-Magnier campaign. The fans were not for backing down, however, and someone else was going to have to act to break the logjam.

Fans' leaders were certainly told Ferguson valued their support, some of them by the manager personally. But he may well have deduced, or been told by advisers, or been warned indirectly by Coolmore or the United board, that if anything went badly wrong at Cheltenham – had there been fights or injuries, for instance – then *he* would be held responsible by people within United and not just by Magnier and J.P. McManus. Ferguson duly chose to speak out against the fans' protest, and in doing so earned himself kudos but the disdain of some senior supporters.

The statement which effectively ended the Rock Of Gibraltar Affair was issued by Ferguson, who took great pains to get it on the radio, and he read it himself to astonished reporters who could not recall the last time the manager had spoken a civil word to them, far less given them an exclusive interview. He said:

> The reputation of Manchester United is paramount to my thinking. The private dispute I have is just that and I don't want to exacerbate the whole thing. Cheltenham is such a great festival and I don't want it marred in any way. There is a lot of concern about what could happen and I would ask supporters to refrain from any form of protest. I am strongly opposed to any violent, unlawful or disruptive behaviour which may reflect badly on the club and its supporters in general.

United added their own statement: 'Sir Alex also knows that this is the view of the Manchester United board, who have previously urged fans not to participate in any disruptive or criminal activities.'

Ferguson's appeal was greeted by shocked fans with something akin to despair. They felt they had been stabbed in the back by Ferguson. The MEC asked 'Sir Alex Ferguson to refrain from giving his name to any form of statement opposing action by United supporters'.

OBJECTIONS AND INQUIRIES

A shell-shocked Sean Murphy called off his group's protest. The statement issued by Ferguson came as a complete slap in the face to his most ardent supporters, and at least one fans' leader challenged the manager over his altered stance.

The fans also began to listen to the other side, to Coolmore's arguments. Some who were already no great worshippers of Ferguson now turned against him completely. One well-known figure in the movement told me that from being a staunch Ferguson supporter, he was now of the opinion that the manager should go quietly and soon. 'This is not over, there will be other questions, and I don't think Alex will have the answers,' he said, in meaningful tones.

Sean Murphy was himself threatened with violence by hard-liners for calling off the protest but he was totally disillusioned by then. He has spoken out for the first time since then especially for this book: 'The planned protest at Cheltenham was an action formed out of anger towards the powers-that-be at Cubic Expression. We felt that these people were bullying our manager and destabilising our football club. We had to act and act in a big way. For obvious reasons, Cheltenham offered my group the opportunity to gain maximum exposure and cause J.P. and Magnier a lot of embarrassment – that was always the aim, to embarrass them, nothing more! – and force them out of our club.

'From an early point, I was contacted by people involved within the different fan groups in Manchester. These were people I had never met but grew to trust and befriend over this period. These people were connected, seriously connected, at Old Trafford all the way to the top. They advised me and guided me on many issues around the protest including media relations. I was advised that Sir Alex was grateful for our help and I was assured that he would not make any public call for the protest to be stopped. I believed this.

'Sir Alex contacted me after being given my contact details through a fan representative (one of the connected people) and we discussed the protest and my plans for Cheltenham. We also discussed other issues around The Rock case and he assured me that the case was nearly at an end and that he felt the pressure on the club would end thereafter. He then dropped the bombshell that the protest must be cancelled.

'I was gutted really. This wasn't just about his personal argument with Magnier about The Rock; this was about a very powerful secretive man attempting to rock my club to the core, and now the protest had been hijacked by Sir Alex. Our support for him was our support for our club, not the other way round. The next day, Sir Alex made a press statement asking for the protest to be cancelled. To say we were angry and upset is an understatement – we were raging.

'He let me down – he revealed that he had spoken to me after we agreed we would do no such thing. I hadn't even informed the other members of United4Action and they felt betrayed by me. I was not popular in Manchester and had "friendly" warnings to stay away.

'Maybe, looking back, I was naive. After all, look how he treated his so-called "son" David Beckham. Other fans and I are left wondering who really destabilised Old Trafford, who really brought the club into the war over The Rock, and who was letting the fans down.

'Quite simply, one great racehorse, two powerful men, one massive mess. And who suffered most of all during this period? The millions of Manchester United fans worldwide, myself included.'

Murphy's frustration is shared by other groups and leading individuals among the United supporters. But at least the trouble was almost over. Sir Alex Ferguson had run up the white flag.

A key figure at this time was Celtic director and United shareholder Dermot Desmond. He had intervened at a crucial point to offer to act as peacemaker, and after meeting Ferguson it was he who paved the way for a rapprochement between Magnier and the manager. It was a role for which he was publicly thanked by Ferguson, though exactly how Desmond managed to negotiate a way out of the impasse is not yet known as he, too, refused to comment.

Ferguson was able to get out of the affair with a large sum of money and, thanks to his Cheltenham stance, his honour virtually intact. In return, he admitted that there had been a 'misunderstanding'. That was seen as Ferguson-speak for 'I was wrong' and there was unanimous agreement that Magnier had won the poker game hands down.

OBJECTIONS AND INQUIRIES

Almost as soon as it arrived to dominate the sporting scene, the Rock Of Gibraltar Affair was over, or so the antagonists would wish us to believe. Sir Alex Ferguson got his £2.5 million tax free – less than he had been offered in 2003 – Magnier kept all of the horse, and both sides signed confidentiality agreements, which they have honoured.

Yet the issues which were raised as a result of Ferguson's claim over Rocky still rumble on. A BBC documentary sparked even more huge headlines, with reporter Alex Millar alleging that Jason Ferguson was given privileged access to United because of his father's position. As expected, United's internal inquiry found no evidence of wrongdoing, but in a move that was seen as a slight against his father, the club banned Jason Ferguson's Elite agency from acting for the club. Elite may no longer be used by United but they still have 13 of the club's players on their books. Legally, they cannot be stopped from acting as agents for the players. Transfer issues may yet surface again to damage the Ferguson family.

So what is the conclusion to this saga which, frankly, would not have happened had Rock Of Gibraltar not been so darned brilliant? Surprisingly, some good may come of this. Football itself is now utterly changed. Fans are organised in mass movements that have a dynamic of their own. The real sleeping giants of football, the multitude of folk who pay their money and invest their dreams in their clubs, have slowly but surely begun to revolutionise football. All over Britain the risings are there, inspired by threats to that thing fans always love – their football club.

There are now more than 100 supporters' trusts in England, Wales and Scotland. Around 60 of them have bought shares in their clubs, from nominal holdings to complete ownership of the club. Some 38 football clubs have recognised the importance of the trust movement by bringing a supporters' representative onto their board, and those who have resisted such a sensible move – mostly public limited companies such as United and Celtic – are slowly losing the argument. Four senior clubs are now owned by trusts – Lincoln City, Brentford and Chesterfield in the Football League and Clyde in Scotland's First Division. The last-named club was denied promotion to the Scottish Premier League only on the last day of the 2003–04 season, otherwise it would have been the first trust-owned club in a top-flight league in the UK.

It is estimated that 15 senior British clubs might well have gone to the wall in recent years if trusts had not weighed in with cash and commitment. The extraordinary saga of Dundee FC, which went bust owing £23 million on a turnover of less than £5 million, saw a monumental campaign by its supporters to save the club. The Dee4Life movement raised £160,000 in less than six months, which made a crucial difference as the club struggled in administration.

No one is suggesting that Manchester United are in money trouble and need financial salvation from its fans. But say there was a director on the board to represent the fans, and Magnier and McManus had been able to consult him directly – might they not have known much sooner that their baiting of Ferguson would prove so unpopular and damaging to them? More importantly, would they not have been able to get their message across to the supporters that they were no threat to the club?

The targeting of Cheltenham and the vandalism to the Magnier family home in Cork were reprehensible, but if Cubic Expression had been able to consult fans or been able to state their case directly to a fans' representative, much of the anguish might have been avoided. Perhaps the best news of all is that Shareholders United have gained so many new members and, working with other groups, this massive association will never be ignored and may eventually gain enough backing to ensure that its members' wishes as fans and shareholders are given priority – which is how it should be.

Supporter passion allied to shrewd organisation and increasing adroitness in handling the media means that fan power is now a genuine force in the land. The supporters – the consumers – have finally realised their powers, and no club director can afford to ignore them. At least Magnier and McManus avoided physical harm, unlike Chris Robinson, chief executive of Heart of Midlothian FC, who was assaulted after he announced plans to sell the Edinburgh club's Tynecastle Stadium to meet its debts. That attack was utterly deplorable, but all club directors are now

OBJECTIONS AND INQUIRIES

aware that fans are no respecters of authority and, thanks largely to the internet, they can get themselves well informed and well organised if they do not like what directors are doing to their club. It's personal, now. This mass phenomenon of fans campaigning for more say in their clubs got under way some years ago, but after Rock Of Gibraltar's genes brought chaos to the word's biggest football club, it is now unstoppable. Any rich man thinking of buying a football club or running one at present should be aware that he must deal with the supporters as well as the directors and shareholders of the club. After all, ultimately the fans pay the wages.

The great pity for Sir Alex Ferguson is that his conduct has disillusioned many influential people in the United fans' groups. It remains to be seen whether those individuals keep their counsel. They may yet tell everything they know in public.

So what about the relationship between Ferguson and his erstwhile friends from across the Irish Sea? When I started to research this book, I will admit my sympathies lay with Sir Alex Ferguson, not least because I had met and spoken to him, and quite liked him, largely because of his passion for racing. It also seemed to me that the mega-rich Magnier had taken a JCB piledriver to crack a nut. But as I found out more, my sympathies for Ferguson evaporated, like those of the loyal fans who backed him. Whatever his motivation, Ferguson made monumental errors of judgement.

The single most important mistake he made was to go to court with a case he had little chance of winning, because in plain English, no money or any binding contracts about ownership had changed hands. It was his word against that of John Magnier. The key witness was Mike Dillon and he had already made it clear that, for whatever reason, he would not be backing the manager's version in court.

It may also be that Ferguson's renowned parsimony has cost him many millions, for legal experts have confirmed that if Ferguson had paid out even a reasonable sum for his share of the expenditure on Rocky – say the infamous 120,000 guineas that was often quoted – then he could have claimed in court that he had a formal contract as evidenced by the fact that money had changed hands. But none did, so any claim that a contract had existed would have been met with considerable doubt on the part of the court.

Ferguson's recollection about the basis of his ownership of Rock Of Gibraltar can also be questioned. He told people – me, for instance – that he had bought the horse. Undoubtedly, rumours circulated about the amount he 'paid' for the horse, and he did little to stop them. Dozens of journalists and, as a consequence, the public at large, were led to believe that Alex Ferguson paid his share for Rocky and was therefore due half of the breeding rights. In fact, the first premise was incorrect and the second highly debatable. He should have corrected the false impressions that were being given, because that led to many reports in which the errors were repeated. A psychologist who studied various accounts of the affair told me that Ferguson may perhaps have deluded himself that he really did own the horse, and finally boxed himself into a corner and found himself unable to admit anything to the contrary. In the absence of Ferguson's own account, such explanations must remain speculation.

But, lest anyone feel too sorry for him, let it not be forgotten that Sir Alex Ferguson has pocketed £2.5 million of Coolmore's money for his trouble. Remember that Landseer or Hawk Wing might well have run in the Gimcrack instead of Rocky, and Ferguson might never, ever have led Rocky into any winner's circle.

For that is the fundamental point about Rocky and Ferguson – the horse was chosen *for* him, not *by* him. Ferguson also played no serious part in the decisions affecting its career, as he admitted, and his main role appears to have been to act the 'owner', which, it must be said, he did to Oscar-winning proportions. He deserved to be rewarded for helping the horse's profile, and it could be argued that he became the highest paid cheerleader in history.

Coolmore's people can also argue till they are blue in the face that Ferguson did not add a penny to Rocky's worth, but that is not the point – Coolmore was happy to use the Ferguson name and the manager's considerable presence as it suited them, and they also concealed the truth about the ownership situation, which was a sin of omission. Coolmore did eventually acknowledge that Ferguson had played a role in Rocky's career, and that realisation

OBJECTIONS AND INQUIRIES

– not the threat of court action – is what led Magnier to eventually make his payment to Ferguson.

John Magnier also made palpable errors. His desire to have Ferguson make the Gimcrack Speech was laudable to those who think the racing establishment should be taken down a peg or two, but he should have thought through the implications of bringing on board such a high-profile and difficult figure as Ferguson, especially at a time when he was investing heavily in United. Their arrangements were not suspicious or mutually beneficial – the eventual falling-out proved that.

Nor do the assertions that the matter is over and done with hold any water. The situation of shattered trust is at best unpleasant, and Magnier might yet decide to ask awkward questions about employees using company time and facilities to brief the press or his opponents among the pro-Ferguson fans. Both sides say the matter is closed, but the question must be asked: is the situation ever likely to be resolved without one or other principals leaving Old Trafford?

To avoid that ending, it must be realised by all involved that mistakes were made by a lot of people on both sides. Ferguson's advisers in particular have let down their man, while John Magnier has little excuse for failing to realise the level of publicity that his actions would attract. Mike Dillon has lost a good friend and suffered the wrong sort of exposure – the public relations man became at least part of the story – but his motivation was sound. Had there been no dispute, he would now be hailed as a genius for raising racing's profile.

Above all, Sir Alex Ferguson has to ask himself why he carried on his case so stubbornly, why he risked everything when he seemed so unlikely to succeed. Why did he – and Magnier for that matter – allow so many people to go on thinking everything was rosy between him and his 'friend' when both men knew it was not?

For the reams of misinformation are the cause of the main damage arising from this extraordinary saga. The credibility of Ferguson has been sorely undermined, and the reputation of Magnier has also been altered – he is also now, whether he likes it or not, a public figure, a celebrity of sorts, and that will pain him more than anything. He has already suffered a family upset. Wearing his wife's dark blue colours, his son, John Paul, brilliantly rode his parents' horse, Rhinestone Cowboy, to a memorable victory in the Martell Cognac Hurdle at Aintree on Grand National Day, 2004. Magnier was not in the winning circle to greet his son after the finest achievement of the young jockey's career, having been advised to stay out of the public eye at Aintree. That will have hurt a man who loves his children.

But, strange to say, if they learn the lessons of the Rock Of Gibraltar Affair, the future may be brighter for Ferguson, Magnier, McManus and United. Ferguson's entire career shows that when he is permitted to do what he does better than anyone in British football history, i.e. manage and coach a football team, then he works wonders. It is no coincidence that his greatest successes – when he took Aberdeen to the Cup-Winners' Cup and United to that trophy and the European Cup itself – came after periods of relative stability off the field which allowed his best talents to flourish.

A Ferguson without distractions, and even possibly with them, will always be a match for Arsene Wenger and Jose Mourinho at Arsenal and Chelsea respectively. Indeed, he will be a match, or better, for any manager in the world. United's corporate governance has already improved since Cubic Expression finalised its spending spree, and the club is already being run more effectively. Magnier's involvement should also mean that Ferguson will stay well away from the boardroom.

Magnier's business acumen gained in another sport has seen him become a world leader in that field. He has invested in other industries and can be a well-informed, helpful and positive force. He and J.P. McManus have too much money – even for them – invested in United not to want the club to move on and succeed. And why shouldn't United's board listen to their ideas? Does the club's habitual arrogance preclude a fresh viewpoint being brought to bear?

Magnier and McManus have already helped United by causing the removal of the baleful influence of some agents from the club. No chief executive or club director at Old Trafford will ever sanction massive transfer fees or payments to agents again – at least, not without knowing they will have to justify the outlays to the largest shareholders. That alone means that United have ceased to be the dripping roast that so many fed off.

Furthermore, the two Irishmen have connections that even giants like United could use, and they remain adamant that they are in the club for long-term gain. Consider this – they could have gone to the market at any time in the first half of 2004 and made a serious profit on their investment. And it is worth repeating that, since late in 2003, they could have called EGMs, sacked Ferguson, demanded and been given seats on the board, or mounted that takeover everyone was so sure was the real reason for Mag and Mac buying into United. Dermot Desmond and Harry Dobson could have backed them, and other institutional investors could have done so too. But, at the time of writing in the summer of 2004, they have no plans for any sale or purchase of United, and my sources indicate they will NOT mount a takeover and will NOT try to get Ferguson sacked now that the case is over, unless real venality on the part of the manager is exposed, and none has been remotely suggested.

If Magnier and McManus ask the board for directors to represent their interests then that is their prerogative – it is the custom of most large companies to have large shareholding represented, and that director might well be the impetus the boardroom needs to refresh its act. Furthermore, as long as Mag and Mac stay, no other individual can buy United. Malcolm Glazer has upped his stake to nearly a fifth of the club, but that is still not enough to give him a platform for a takeover while Magnier and McManus retain their holding. They control the future, and they want success. They may well sell up in years to come, but it won't be at a price which values United at anything less than the £1 billion they consider the club is worth.

In the mean time, they want trophies, because that increases shareholder value. Ferguson also wants more success. Manchester United may well have won the FA Cup of 2004, and that is always a special achievement for any side, but for United the true measure of their worth is the test set them by Sir Matt Busby and Sir Alex Ferguson – United must compete for, and win, the European Cup. Ferguson is once again building a young team at Old Trafford, and he is arguably the only man who can deliver the glory again.

Similarly, Magnier's Coolmore Stud has a whole new raft of stallions, even if Ballydoyle has recently misfired by its own high standards, and there appears to be no real threat to Ireland's tax breaks for breeders. As for J.P. McManus, he already has the kind of career-affirming tribute that probably means more to him than anything – the council in his beloved home city of Limerick has named part of its civic complex Istabraq Hall.

The achievements of Sir Alex Ferguson and John Magnier will live on long after they are dead. When their human faults are consigned to our collective memory's dustbin, their feats will be recalled with wonder, if only at the sheer prolonged efforts they have taken to achieve them.

It is probably beyond Ferguson and Magnier to forget everything that has happened over Rocky, and they are unlikely to be friends again, but truly great people have the capacity to forgive and move on. These two men, so great in so many ways, can surely reach a working accommodation for the good of Manchester United which benefits them, too. One day, they may even look back and wonder what all the fuss was about . . . but I doubt it.

Ferguson has also not lost his love of racing or a gamble. The colt Gatwick, whose public appearance at Mick Channon's yard in February 2003 can now be seen to be the first public sign of the breakup between Ferguson and Magnier, improved vastly as a three year old. It won two valuable handicaps – including one on the day United beat Millwall in the 2004 FA Cup final – and nearly £90,000 inside five days in May. The owners, led by Henry Ponsonby, were persuaded by trainer Mick Channon and Ferguson to stump up a £75,000 'late supplement charge' to enter it at the last moment in the Epsom Derby of 2004. The favourite at that point was Yeats, owned by Magnier, and the papers loved the possibility of Ferguson's horse taking on Magnier's. Maybe that idea attracted the United manager to the race, too. In the event, Yeats pulled out injured three days before the big race was won by North Light, with Gatwick clearly failing to stay the twelve furlongs and trailing in tenth, losing the Ponsonby syndicate its entry fee. Not a good result, but the horse has already recovered its

OBJECTIONS AND INQUIRIES

25,000 guineas cost, and looks to have a decent future, perhaps in Group 3 races or top handicaps. It would have been a pity if Ferguson's experience of ownership had ended with Rocky, as he has much to offer the sport, and at least with Channon he is with a friendly face.

Meanwhile, the cause of all the fuss is said to be happier than ever and siring foals on two continents – an amazing 152 mares were sent to him in Australia alone in 2003. His magnificence has not been besmirched in any way by this human imbroglio, and if anything, his reputation has been enhanced – for what kind of animal could have inspired such a battle between giants?

After much reflection, I'm prepared to give my verdict on Rock Of Gibraltar, for what it's worth. He was not the greatest racehorse I've ever seen on the Flat – as Dancing Brave holds that place in my heart – but, without any shadow of a doubt, he is the best *racing* horse I've ever seen.

This difference is important yet subtle, and perhaps accounts for the remarkable fact that hardly any two pundits agreed on Rocky's merits as a racehorse throughout his track career.

The problem was that he won some of his races at a canter and never really showed just how superior he was to his opponents in race after race. Michael Kinane, who was his jockey in all but one race, often deliberately held up Rocky to make full use of his ability to accelerate. In my opinion, if Kinane had made more use of Rocky in, say, the Group 1 Sussex Stakes at Goodwood in 2002, he would undoubtedly have scorched clear of the field and been acclaimed as a truly superlative horse.

The only mystery to his legions of fans is why anyone ever questioned that status, but those who did cavil were usually hung up on the ratings system, and though I'd rather hammer nails through my cheekbones than get into an argument with ratings junkies, some of their claims must be countered.

At his retirement in 2002, Rocky was officially rated that year's 'world champion' in the International Classifications at 128 lbs. This rating is a full 13 lbs behind the leading horse in the ratings of the last two decades, Dancing Brave, who broke the course record in winning the Prix de l'Arc de Triomphe in 1986. Rocky was also rated 10 lbs behind the Classification's best miler of recent history, El Gran Senor, winner of the 2,000 Guineas in 1984. Many pundits said Rocky's rating was still too high, not least because he was mysteriously moved up 4 lbs shortly before he went off to stud. The higher the rating, the more you can charge in stud fees, so the implication was that Rocky's owners were being done a favour because of his fame with the public rather than anything he had done on the course.

Other experts had a more justifiable argument, saying that Rocky was lucky to win at least two of his races – the Darley Dewhurst Stakes and the Sagitta 2,000 Guineas, and so he was. Nor would anyone, least of all Aidan O'Brien, quibble with the statement that you need luck to stay intact for two whole seasons, as Rocky did. But that assertion about good fortune forgets that Rocky also had monumental bad luck in the Coventry Stakes and the Breeders' Cup Mile, which latter race would have stretched his world record to eight Group 1 victories in a row. His own strength and natural vigour also counted for much more than luck in his make-up.

Nevertheless, despite all the arguments, Rocky still ended his career as the highest-rated horse in the world, both in the International Classification and by Timeform, the world's leading independent assessors of racehorse form, who had rated him at 133.

In Rock Of Gibraltar's case, I think the ratings experts will never agree on his exact mark or how he related to other champions of the past. The plain truth, though, is that statistics don't win races, *horses* win races. This book, if anything, has surely shown why the carpers are wrong and why Rock Of Gibraltar is one of the all-time greats of the Turf.

You will recall that Rock Of Gibraltar had won two Group 1 races by the end of his juvenile year, but still suffered by comparison with his outstanding stable companions, Johannesburg and Hawk Wing. It is Hawk Wing, I believe, who is the pointer to the true stellar merit of Rock Of Gibraltar.

At two, Hawk Wing had broken the all-aged course record at The Curragh. It was a measure of the massive anticipation that had been felt about him at the start of the season that most commentators concluded at the end of 2002 that Hawk Wing had

OBJECTIONS AND INQUIRIES

suffered a disappointing year. At three, he 'only' won the Group 1 Eclipse and was second in the 2,000 Guineas, the Derby, the Irish Champion Stakes and the Queen Elizabeth II Stakes at Ascot – a record that most horses could never aspire to.

In his first race at the age of four, Aidan O'Brien and Mick Kinane decided it was time for the horse to show everyone how brilliant he was. No one who saw the Group 1 Juddmonte Lockinge Stakes at Newbury on 17 May 2003 will ever forget that race. Did I call it a race? It needs other horses to make it a race, and they were having a battle all of their own while Hawk Wing was fighting only the dictates of history. Apart, perhaps, from Shergar in the Derby of 1981, no horse had ever reduced a Group 1 race in Britain to the status of a hack gallop. Hawk Wing did so that day.

The other five contestants included three Group 1 winners and one who would later win a Group 1. Domedriver, Rock Of Gibraltar's conqueror in the previous year's Breeders' Cup Mile, was there. Where Or When had beaten Hawk Wing in the Queen Elizabeth II Stakes, Olden Times had won the Prix Jean Prat and Reel Buddy would go on to win the Sussex Stakes. The weakest horse in the race was Tillerman and he had won the Group 2 Celebration Mile at Goodwood.

It was then that greatness was thrust upon Hawk Wing by accident rather than design, because it was expected that Desert Deer would make the running as he normally did and Hawk Wing would come from behind to win. But Desert Deer was pulled out of the race behind the stalls, and in pouring rain, though the ground remained firm, it was Hawk Wing who surprisingly leapt to the front from the off, stayed there and just kept going and going. It was not supposed to happen – horses running so fast were not supposed to be able to last out the straight, stiff Newbury mile. But the further he went, the faster Hawk Wing flew.

He carried his head strangely high and drifted off a straight line, otherwise Hawk Wing might have won by more. But by the line he was an extraordinary eleven lengths clear, with Where Or When in second, itself eight lengths ahead of Olden Times and the rest trailing back to Tillerman – a Group 2 winner, don't forget – who finished some 26 lengths in arrears. Hawk Wing had produced what was, by common consent, the finest performance over a mile

ROCK OF GIBRALTAR

since the heyday of Brigadier Gerard some three decades previously. His winning margin was also a record for a Group 1 race in the entire 30-odd year history of such races.

The next issue of the *Racing Post* gave up its entire front page to a picture of Hawk Wing sailing home clear with the rest of the field a blur in the background and a one-word headline right across the page – 'ASTOUNDING'.

It was all of that and more. Mick Kinane was almost breathless with excitement as he stepped down from Hawk Wing's back. He was trying to stay cool but looked like a teenager who had just taken a Porsche for a test drive. He also had a message for the horse's detractors, saying, 'Quite a few people have said unkind things about Hawk Wing, but he did the talking today and put paid to all that.'

The official handicappers from the BHB and the Turf Club gave Hawk Wing an immediate rating of 137, just 1 lb behind El Gran Senor. Timeform rated him at 138 lbs, 6 lbs behind the rating they gave Brigadier Gerard in 1972. The *Evening Standard* reported, however, that at least one expert at Timeform wanted to rate him as 156 – their highest ever. After Hawk Wing was forced to retire due to an injury sustained in his very next race – the Queen Anne Stakes at Royal Ascot in June 2003 – the International Classifications panel downgraded Hawk Wing to 133 as their mark for the season. This was still a whole 5 lbs higher than Rock Of Gibraltar was rated at his peak the previous year.

Aye, there's the rub – leaving aside Hawk Wing's final injury-hit race at Ascot, only one horse twice managed to finish in front of him, and that was Rock Of Gibraltar. On 1 July 2001, in the Anheuser Busch Railway Stakes at The Curragh, Rocky became the only horse to beat Hawk Wing in the latter's two-year-old career, and he did so quite comfortably by two lengths. Luck of the draw or not, in the Sagitta 2,000 Guineas of 2002, Rock Of Gibraltar finished a clear neck ahead of Hawk Wing to win that Classic in a fast time.

Yet, rated at their highest, Rocky was still considered by the experts to be 5 lbs or more in arrears of Hawk Wing. Alex Ferguson was not the only punter to scratch his head and wonder at that discrepancy. And for those of you who detect conspiracy theories

OBJECTIONS AND INQUIRIES

everywhere, or are possessed of that peculiar paranoia which is often displayed down Old Trafford way, please be assured that none of the handicappers involved was a Manchester City or Arsenal fan.

Hawk Wing was so imperious in his Lockinge victory that it can be safely concluded that any horse who beat him at level weights on reasonably sound turf must have been extra special himself. The only horse to do so twice in an equal contest was Rocky. I rest my case – and that's enough statistics.

For the true measurement of Rock Of Gibraltar's greatness was the way he captured the imagination not just of racing fans, but of the public at large in the UK and Ireland. His juvenile season had been a wonderful antidote to the gloom caused largely by foot-and-mouth disease, particularly late in the season when the newspapers were full of pictures of Sir Alex Ferguson leading in his star.

Against the dismal background of inquiries into racing's integrity, the sport needed even more heroes on the track in 2002, and one colt just kept on providing the right sort of headlines – winning the Sagitta 2,000 Guineas, the Entenmann's Irish 2,000 Guineas, the St James's Palace Stakes at Royal Ascot, the Sussex Stakes at Glorious Goodwood and finally the world record Group 1 victory in the NetJets Prix du Moulin at Longchamp. He was the 'tough of the track' who kept on improving with every race, drawing the admiration of the racing public and experts alike. O'Brien's fellow trainers and the opposing jockeys, for instance, could often be seen admiring him in the parade ring and winner's circle, trying to figure out why he was so good.

Race after race, Rock Of Gibraltar repaid the faith shown in him above all by Aidan O'Brien. How the Maestro needed his Rock. For remember that O'Brien virtually had to shut up shop for several weeks as coughing reverberated round the yard. It was a desperate time for the young trainer, made all the more wretched as it happened just after his glorious record-breaking season. Yet in adversity is our true worth found, and O'Brien had the courage to keep Rock Of Gibraltar in training when it might have been easier – and more financially prudent as a sub-par display could have damaged his stud value – to quietly turn him out to grass and announce his retirement some time later.

His faith in Rocky never wavered. The public shared that faith and latched on to Rocky as they have done with very few racehorses in such a short career. The great favourites of recent years on the Flat have tended to be sprinters or stayers such as the fabulous filly Lochsong and the ill-fated Persian Punch, both of whom took time to reach heroic status. Lochsong ran 27 times in 4 seasons while Persian Punch ran 63 times over 9 seasons, and it is no disrespect to two wonderful animals to say they were not always running against Group 1 horses. Largely because so many champions are retired to stud early or get injured, the public rarely gets the chance to become attached to a Classic winner. Yet Rocky became a massive favourite, achieving what is known as 'crossover', when people not normally interested in racing learn a horse's name and maybe even have a flutter on it.

The horse to which most people compare Rocky is Giant's Causeway – O'Brien's hero of the 2000 season, who had been the first horse since Nijinsky in 1970 to win five Group 1 races in a single season. This record was equalled by Rock Of Gibraltar only two years later, though Giant's Causeway never managed a Classic in his run. It wasn't just that Giant's Causeway won race after race, it was his courageous style of running which made him rightly famous. His never-say-die exploits won him the nickname the Iron Horse, and he truly deserved it. But if Giant's Causeway was the Iron Horse, then Rock Of Gibraltar was surely the Steel Steed.

He won races by as much as he pleased – he won them by a neck, he won them by five lengths and he won them on all sorts of going and always with great heart and courage. For it was racing and not time trials that he loved. Even that unfortunate second place in the Breeders' Cup Mile did not dent his popularity – the British have always loved an unlucky loser.

Throughout that *annus mirabilis*, partly due to Ferguson, Rocky enjoyed the kind of media attention which only football stars normally get. In all his races, Rock Of Gibraltar had displayed the assets of a true champion racehorse – genuine sustained speed and sheer courage, and the will to win that any horse must have if it is to stand apart from the herd.

OBJECTIONS AND INQUIRIES

Now he is in heaven on earth for a horse. His first year at stud went well. His fertility rate was above average and he is on course to have earned around £20 million in stud fees by the end of his second year. An Irish expert who has seen a couple of Rock's foals has pronounced them 'very fine'. An even better judge is Lester Piggott. Interviewed briefly – as with all Piggott interviews – for this book, the greatest jockey judge of horses confirmed that he had a share in a foal which had been sired by Rock Of Gibraltar in his first season at stud and the youngster 'is good, looks very good. It's a bit early to tell, but he definitely looks good and I think he's going to be fine'.

That news is a boost not just for Coolmore but for everyone who wants to see the thoroughbred improve. For it is no secret in racing that many people fear for the future of the thoroughbred racehorse as a species. Allegations made by various animal rights activists that inbreeding and dependence on fewer bloodlines have caused endemic infirmities in the species have yet to be fully answered, and there is an understandable reluctance on the part of breeding organisations to commission research into a growing problem which is certainly perceived by many people within racing as real.

Trainer Ian Balding, responsible for Brigadier Gerard's fantastic career in 1971 and 1972, spoke out on his fears in 2003, saying, 'There is no doubt in my mind that the current racehorse is much more fragile than it used to be. In the 1970s, 90 to 95 per cent of our two year olds actually made the racecourse in their first season; by the 1980s, that dropped to about 75 or 80 per cent, and in the 1990s just 65 or 70 per cent were actually getting a run in their two-year-old seasons.'

Balding mainly blamed changing methods in training and breeding, but added, 'I do feel also that we have a diminished resistance to disease. That has got worse rather than better, in spite of the advances in veterinary science.'

In the absence of verifiable facts and figures about injuries and illnesses in racehorses, fears will continue to be expressed about inbreeding and dependence on too few stallions being the cause of the problems. One defence against potential problems caused by inbreeding is to widen the gene pool by increasing the number of stallions and limiting the number of closely related mares they can cover, but the best defence of all is to breed from animals who have been tough, strong, fast and consistently fit and well. Such stallions may not pass all of those qualities on to their offspring, but if their progeny flourish and cease to suffer from the problems identified by Balding and others, then the species will not only survive but improve.

This is why the new crop of stallions at Coolmore's three branches in Ireland, Kentucky and Australia are so important. The major arrivals within the last three years are all proven class animals and must surely bring their own special essence into the breed. Given Coolmore's virtual stranglehold on the top rank of breeding, it can be argued that Golan, Galileo, Hawk Wing, the mighty French champion Montjeu, Derby winner High Chaparral, the electric Australian sprinter Choisir, Kentucky Derby hero Fusaichi Pegasus and especially Giant's Causeway and Rock Of Gibraltar all have a massive job – no, a duty – to perform, and it is nothing less than safeguarding the future of their species.

A tall order? Overstating the case? Possibly, but then Rock Of Gibraltar has already been the subject and indeed the cause of more ballyhoo than any horse since the one that rolled into the city of Troy three millennia ago. And just as he excelled on the track, so he appears to be living up to expectations at stud.

Owners and breeders seem convinced that Rock Of Gibraltar is indeed the heir to the ill-fated Danehill. The quality of mare being sent to him has been testament to that feeling. The brilliant New Zealand-born Sunline, twice winner of the Cox Plate, was sent to Rocky for her first covering – the equine equivalent of football's George Best cuddling up with Miss World – and the prospect of owning a foal from two such champions is the sort of thing which keeps a breeder awake at night.

His stud career will be worth monitoring, but how we miss him on the track. At the time of writing, it is almost two years since he ceased to race, and Rock Of Gibraltar is sadly missed. We appreciate now that he was a hero who was also a talking horse in the best sense of that word – we never stopped talking about him. The more reflection there is on his career, the more people will conclude that he was truly one in a million. For two glorious seasons, he brought to the sport something all of his own making – sheer, unadulterated racing magic. If he never sees another mare, Rocky will never be forgotten for what he did on the racecourse.

Don't take my word for it. The major players in the sport who admired the horse when he was racing have not changed their views one whit.

Frankie Dettori told me: 'I raced against him several times and he was simply an amazing horse. It took Michael [Kinane] two or three times to find out what he was really all about. I caught him by surprise with Dubai Destination at Doncaster, I played a cat and mouse game with him and made him commit before he wanted to, and I nailed him. Mind you, I had a good horse under me.

'I think it was from that day on that he really worked out how to ride the horse, that he was best when he came on the scene last. The horse also would go and pick up anything in two or three strides. That was his great strength. If it was a one-on-one race he would beat anything, that's what I thought of him.

'In the 2,000 Guineas, the best horse wins. There is no real draw bias at Newmarket and I sometimes think trainers use that as an excuse. The first two were the two best horses in that race and Rock Of Gibraltar was the better of them.

'In the Sussex Stakes, I was on Noverre and my horse ran a solid race, but basically Rock Of Gibraltar was better. There were only a few runners, he really only had me to beat, so Michael just kept him handy, pressed the button and beat me well. As I said, in a one-on-one race, he would beat anything.

'I was not surprised when he got the world record as he was easily the best miler at the time, and the reason he got beaten in America was the track – Arlington is one of the tightest tracks in the world, the straight is only 200 metres or so, and the winner got a dream run on the inside.'

Lester Piggott was happy to share his view. 'He was a great racehorse, there's no doubt about that. He was a racing machine.'

Mark Johnston's formidable talents have been brought to the fore by the brilliance of his work with Attraction, 2004's new superstar of racing. The filly has brought him two Classics, with the historic first double of English and Irish 1,000 Guineas. Like

Rocky, Attraction is a miler, and asked which horse's feats he would most like to see her emulate, Johnston immediately mentioned Rock Of Gibraltar: 'He was the greatest thing we've seen in years and I just cannot understand why people kept trying to knock his record. He could only beat what he raced, and he did that better than any horse I've seen in years. I have no doubt he could have won races by further, and he was unlucky in Chicago, or else he might have gained the acclaim I feel he deserved. But you just cannot argue with a world record, and I feel that, in years to come, people will look back and realise just how great he was.'

I believe Johnston's verdict will be borne out in the future. But even if the so-called experts do take a kinder revisionist view, there will still be no words of tribute to surpass those of Mick Kinane – Rock Of Gibraltar was indeed the ultimate racehorse.

Me? I will picture a bay colt, handsome and happy, with the focus of a boxer, sleek-maned in the wind, as he courses across the meadows of my mind in a summer that is always sunlit, leaving his fellows and all humanity behind, rendering us spellbound by his intrinsic champion-ness.

On his back is Kinane, immobile and sure, both of them in that zone where only those touched by greatness can go, the rider awaiting the precise instant, preparing the correct gesture, so that no detail will sully the image of his mount in its transcendence.

The rest of the herd toil to match these superior beings. Their sweat goes flying, hooves start faltering, jockeys begin to mouth curses as Kinane gives the merest hint of a smile, his eyes betraying only the certainty that *he* is the one upon the ultimate racing horse.

The noise of the crowd, the congregation ready for worship, greets Bayard as his jockey draws him to the outside of a pack of magnificent animals who all of a sudden seem to start waddling like ducks across a mudflat.

Kinane cocks his wrists and slowly releases a millimetre of rein. The whole panoply is crystallised, as if the vision of an inner eye has frozen the frame at the precise nanosecond where Rock Of Gibraltar becomes transfigured, glowing with an intensity of brilliant light you see only in the sun of Turner's translucent dawns.

OBJECTIONS AND INQUIRIES

Magnanimous in his great-heartedness, Rocky invites us to step outside ourselves, and achieve communion with something metaphysical, become one with the good, the true and the beautiful. We anticipate the magic – breathing suspended, concentration total. Share with him, and we can all be heroes, just for one speck of the day.

This is the instant of time we *fanatics* live for, the smile on the face of the Tiger as he strokes the golf ball with perfect angle and velocity, the deft flick of Zidane past the despairing dive of the goalkeeper, Muhammad's right hook dropping on Foreman's jaw under an African sky, O'Driscoll's feinting jink sending entire nations the wrong way, the killing volley dropped by McEnroe an inch over the net on a south London lawn. This is the consummation of artistry and physicality which 'mere games' render to an often unknowing species of hairless ape that only appreciates the quintessence of sport, or any other activity, long after it has gone.

It is the apotheosis of sport, in its own way a moment as perfect as the first smile on the face of your child.

The eyes of Kinane blink once and he mouths a long, slow syllable – 'go'. Beneath him, the heart of Bayard instantaneously expands, the muscles ripple from neck to tail, the ears attain the perpendicular, the nostrils flare as the lungs suck in the necessary oxygen. The hooves are flung a few inches further forward, the magnificent head strains, forward and down, while the eye of the horse says so much – this is my territory, my life, my *purpose*.

For Rock Of Gibraltar, it is the call to victory. In the blink of an eye he is moving ahead, and everything else stands still as if the rest of existence is in awe of the sheer perfection of him.

And then he is gone.

Whoosh.

APPENDIX

Key to Race Reports

Details at the start of each race report are given as follows: location of race; date and time (including actual off time if different from scheduled start time); name of race; distance of race; official state of going at time; number competing; finishing order (first six only); horses which also ran; time taken by winner; winning owner or owners.

For each of the first six horses, the following details are given: name; age (if an all-aged race) and weight (total carried) in usual racing form, i.e. 3-9-2 equals aged three and carrying 9 st. 2 lb; jockey (apprentice allowances stated if carried); price (declared starting price); distance (behind horse in front, in lengths – see ry for other abbreviations); trainer.

Glossary of Racing Terms

Racing has a language all of its own and since not every reader will understand the argot, I have provided a glossary of those terms which may not be fully understood or which have not been explained in the book.

ALL-WEATHER: Most races are run on turf racecourses, but Britain now has three courses – at Lingfield, Southwell and Wolverhampton, with more on the way – which have all-weather artificial surfaces.

ANTE-POST (ODDS): Most bookmakers offer odds on major races considerably in advance of the event, termed ante-post odds. These can be very lucrative for the punters because the odds offered are usually more rewarding than those offered on the day of the race. They can also be dangerous, as most ante-post bets are lost if the horse does not run, and obviously ante-post bets do not take account of the weather or the going on the day.

BEAKS: From the slang for judges, the beaks in racing are the racecourse stewards or the Jockey Club's senior stewards who have the power to rule on misconduct by a trainer, owner or jockey.

BETTING MARKET: Though the big bookmaking chains often detest the system, the 'market' is determined by the amount bet at the racecourse where a particular race is held. Contrary to popular belief, the market usually does accurately reflect the amount bet on a race. A horse's odds are said to 'drift' or lengthen when they become larger, e.g. move from 8–1 to 10–1, because fewer people are betting on it. Conversely, the odds 'harden' or 'shorten' when more people bet on it.

BLUE RIBAND: Originally the Blue Ribbon, because Lord George Bentinck once challenged Benjamin Disraeli on his knowledge of the Derby, and Disraeli, who had recently received the Order of the Garter with its bright blue sash, replied that it was the 'blue ribbon' of the Turf. This description of the Derby caught on and the variant term Blue Riband, meaning the top honour or rank, came into general use because for decades a 'blue riband' was the award given to the fastest ship to cross the Atlantic. The Blue Riband is also a popular and delicious biscuit beloved of this author.

BRIDLE (as in 'on' or 'off the bridle'): When a horse is running well in a race and not having to make its best effort it is said to be 'on the bridle', because the jockey is not having to use the horse's headgear to force it to run quicker. When the jockey has to ask for more effort from his mount, it is said to be 'off the bridle'.

DISTANCE: (1) The length of a race. In deference to Britain's foundation of the sport, most countries use the Imperial measurements of miles and furlongs. There are 8 furlongs in a mile, and 220 yards in a furlong. The minimum distance for a Flat race is five furlongs, and the maximum in Britain is two miles six furlongs. Two miles is the shortest distance over hurdles and steeplechase fences, while the longest distance of any race in Britain is the Grand National at Aintree at four miles four furlongs.

Confusingly, some races start at non-standard distances, usually for historical reasons or because starting stalls cannot be placed exactly at a furlong pole.

The French, as always, do their own thing, and run their races over metric distances. Fortunately, though, it is simple to

GLOSSARY OF RACING TERMS

convert their distances to Imperial measures – just divide by 200 to get the number of furlongs.

To add further confusion, reports and commentaries often mention races being 'down to the distance' or 'at the distance', which is a conventional term for one furlong from the winning post.

(2): The amount by which a race is won, or a horse finishes in front of the next horse, and is usually described in lengths, e.g. 'won by three lengths' means the winner was three times his or her own length in front of the second horse, and so on down through the runners.

The usual abbreviations for standard British winning distances in ascending order are sh hd for short head, hd for head, nk for neck, l for one length and fractions thereof, and dist for distance, meaning the race was won by more than 25 lengths. Other countries mostly follow these definitions, but there can be differences – in America, for instance, the shortest winning distance is a nose.

DRAW: The stall number allocated to a horse, e.g. Rock Of Gibraltar was drawn 22 in the 2,000 Guineas at Newmarket. The draw can be very significant because some racecourses have a topography which favours one side or the other. For instance, on the famous Roodeye course at Chester, horses drawn in low-numbered stalls often have a distinct advantage. The effect of the draw can also change with the weather, as the ground may end up softer on one side or the other.

EACH-WAY: The practice of betting a horse to win and/or reach a place, i.e. first, and usually second or third, though fourth place is allowed in handicap races with 16 runners or more. British bookmakers insist that you can only bet 'to place' if you also bet to win, hence each-way, though really it should be 'either way'.

EASING DOWN: When a horse has clearly won a race a jockey will often 'ease down', i.e. let him or her run a bit more slowly to conserve his energy. It can be a dangerous practice – even the best jockeys such as Keiren Fallon and Willie Carson have eased down their mounts only to be caught by a fast finisher.

FIELD: the totality of horses in a race, e.g. 'in a field of 22' or 'ahead of the field'.

FILLED OUT: When a young horse develops into a mature colt or filly it is said to have 'filled out' as its size and musculature increases.

FORM OR FORMLINE: Racing fans soon learn to 'read the form', which is the record of past performances by horses in a race. A formline or 'line' is simply a possible clue from a previous race as to how a horse may perform, e.g. if a horse has finished well behind another horse in a previous race then the formline would suggest it will do so again. Horses being fickle creatures, form is often of no use whatsoever in pre-judging a race.

THE GALLOPS: The places where trainers take their horses to maintain their fitness with daily workouts, and where they supposedly teach the horses how to race. Some trainers have private gallops, often with an all-weather surface, while some use communal gallops, such as those at Newmarket and Middleham Moor in North Yorkshire.

GELDING: The practice of castrating a horse to improve its temperament and remove its inclination to misbehave with fillies. It is usually only done when it is clear that a horse is not going to be good enough to have a career at stud.

GROUND: The condition of the turf for a race. It can vary from heavy, i.e. rain-sodden, to firm or even hard. Like humans at play on grass, horses often have their preferences for either soft or firmer 'going', which is another term for the state of the ground. It goes without saying that the firmer the ground, the faster the race.

HACKING UP: When a horse wins easily, it is said to have done so 'hacking up' or 'at hack gallop', which simply means that it did not need to exert great effort or produce a full or all-out gallop to win.

HANDS AND HEELS: When a jockey knows his horse is going well, he never reverts to the whip and uses the reins and the stirrups to cajole his mount to victory.

JUVENILE: In a typical career on track, a horse will start to race at two years old, which is known as its juvenile stage or season. If it is a quality horse and races at the age of three, that is often known as its Classic season.

KEPT GOING: As in 'kept going all the way to the line'. Many horses

GLOSSARY OF RACING TERMS

tire dramatically or 'fade away' as they come to the end of a race, so it is usually a good sign that a horse 'kept going'.

KICK: As in 'kicking again'. When a horse starts to make its challenge, usually towards the end of a race, it is said to 'kick' or 'kick on', though the only thing being kicked is the horse itself, as the jockey uses his or her stirrups to ask the horse for more effort.

MAIDEN: A horse which has not yet won a race, or a race for horses which have not yet won. A horse winning its first race is said to have 'won its maiden'. Perhaps confusingly, the term applies to horses of both sexes and is nothing whatsoever to do with maids or damsels.

ONE FOR THE JUDGE: In a close finish to a race, the official judge will decide the winner, usually using the latest camera and video systems. Hence, the closest finishes are said to be 'one for the judge'.

ON THE NOSE: Betting on a horse to win rather than to finish in a place or each-way.

PADDOCK: Though paddocks and parade rings can often be one and the same, most courses usually have a separate area beside the saddling enclosure where horses are prepared for a race by trainers and grooms prior to entering the parade ring.

PARADE RING: Prior to every race, horses must be seen in this area, which is usually behind the stands on most racecourses. It is an integral part of the pre-race ritual that a horse is seen to be mounted by its jockey in the parade ring, and stewards must give permission if a horse and jockey want to leave the parade ring early.

PARI-MUTUEL: The French name for a pool betting system, in which the total amount bet on the race is shared out among the winning punters, less a deduction for the management of the system and a contribution to the administration of racing. France's pari-mutuel is not strictly an equivalent to Britain's Tote as the latter also acts as a normal bookmaker with betting shops around the country.

POINT-TO-POINTERS: A form of racing over jumps which is less prestigious than National Hunt, and has regulations of its own, but is hugely popular in many parts of Britain and Ireland. The term refers to the horses that run in 'point-to-point' races, which, as the name suggests, were originally run from one point to another on a map. Many 'point-to-pointers' move up to enjoy good careers as National Hunt horses when they are said to run 'under Rules', i.e. the formal rules of racing as superintended by the Jockey Club.

POSITION: Where a horse is at any given time in a race. A horse is said to be in a good or handy position if it is up with or just behind the leaders. If the horse makes its run in what is usually the best position nearest to the running rail alongside the track, it is said to be in the 'rails position'.

PULLING UP: When a horse has run its race and can give no more effort or is clearly not going to win or reach a place, the jockey will often pull on the reins to stop it racing, or the horse itself just stops of its own accord. Sometimes, a horse will be 'pulled up' because it is injured, or a horse will win so easily that it is said to win 'pulling up'.

RACE FIXING: The vast majority of racing is a clean sport, and most races are not 'fixed'. Sadly, there are a few evil miscreants who have tried to fix the results of races over the years, usually by drugging horses or bribing jockeys to lose, but these people are very few in number. They should be shot, by the way.

RAG: The horse who is presumed to be the worst in the race.

RIDDEN: You might think all horses are ridden from start to finish, and obviously they are. But the term 'ridden' is a convenient shorthand for the time in the race when a jockey calls on a horse to put its best foot forward. Similarly, when a horse is made to exert full effort all the way to the finishing post, the jockey is said to have 'ridden it out'.

RUN GREEN: When a young or inexperienced horse behaves badly on course, for example when swerving off a straight line, it is said to have 'run green'.

SHOOK THE REINS: Jockeys who are confident that their horse will respond to their urgings will merely use the reins and bridle to convey their instructions to their mount, hence 'shaking the reins'.

SIDE: On most courses, there are two distinct 'sides': the stands or near side and the far side – in other words, the one further away

GLOSSARY OF RACING TERMS

from the stands. This convention is followed even when temporary stands are erected on the far side, giving two stands sides.

STAYING: Most horses have an optimum distance. In the case of Rock Of Gibraltar, that was a mile, but when he was young he was so speedy that there was a worry that he would not be able to last out the full-mile distance and might be a six-furlong sprinter. 'Lasting out the distance' in racing parlance is known as staying. In the final analysis, Rock Of Gibraltar could not only 'stay' a mile but might even have 'stayed' further.

Similarly, in a race, a horse is said to have 'stayed on strongly' if he kept going at top speed for the full distance, or else he or she 'didn't stay', which is an all too common excuse for defeat when a trainer has not yet worked out a horse's maximum distance.

STEWARDS' INQUIRY: The stewards are supposedly experts – to be fair, most of them are – who are responsible for ensuring that the rules of racing are observed by horses and jockeys during a race. If the stewards decide that a rule may have been broken, for instance when horses bump each other, they will immediately call an inquiry, interview the jockeys involved and either disqualify culprits and place them behind the horse who was disadvantaged or let the result stand. The key question they always ask is, 'Was the result affected?' Stewards can also suspend jockeys from riding if they think the rider was guilty of careless or irresponsible behaviour.

TIGHT REIN: When a jockey knows that his horse needs to be held back to give its maximum effort late in the race, or sure his horse has more energy than the others in the field and it needs to be conserved, he or she will keep the reins gripped in such a way that the horse knows it must hold back from charging ahead. It is said to be 'on a tight rein'.

TOTE OR TOTALISATOR: In Britain, the Tote is the national pool betting system set up by law to contribute to racing's administrative costs, such as prize money. Unlike bookmakers, the Tote's profits go back into racing. Tote is simply short for totalisator, and the affectionate nickname for this form of betting, in which you only find out your 'odds' after the race is

ROCK OF GIBRALTAR

over, is the Nanny, or Nanny Goat. Rhyming slang is popular in racing.

TRAIN ON: Unless they are competing on the all-weather circuit, horses tend to be given a break from racing over winter, and their trainers take on the task of keeping them fit and exercised. From the age of two to three, and from three to four, horses can sometimes improve or deteriorate, just as sporting prowess increases or decreases with humans as they move from adolescence to adulthood. A horse which maintains its standards or improves at the age of three or four is said to have 'trained on'.